Basic Materials
in
Music Theory

Answer Cover

Note: To create the Answer Cover, tear out the entire page at the perforation and fold to size, or cut keyboard portion off along dotted line.

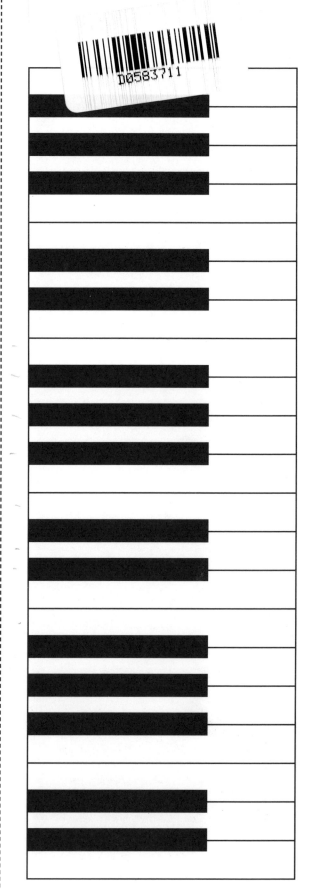

Basic Materials
in
Music Theory

Basic Materials

in

Music Theory

A Programed Course

TWELFTH EDITION

Paul O. Harder

Late, of Michigan State University

Greg A Steinke

Independent Composer/Musician

Prentice Hall
Upper Saddle River   London   Singapore
Toronto   Tokyo   Sydney   Hong Kong   Mexico City

Editor-in-Chief: Sarah Touborg
Executive Editor: Richard Carlin
Project Manager: Sarah Holle
Editorial Assistant: Emma Gibbons
Director of Marketing: Tim Stookesberry
Senior Marketing Manager: Kate Mitchell
Marketing Assistant: Jennifer Lang
Senior Managing Editor: Mary Rottino
Production Editor: Emilcomp/Prepare
Project Management Liaison: Joe Scordato
Senior Operations Supervisor: Brian Mackey

Cover Designer: Margaret Kenselaar
Creative Director: Jayne Conte
Cover Photo: Jane Burton / Dorling Kindersley Media Library
Manager, Cover Visual Research and Permissions: Karen Sanatar
Composition: Emilcomp/Prepare
Full-Service Management: Emilcomp/Prepare
Printer/Binder: Edwards Brothers Malloy
Cover Printer: Edwards Brothers Malloy
Recording Engineer: Greg A Steinke
Recording Performer: Elizabeth Honer

Credits and acknowledgments borrowed from other sources and reproduced, with permission, in this textbook appear on appropriate page within text. Musical examples completed using *Notewriter*™, *NoteAbilityPro*™, and *Finale 2008*™.

Library of Congress Cataloging-in-Publication Data

Harder, Paul O.
    Basic materials in music theory : a programed course / Paul O. Harder, Greg A Steinke. — 12th ed.
      p. cm.
    Includes bibliographical references and index.
    ISBN 0-205-65420-7
      1. Music theory—Programmed instruction. I. Steinke, Greg A, Title.

MT6.H255B4 2010
781'.076—dc22

2008024352

10 9 8 7

Prentice Hall
is an imprint of

ISBN 0-205-65420-7

ISBN: 978-0-205-65420-8

Contents

4.0

5.0

6.0

7.0

Preface to the Twelfth Edition

It is always a challenging task to revise a book that has already enjoyed many years of success. It is an honor to be asked to undertake this latest revision of what has now been many editions. I have had a deep belief in these books ever since I first used them as a young theory teacher in 1967 when they were first available. With a great deal of history behind me, and the highest respect and regard for all of Paul Harder's diligent efforts, I again offer various revisions and enhancements, which I believe keep to the original spirit of Dr. Harder's programed concept, and that I hope all users will find helpful as they work through these pages.

In making the revisions, I have responded to comments and suggestions from reviewers and current users of the book. Earlier revisions have contained additions made to the supplementary exercises and to the appendix material. In selected places throughout the book, I have continued to clarify definitions or to demonstrate to the reader that there are always alternatives to the ideas presented and that the reader should explore those alternatives either independently or in class with the instructor. Therefore, this edition sees a number of small changes throughout the book. I hope that the differences in theoretical and analytical approaches (which, I know, will always be there) work comfortably with previous editions and also provide many interesting points of discussion in class. I'm quite sure that Dr. Harder never intended this volume to be the final, definitive answer but, rather, to provide an informed point of departure for exploring the many anomalies that are always to be found in musics everywhere.

The exposition of the material is accomplished through a step-by-step process. To some, this approach may seem mechanical, but it does ensure, in general, a good understanding of the basic tenets of the materials of the so-called common-practice period in music. I emphasize that this approach does not preclude the presentation of alternatives or the exploration of other ways in which composers may work with various cause-and-effect relationships, rather than following any set of "rules." A rich learning experience can be created for instructors and students alike as they explore together the many exceptions to the so-called rules or principles. This allows them to ultimately link all that they study to actual musical literature or to create many varieties of assignments to solidify the understanding of the basic framework presented in these pages.

The reviser continues to be grateful to both The Paul Harder Estate and Pearson Education for providing helpful comments and support throughout the revision process. I am also indebted to the late Mildred Harder for having provided me access to all notes and support materials Dr. Harder used in the original creation of his book and for her past comments and moral support. I also thank colleagues Dr. David Stech, Dr. Margaret Mayer, Dr. Deborah Kavasch, Dr. Tim Smith, Dr. David Sills, Prof. David Foley, and Dr. Lewis Strouse, among many, for their comments, encouragement, and assistance on revision ideas over past editions. While a number of reviewers provided very helpful suggestions for this edition, I specifically thank Jessica Howard (San Antonio College, San Antonio, TX), and Mauro Botelho (Davidson College, Davidson, NC). I also thank Debra Nichols, who copyedited this edition and provided many helpful changes and suggestions. I am grateful to all concerned and am most appreciative of the help they have provided. I hope users of this volume will find many hours of rich, musical learning to enhance their developing musicianship.

GAS

Preface to the Sixth Edition

Thorough grounding in music fundamentals is necessary for serious study of music. Unless one understands the vocabulary of music terminology, it is impossible even to converse knowingly about music. This book provides training that goes beyond vocabulary; it gives students a functional understanding of matters related to the basic materials of music: time and sound. Exercises incorporated with factual material teach not only how to write and interpret various musical symbols, but also how to construct scales, intervals, and triads.

This book employs a learning system called programed instruction, a method that results in quick, thorough learning with little or no help from the instructor. Students may work at their own pace and repeat any set of drills as many times as necessary. Comprehension of the material is subject to constant evaluation, so a missed concept or error of judgment is isolated quickly, before damage is done.

Because this book provides self-paced learning and requires little supplementation, it is ideal for use as a beginning text in a course devoted to the study of tonal harmony. It is also useful in the applied studio and for a quick review before proceeding with more advanced work.

This new edition incorporates many suggestions that have been made by both students and instructors. The acoustical knowledge contained in Chapter 1.0 has been completely revised to employ terminology that has recently come into general use. Also, the order of chapters has been adjusted to provide a more logical sequence. All mastery frames have been rewritten to assess achievement more thoroughly. The supplementary assignments are all new.

The organization and methods used in this book are the product of practical classroom experiences over a period of many years. They reflect the experimentation and free exchange of ideas between faculty and students at Michigan State University and California State University, Stanislaus.

Paul O. Harder
(1923–1986)

How to Use This Text

A programed text is designed to induce you to take an active part in the learning process. As you use this book you will, in effect, reason your way through the program with the text serving as a tutor. The subject matter is organized into a series of segments called *frames*. Most frames require a written response that you are to supply after having read and concentrated on the information given. A programed text allows you to check each response immediately, so that false concepts do not take root and your attention is focused on "right thinking." Since each frame builds upon the knowledge conveyed by previous ones, you must work your way through the program by taking each frame in sequence. With a reasonable amount of concentration, you should make few mistakes, for each successive step in the program is very small.

A glance at the first page will show that it is divided into two parts. The correct answers appear on the left side. *These should be covered with the Answer Cover, a ruler, a slip of paper, or the hand.* Check your response to a given frame by uncovering the appropriate answer. *Your answer need not always be exactly the same as that supplied by the text.* Use your common sense to decide if your answer approximates the meaning of the one given. If you should make an excessive number of errors, repeat several of the preceding frames until your comprehension is improved. If this fails to remedy your difficulty, you should seek help from your instructor or knowledgeable colleague.

Following each chapter summary, you will find a short series of Mastery Frames. These frames will help you assess your comprehension of the key points of the chapter. *Do not continue unless your handling of the Mastery Frames assures your mastery of the preceding material.* Along with the correct answers on the left side of the frame are references to the specific frames in the main part of the chapter that cover that subject. These references are in parentheses. This arrangement allows you to focus remedial study on the points missed. Because the Mastery Frames are concerned with the essential matters covered in each chapter, you will find that they are useful for later review. There are also Supplementary Assignments, which are intended primarily for use in a classroom setting. The answers to these assignments are contained in the *Instructor's Manual for Harder and Steinke Basic Materials in Music Theory*, which is available upon request from the publisher. In all chapters Supplementary Activities also are given. These can be carried out in class or by the student alone, or with a colleague.

This book concentrates on the *knowledge* of music fundamentals. Knowledge alone, however, is but one aspect of your musical development. To be useful, knowledge about music must be related to the actual experience of music as *sound*. To that end, Ear-Training Activities appear at the end of each chapter. These exercises are designed for self-study; they are coordinated with the text but are not meant to be all-inclusive. They are intended to supplement other ear-training experiences. Do not approach the study of music fundamentals as merely the acquisition of knowledge; bring to bear your musical experiences as both a performer and a listener. Try to sing or play each item as it is presented. In this way, the relation of symbols to sound will become real and functional.

A ⊙ beside a frame, example, or ear-training exercise indicates that the music is reproduced on the compact disc. The short samples on the disc are offered to demonstrate how a particular exercise might be practiced or utilized to develop that particular ear-training skill. Remember, however, these exercises are meant to supplement other, more comprehensive ear-training experiences. (For in-depth study of ear training, you can reference the Ear Training section of the *Bibliography for Further Study*, pp. 378–379.)

About the Authors

Dr. Paul O. Harder (1923–1986) received a Master of Music degree in Music Theory from the Eastman School of Music, University of Rochester, where he performed as oboist with the Rochester Philharmonic Orchestra. Later, as a fellowship student at the University of Iowa, he received his Ph.D. in Music Composition. He studied composition with Mlle. Nadia Boulanger at the École des Beaux Arts de Fontainebleau, France, and at the Royal Academy of Music in Copenhagen, Denmark.

Dr. Harder held the post of Chairman of Music Theory at Michigan State University before becoming Assistant Vice President and Professor of Music at California State University, Stanislaus. He was a Professor Emeritus at Michigan State University.

In addition to approximately fifty compositions for a variety of media including orchestra, band, chorus, and chamber groups, Dr. Harder was the author of *Harmonic Materials in Tonal Music,* Parts I and II, through the fifth edition; *Basic Materials in Music Theory,* through the sixth edition; *Music Manuscript Techniques,* Parts I and II; *Bridge to Twentieth Century Music,* through the first edition; and as co-author (with H. Owen Reed), *Basic Contrapuntal Techniques.* All were published by Allyn & Bacon (see the Bibliography)

Dr. Greg A Steinke (b. 1942) holds a Bachelor of Music degree from Oberlin Conservatory, a Master of Music degree from Michigan State University, a Master of Fine Arts degree from the University of Iowa, and a Doctor of Philosophy degree from Michigan State University.

Dr. Steinke retired in June 2001 as Chair of the Art and Music Departments, Associate Dean for Undergraduate Studies, and as holder of the Joseph Naumes Endowed Chair in Music at Marylhurst University in Oregon. Formerly, he was Dean of the College of Fine Arts and Professor of Music at Millikin University, Director of the School of Music and Professor of Music at Ball State University, Assistant Director of the School of Music at the University of Arizona, Chairman of the Music Department at San Diego State University, Director of the School of Music at the University of Idaho, Chairman of the Music Department at Linfield College, and a faculty member at Northern Arizona University, The Evergreen State College, California State University, Northridge, and the University of Maryland. Currently, he is a freelance composer, writer, oboist, and conductor.

Dr. Steinke is the author of numerous articles, has done the revisions to Paul Harder's *Basic Materials in Music Theory* (seventh through twelfth editions), *Harmonic Materials in Tonal Music,* (sixth through tenth editions), *Bridge to Twentieth Century Music* (revised edition), and, with H. Owen Reed, *Basic Contrapuntal Techniques* (revised edition, Alfred Music). He holds membership in a number of professional organizations and served for nine years (three terms, 1988–97) as the President and National Chairman of the Society of Composers, Inc. Professor Steinke is active as a composer of chamber and symphonic music with a number of published works, as a speaker on interdisciplinary arts, and as an oboe soloist specializing in contemporary music.

Basic Materials
in
Music Theory

Chapter 1.0
The Basic Materials of Music: Time and Sound

Time and sound are the basic materials from which music is made. In music, time is organized into patterns of duration. Sound consists of several characteristics, each of which contributes in its own way to the music. Further, the sounds of music are organized to convey an aesthetic or artistic purpose. The objective of this book is to acquaint the reader with the terms and the systems of notation that apply to the organization of time and the properties of sound generally found in the context of American and European art music. Many of these concepts and principles can also be utilized in studying and discussing other musics of the world.

This chapter will help lay the groundwork for understanding the more complex materials of music. The discussion that follows presents some of the scientific parts of music. This aspect of music study is known as ACOUSTICS.

1.1   The source of sound is a VIBRATING OBJECT. Any object that can be made to vibrate will produce sound. *Vibrating objects* that are familiar to musicians include strings, columns of air, and metal or wooden bars or plates.

sound

A *vibrating object* is the source of _____.

1.2   A vibrating object generates energy that is transmitted to the ear by vibrational disturbances called SOUND WAVES. These waves are transmitted as alternate compressions and rarefactions of the molecules in the atmosphere.
   Sound waves transmit energy from the vibrating object

ear

to the _____.

1.3   A simple *sound wave* may be represented as follows:

One Cycle (pitch)

Time ⟶

One complete oscillation both above and below the central axis is called a CYCLE. The example measures the *cycle* from one peak to another. How many *cycles* are represented if measured at the central axis itself?

Six

_____

1.4   One complete oscillation of a sound wave is called a

cycle

_____.

1.5   Sounds are perceived subjectively as being relatively "high" or "low." This property of sound is called PITCH. The speed at which an object vibrates is affected by the object's physical nature, including its size, shape, and material. The faster the vibrating object vibrates, the "higher" the *pitch*. Conversely, the slower the vibrating body vibrates, the

lower

"_____" the *pitch*.

pitch

1.6   Frequency of vibration determines the _____ of the sound.

Expository Frame

1.7   Frequency of vibration may be expressed as the number of cycles per second. Musicians are familiar with the standard of A = 440. This means that the note A (above middle C) vibrates at 440 cycles per second.

The term *cycle* lately has been supplanted by HERTZ (abbreviation: Hz). This is to honor the nineteenth-century physicist Heinrich Hertz. As discussion proceeds, the term *hertz* will be used instead of *cycle*.

(No response required.)

1.8   Will a *pitch (tone)* whose frequency is 620 *hertz* sound higher or lower than one whose frequency is 310

hertz? _____

Higher

_____

Note: If you are unfamiliar with some basic principles of music notation, you may wish to cover frames 2.1–2.16 from Chapter 2.0 before proceeding.

1.9   When the frequency of a pitch is *doubled,* the resulting tone will be perceived as sounding an OCTAVE *higher.* When the frequency of a pitch is halved, the resulting tone will be

lower

an *octave* _____. *Experience this effect at the piano by playing a note such as C or A in various octaves. Note that pitches an octave apart have the same name.*

1.10   Two simple sound waves are represented below.

Time ⟶

Two vibrations of Wave 1 occur for each vibration of Wave 2. Thus Wave 1 represents a tone whose pitch

higher

(frequency) is one *octave* (higher/lower) _____ than that of Wave 2.

1.11   The tone whose frequency is 440 hertz is called A. The A an octave lower would have a frequency of

220

_____ hertz.

1.12   The tone whose frequency is 261 hertz is called C. The C sounding an octave higher would have a frequency of

522

_____ hertz.

1.13   A tone whose frequency is one-half that of another tone will sound an octave (higher/lower)

lower

_____.

1.14   The frequency of a tone two octaves lower than a

1/4

second tone is (1/2, 1/3, 1/4, 1/8) _____ the frequency of the latter.

1.15   In addition to pitch, music makes use of various degrees of "loudness" or "softness" of sound. This property of sound is called INTENSITY. *Intensity* is determined by the amount of power transmitted to the ear by the sound wave.

   Produce a soft sound by humming or singing; then produce the sound again, but considerably louder.

   Does the louder sound require a greater expenditure

Yes

of energy? _____

1.16   *Intensity* is determined by the amount of energy transmitted from the sound source to the ear and is measured by the AMPLITUDE of the sound wave. Sound waves can be compared to waves on the surface of water: the greater the agitation, the higher the waves.

intensity

   Amplitude is a measurement of _____.

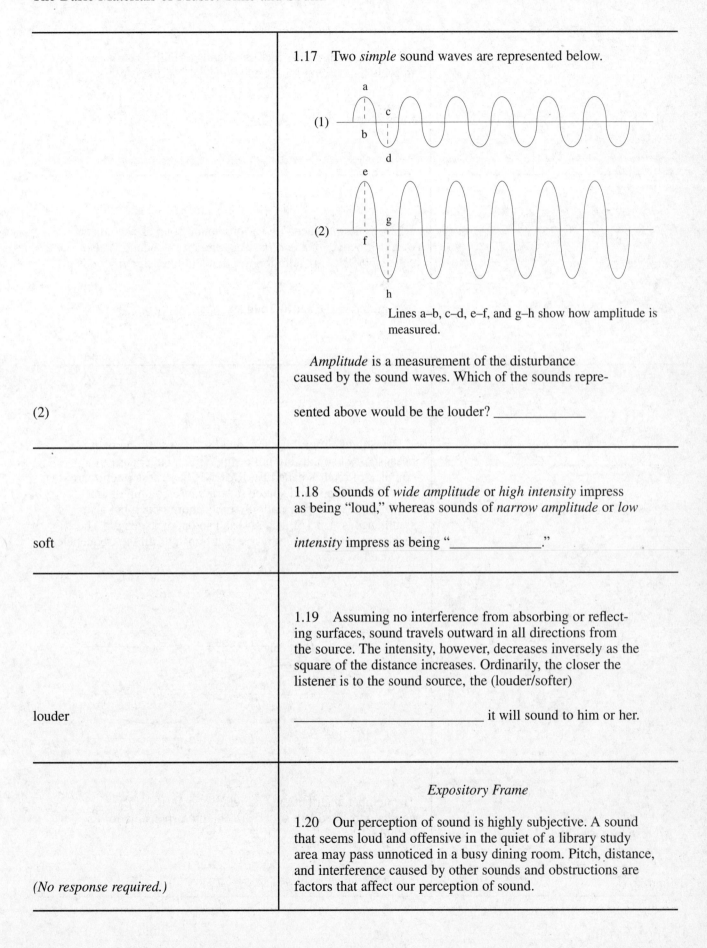

1.17   Two *simple* sound waves are represented below.

Lines a–b, c–d, e–f, and g–h show how amplitude is measured.

Amplitude is a measurement of the disturbance caused by the sound waves. Which of the sounds represented above would be the louder? _____

(2)

1.18   Sounds of *wide amplitude* or *high intensity* impress as being "loud," whereas sounds of *narrow amplitude* or *low intensity* impress as being "_____."

soft

1.19   Assuming no interference from absorbing or reflecting surfaces, sound travels outward in all directions from the source. The intensity, however, decreases inversely as the square of the distance increases. Ordinarily, the closer the listener is to the sound source, the (louder/softer) _____ it will sound to him or her.

louder

Expository Frame

1.20   Our perception of sound is highly subjective. A sound that seems loud and offensive in the quiet of a library study area may pass unnoticed in a busy dining room. Pitch, distance, and interference caused by other sounds and obstructions are factors that affect our perception of sound.

(No response required.)

1.21   Excluding other factors, sounds of high intensity impress us as being loud, and sounds of low intensity

soft

impress us as being _____.

1.22   Tones produced by various sound sources have their own distinctive *tone quality*. This property of sound is also called TIMBRE. In addition to pitch and intensity, *timbre* is

waves

transmitted to the ear by sound _____.

Expository Frame

1.23   Sounds from different sound sources vary in quality because most sounds are not a single pitch but consist of a complex of pitches called HARMONICS.* These pitches are the result of the sound source (a string or a column of air, for example) vibrating not only in its entire length but also simultaneously in 1/2, 1/3, 1/4, and so on, of its length. The result is a complex sound wave that transmits all the frequencies produced by the source.

The number, distribution, and relative intensity of the *harmonics* contained in a sound are chiefly responsible for its *timbre*.

(No response required.)

---

* The term *partials* is also used for these pitches.

1.24 The complex of simultaneously sounding pitches generated from a fundamental that determines the timbre of a tone is called the HARMONIC SERIES. Theoretically, the *harmonic series* extends indefinitely; but for our purposes, the naming of the first eight *harmonics* will suffice.*

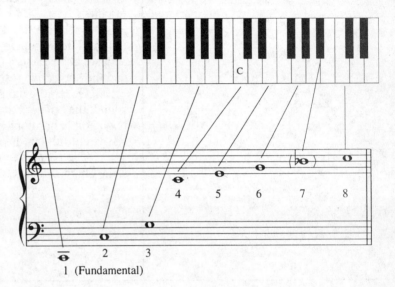

The example above shows that the *harmonic* with

fundamental

the lowest frequency is called the _____.

———————————

* To avoid confusion, the practice of referring to the harmonics other than the first (fundamental) as "overtones" (i.e., notes 2 through 8 above) generally has been abandoned.

1.25 Not all the tones of the *harmonic series* are present in some musical sounds. The tuning fork, for example, produces a "pure" sound consisting of the first *harmonic* only; a closed tube, such as a stopped organ pipe, produces only the odd-numbered *harmonics*.

The number of *harmonics* present and their relative

timbre

intensity determine the _____ of the sound.

1.26 *Timbre* is a technical term that refers to the quality of a sound. *Tone color* is a descriptive term that refers to the same phenomenon. Reference to the visual effect of color is appropriate in the context of sound because sounds often impress us as being "bright" or "dark," or even suggesting specific colors. Some individuals are endowed with "colored hearing," a condition called *synesthesia,* in which sounds produce accompanying visualization of colors.

Factors other than harmonics affect our perception of timbre. These include the physical nature of the sound source, the acoustical characteristics of the place in which the sound is heard, and the subjective response of the listener.

Generally, the greater the number of harmonics present in a sound, the "richer" the effect will be. In comparison, a sound with few audible harmonics will sound "pure." Such a tone may be no less beautiful, but the timbre will be different.

The terms *timbre, tone quality,* and *tone color* refer to the same characteristics of sound.

True

(True/False) _____

Expository Frame

1.27 The harmonic series (shown in frame 1.24) has been introduced here to help explain what causes different timbres. It has importance in other areas of music study, such as harmony and orchestration. Because use of the harmonic series will be made in future study, try to learn its structure and be able to play and write it on any pitch. *This should be possible once intervals, keys, and key signatures have been mastered later on in this study.*

(No response required.)

1.28 The structure of the harmonic series is the same regardless of the pitch of the fundamental—the series of tones is identical.

Is the fundamental considered to be one of the harmonics

Yes

of a sound? _____

(1) pitch (2) intensity (3) timbre *(any order)*	1.29 List the three *properties of sound* that have been examined to this point. (1) _____ (2) _____ (3) _____
(No response required.)	*Expository Frame* 1.30 Since time is one of the basic materials of music, DURATION of sound is an important factor. Even though time is required for the vibrations that produce sound to occur, *duration* is generally not regarded as a property of sound. In music, however, the *duration* of sounds is an important consideration. Patterns of *duration* create the element of music called RHYTHM. Because of its importance to music, *duration* will be included here as the fourth *property of sound*.
rhythm	1.31 The term RHYTHM applies to all aspects of time in music, including *duration*. Music utilizes sounds ranging from very short to very long, and the Western system of notation is designed to indicate with precision the exact duration required. 　　　All aspects of duration are part of the basic element of music called _____.
Time	1.32 Is *rhythm* primarily a matter of time or of sound? _____
(your opinion)	1.33 Can *rhythm* be conceived without sound? _____
duration	1.34 The property of sound that refers to the "length" of tones is called _____.

1.35   The basic materials of music are TIME and SOUND. Durations of sounds are combined to produce rhythm. Duration is one of the properties of sound. Name the other three.

(1) pitch   (1) _____

(2) intensity   (2) _____

(3) timbre   (3) _____
(any order)

Summary

Sound is produced by a *vibrating object* that transmits energy in the form of *sound waves* to the ear. The *four properties of sound* that concern musicians are summarized below:

1. *Pitch* is the perceived "highness" or "lowness" of sound and varies according to the *frequency* of vibration—higher frequencies produce higher pitches. Each time the frequency is doubled, the pitch is raised one *octave.*

2. *Intensity* is the "loudness" or "softness" of a sound and is the result of the *amplitude* of the sound wave. This in turn is a reflection of the amount of energy emanating from the sound source.

3. *Timbre* refers to the "quality" ("brightness" and "darkness") of a sound and results, in part, from the number, relative intensity, and distribution of the *harmonics* present. Other factors, such as the physical nature of the sound source, the acoustics of the listening space, and the subjective response of the listener, may also play a role in the perception of *timbre.*

4. *Duration* and patterns thereof are especially important for musicians because they are concerned with *rhythm*—one of the basic elements of music.

Mastery Frames

vibrating (frames 1.1–1.2)	1–1 The source of sound is a _____ object.
sound waves (1.2)	1–2 Alternate compressions and rarefactions of the molecules in the atmosphere transmit energy in the form of _____ _____ to the ear.
True (1.3–1.4)	1–3 One complete oscillation of a sound wave is called a cycle. (True/False) _____
pitch (1.5–1.6)	1–4 The frequency at which an object vibrates determines the _____ of the sound.
620 (1.7)	1–5 A tone with the frequency of 620 hertz is vibrating at the rate of _____ cycles per second.
octave (1.9–1.14)	1–6 A tone with a frequency twice that of another is said to be an _____ higher.
intensity (1.15)	1–7 The property of sound that refers to the "loudness" or "softness" of a tone is called _____.

True (1.16–1.18)	1–8 Amplitude is a measure of the energy transmitted to the ear. (True/False) _____
timbre (1.22)	1–9 The property of sound that refers to the quality of a tone is called _____.
harmonics (1.23)	1–10 Most musical tones consist of a complex of pitches. Those pitches are called _____.
harmonic (1.24–1.28)	1–11 The entire complex of pitches that constitutes the total sound is called the _____ series.

Supplementary Activities

1. Acoustics may be explored in depth. Please see the *Bibliography for Further Study* under "Acoustics" for a number of references in this area. Consider developing an essay or a series of essays on various acoustics topics—for example, amplitude, frequency, harmonics, and timbre. Or perhaps develop a paper around the history of sound and the people who played a role in this history.

2. If a synthesizer is accessible, try exploring the four properties of sound in actuality by manipulating their parameters and sensing the results.

3. Consider relating what has been found out about the four properties of sound to various pieces of music known. How has each composer manipulated or used these properties to create a particular piece? Is one property stressed or used more than another? Might there be a reason why the composer has done so?

4. Try to seek out pieces that may demonstrate the stressing of one or more properties of sound over the others. Image a piece that might stress a particular property. Then, try to realize that piece in some way.

Supplementary Assignments

ASSIGNMENT 1–1   Name: _____

1. The field of science that is concerned with the phenomena of sound is called _____

   _____.

2. Sound is an auditory sensation caused by vibrations that reach the ear by means of _____

   _____.

3. The source of sound is a _____ object.

4. Name several objects that are capable of producing sound.

   a. _____

   b. _____

   c. _____

   d. _____

5. Name the property of sound that relates to the "highness" or "lowness" of sound._____

6. What determines the pitch of a sound? _____

7. Explain the meaning of the designation "100 hertz."

   _____

   _____

8. Complete the table by providing the missing information.

   Frequency

Two octaves higher	_____
One octave higher	_____
Original tone	440
One octave lower	_____
Two octaves lower	_____

9. Name the property of sound that relates to the volume of sound. _____

   _____

10. What effect does distance have upon the volume of sound?_____

_____

11. The individual pitches that combine to produce a complex sound are called _____.

12. To what does the term *timbre* refer? _____

_____

13. The harmonic series through the eighth harmonic with C as the fundamental is shown below. Write the series on F in the space provided. *(If inexperienced in musical notation, attempt to imitate the pattern from the first line.)*

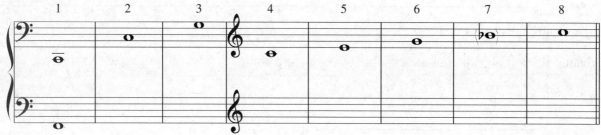

14. Select the item on the right that corresponds to each term on the left. *(Write the appropriate letter.)*

    _____ 1. Amplitude   a. Loudness/softness
    _____ 2. Timbre   b. Partials
    _____ 3. Vibrating object   c. 2:1 frequency ratio
    _____ 4. Harmonics   d. Time
    _____ 5. Pitch   e. Tone quality
    _____ 6. Fundamental   f. Energy transmitted by sound waves
    _____ 7. Duration   g. Cycles per second
    _____ 8. Intensity   h. Transmit sound
    _____ 9. Hertz   i. Highness/lowness
    _____10. Sound waves   j. First harmonic
    _____11. Octave   k. Source of sound

15. Rhythm is concerned with the basic material of music called _____.

16. Which frequency would produce the "higher" tone? _____

    a. 620 vibrations per second   b. 310 vibrations per second

17. A tone whose frequency is double that of another sounds an _____ higher.

Ear-Training Activities

INTRODUCTION

Full musical comprehension requires both the ear and the mind: Sounds and their related symbols must be *sensed* as well as *understood.* An extensive ear-training program is usually needed to develop aural discrimination. These ear-training activities, however, have a more modest objective: to reinforce your understanding of the material presented in this book. The exercises are suggestive rather than comprehensive. In most cases, they do not provide sufficient drill for developing aural mastery. They should, on the other hand, be a useful supplement to class experiences. They also may serve as models for further self-help. (For more comprehensive practice in ear training, please reference the Ear Training section of *Bibliography for Further Study,* pp. 378–379.) The author has listed only a few of the *many* programs to be found via the Internet. A quick search will reveal many programs, some of which are free and/or can be accessed directly from a Web page.

Musicians must become acutely sensitive to sounds and time relations. To develop sensitivity, one must do more than passively listen. Both the sounds and the way those sounds affect a person must be analyzed. By being aware of responses to musical stimuli, mastery of musical expression will be gained.

This book has been designed to help acquire musical knowledge largely on one's own. These ear-training activities are provided to help achieve this goal. The exercises may be used alone or with another person, each checking the other. Working with a partner can be extremely helpful in all the Ear-Training Activities throughout the book. Some exercises may seem simple, even naive, but they serve an important function: to encourage sensitive, critical, and analytical listening.

(Aural demonstrations of the following examples [marked with ⊙] are to be found on the CD accompanying this book.)

1. Tap, or strike with a pencil, any object that happens to be nearby. Listen for differences in effect; analyze responses to these simple stimuli. Are the sounds soothing or stimulating, hard or soft, high or low, short or long?

2. Notice the effect sounds that are nearby or far away have.

3. Pluck a stretched rubber band. Listen to variations of pitch and observe how the rubber band vibrates as the tension is varied.

4. At the piano, play notes that are within vocal range and match their pitches with voice.

5. Play notes outside vocal range and match them within vocal range.

6. Sing octave intervals, both up and down. *(Check yourself at a keyboard.)*

7. Sing the tones of the natural harmonic series on various pitches. Bring the tone within your vocal range as in the following example:

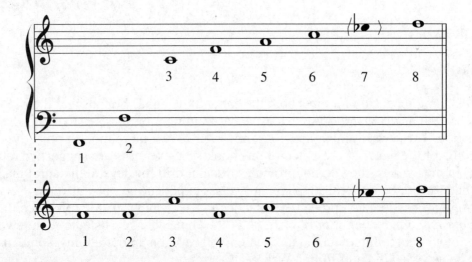

8. Additional practice with these materials could combine exercises from above by singing intervals or patterns of notes at random—sing interval or pattern and check with keyboard, or play interval or pattern and try to match with voice. (Note that specific information on intervals is presented in Chapter 6.0.)

Chapter 2.0
The Notation of Pitch

Various musical terms and symbols are used to refer to the organization of time and the properties of sound. In this chapter, the notation of one aspect of sound, that of pitch, will be illustrated. The European or Western art music system of notation originated many centuries ago when tonal materials were much more limited than they are now. The system was not designed for the highly chromatic music that eventually evolved. The result is that the notation of pitch is unnecessarily complex. Prevalent usage, however, causes even minor changes to be resisted. Modern notation is an imperfect, but nevertheless effective, visual representation of the "high" and "low" effects produced by tones of different pitch.

	2.1 Five parallel horizontal lines with intervening spaces are used to notate the pitch of tones. This device is called a STAFF (plural: staves or staffs). The *staff* is used to notate the property of sound
pitch	called _____.
	2.2 The five horizontal parallel lines with intervening spaces used for the notation of pitch are called the
staff	_____.
seen (and written) *(The effect of a note can be imagined, but this is not an auditory sensation.)*	2.3 The written symbols that represent tones are called NOTES. *Tones* can be heard, whereas *notes* can be _____.

No
(It is the representation of a sound.)

2.4   A *tone* is a musical sound. Is a *note* also a

sound? _____

2.5   The *lines* and *spaces* of the *staff* are numbered from the bottom to the top.

LINES	SPACES
5	
4	4
3	3
2	2
1	1

higher

The fourth space is (higher/lower) _____ than the fourth line.

2.6   The first seven letters of the alphabet (A through G) are used to name the *notes* that are placed on the various lines and spaces of the staff.

Signs are placed at the left on the *staff* to identify a particular line. These signs are called CLEFS.

A *clef* sign is used to name a particular line of

staff

the _____.

2.7   The modern *clef* signs are stylized forms of the Gothic letters G, F, and C. The TREBLE CLEF establishes the location of the note G on the second line of the staff, that passes through the lower curved half of the clef sign.

The *treble clef* identifies the second line of the staff as

G

_____.

2.8   Write the *treble clef* several times.

(etc.)

2.9   Reference to the note established by the clef establishes the location of other notes.

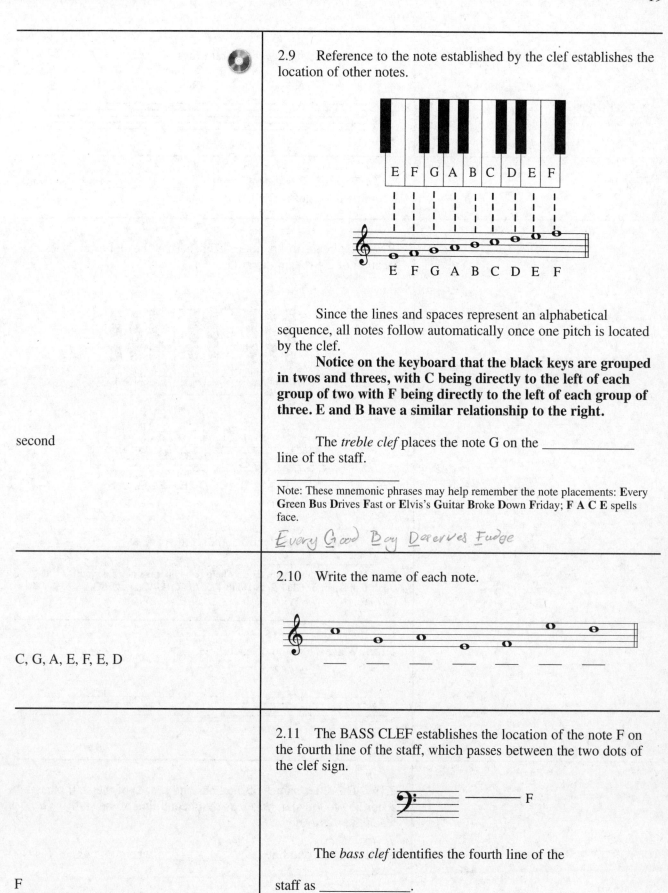

Since the lines and spaces represent an alphabetical sequence, all notes follow automatically once one pitch is located by the clef.

Notice on the keyboard that the black keys are grouped in twos and threes, with C being directly to the left of each group of two with F being directly to the left of each group of three. E and B have a similar relationship to the right.

second

The *treble clef* places the note G on the _____ line of the staff.

_____

Note: These mnemonic phrases may help remember the note placements: **E**very **G**reen **B**us **D**rives **F**ast or **E**lvis's **G**uitar **B**roke **D**own **F**riday; **F A C E** spells face.

Every Good Boy Deserves Fudge

2.10   Write the name of each note.

C, G, A, E, F, E, D

—   —   —   —   —   —   —

2.11   The BASS CLEF establishes the location of the note F on the fourth line of the staff, which passes between the two dots of the clef sign.

F

The *bass clef* identifies the fourth line of the staff as _____.

2.12   Write the *bass clef* several times.

𝄢 𝄢 𝄢 (etc.)

fourth

2.13   The note F is located on the _____ line of the staff when the bass clef is used.

2.14   Reference to the note established by the clef establishes the location of the remaining notes.

G A B C D E F G A

G A B C D E F G A

E

The *bass clef* identifies the third space as _____.

Note: These mnemonic phrases may help remember the notes: **G**ood **B**urritos **D**on't **F**all **A**part or **G**lad **B**ags **D**on't **F**all **A**part; **A**ll **C**ows **E**at **G**rass or **A**ll **C**ars **E**at **G**as.

2.15   Write the name of each note.

D, A, G, E, F, G, C

2.16   The letter names of the lines and spaces of the staff change according to the clef. Whereas the second line of the staff is G when the *treble clef*

B

is used, the second line is _____ when the *bass clef* is used.

2.17   Write the name of each note.

C, E, G, A, F, E

2.18   The C-CLEF establishes the location of the note C.*

The line that passes through the center of the

C-clef is _____.

C

---

* This note is actually "middle C." The precise meaning of this term is explained later in this chapter. (See frames 2.35–2.36.)

2.19   The C-clef can be placed on various lines of the staff.

TENOR CLEF (4th line)   ALTO CLEF (3rd line)

MEZZO-SOPRANO CLEF   SOPRANO CLEF
(2nd line)   (1st line)

The C-clef is not always located on the same line, but in each case the line that passes through the center

C

of the clef is _____.

Note: There are other usages of each of these clefs (treble, bass, and C) if one examines the entire musical literature. What is presented in this text represents the most common usages today.

2.20   In modern notation, the ALTO CLEF is used mainly by the viola and occasionally by the trombone. The TENOR CLEF is used by the violoncello, the trombone, and the bassoon. Other C-clefs are found mainly in older editions of choral music and are seldom used today.*

Write the *alto clef* several times.

* The C-clefs are introduced here to enable interpretation of them if necessary, since they are used in much instrumental music. There is also a non-pitched clef that may be used for percussion and other non-pitched musical situations:

(etc.)

The third

2.21   On which line of the staff does the note C occur when the *alto clef* is used? _____

2.22   Write the name of each note.

B, E, G, F, A, G, D

2.23   Write the *tenor clef* several times.

(etc.)

The fourth

2.24   On which line of the staff does the note C occur when the *tenor clef* is used? _____

2.25   Write the name of each note.

G, E, C, A, D, E, B

bass

2.26   The three clefs used in modern music notation

are the C-clef, the treble clef, and the _____ clef.

2.27   The range of a *staff* may be extended by the use of
LEDGER LINES.* These lines are added above or below a staff
and are spaced the same as the lines of the staff itself. The
alphabetical succession of notes continues as on the staff.

staff

     Ledger lines are used to extend the range of

the _____.

_____

* The spelling *leger lines* is occasionally used.

2.28   Extension of the staff by means of ledger lines is shown
below.

     The note on the second ledger line above the staff

C

when the treble clef is used is _____.

2.29   Extension of the staff by means of ledger lines is shown
below.

     The note on the second space below the staff

D

when the bass clef is used is _____.

2.30   Write the name of each note.

(1) A, C, B, G, D
(2) G, D, B, A, C

2.31   Write the name of each note.

(1) D, B, C, F, E
(2) C, B, E, F, D

2.32   Write the name of each note.

B, C, C, B, D, A

2.33   Write the name of each note.

A, B, C, D, B, C

2.34   The treble and bass clefs are placed on two staves connected at the left by a vertical line and a brace to form the GRAND STAFF.

The *grand staff* is used for the notation of piano music, and is useful for other purposes, since it is capable of representing the full range of virtually all musical media. The grand staff employs the

treble, bass
(any order)

_____ clef and the _____ clef.

2.35   A note placed on the first ledger line above the bass staff represents the same pitch as a note placed on the first ledger line below the treble staff. This note is called MIDDLE C.

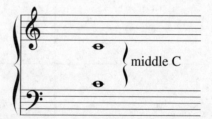

middle C

Middle C derives its name from the fact that

grand

it is located in the middle of the _____ staff.

This note is also approximately in the middle of the piano keyboard. Locate this note at the piano.

2.36   Notes in addition to *middle C* can be notated on either the
treble staff or the bass staff.
Rewrite the notes on the bass staff so they will *sound
the same*.

2.37   Rewrite the notes on the treble staff so they will *sound
the same*.

2.38   Rewrite the notes on the alto staff so they will *sound
the same*.

2.39   Rewrite the notes on the bass staff so they will *sound the same*.

2.40   Rewrite the notes on the tenor staff so they will *sound the same*.

2.41   Rewrite the notes on the treble staff so they will *sound the same*.

2.42   It is impractical to use more than three or four ledger lines, since notes become more difficult to read as the number of ledger lines increases. To avoid the excessive use of ledger lines, the treble staff may be extended upward and the bass staff extended downward by the use of the OTTAVA sign (*8 ---,* *8va ---,* or sometimes *8ve ---,*; and conversely *8 ---',* *8vb ---',* or sometimes *8ve ---').** Notes over which the *ottava* sign is placed sound an octave higher than written; notes below which the *ottava* sign is placed sound an octave lower than written.

The *ottava* sign is used to avoid the excessive

ledger lines   use of _____ _____.

---

* Recent practice tends to give preference to *8 ---,* or *8 ---'.*

2.43   Observe the use of the ottava sign below.

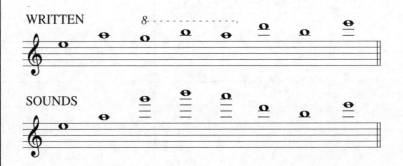

WRITTEN

SOUNDS

The dotted line following the *8* indicates the notes affected by the sign.

All notes over which the ottava sign appears are

higher   to be played an octave _____.

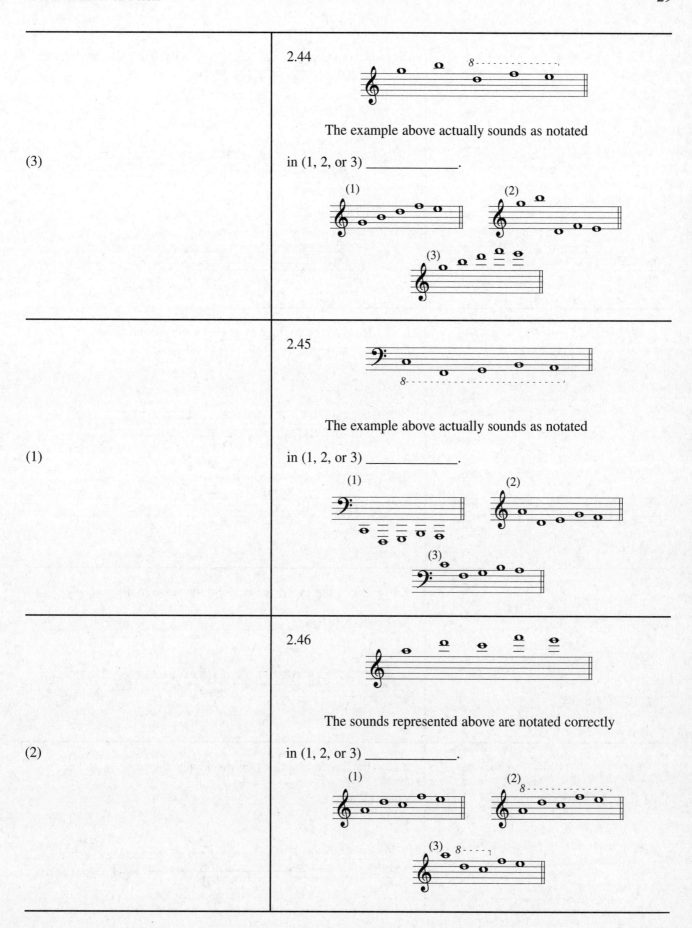

2.44

The example above actually sounds as notated

in (1, 2, or 3) _____.

(1)   (2)

(3)

2.45

The example above actually sounds as notated

in (1, 2, or 3) _____.

(1)   (2)

(3)

2.46

The sounds represented above are notated correctly

in (1, 2, or 3) _____.

(1)   (2)

(3)

(3)

(1)

(2)

2.47   Rewrite the passage below so it will *sound the same*. Avoid all use of ledger lines. *(Use the ottava sign.)*

2.48   Rewrite the passage below so it will *sound the same*. *(Use the ottava sign only for those notes that lie below the staff.)*

True

2.49   Each note as written below notates the *same pitch*. (True/False) _____

True

2.50   Each note as written below notates the *same pitch*. (True/False) _____

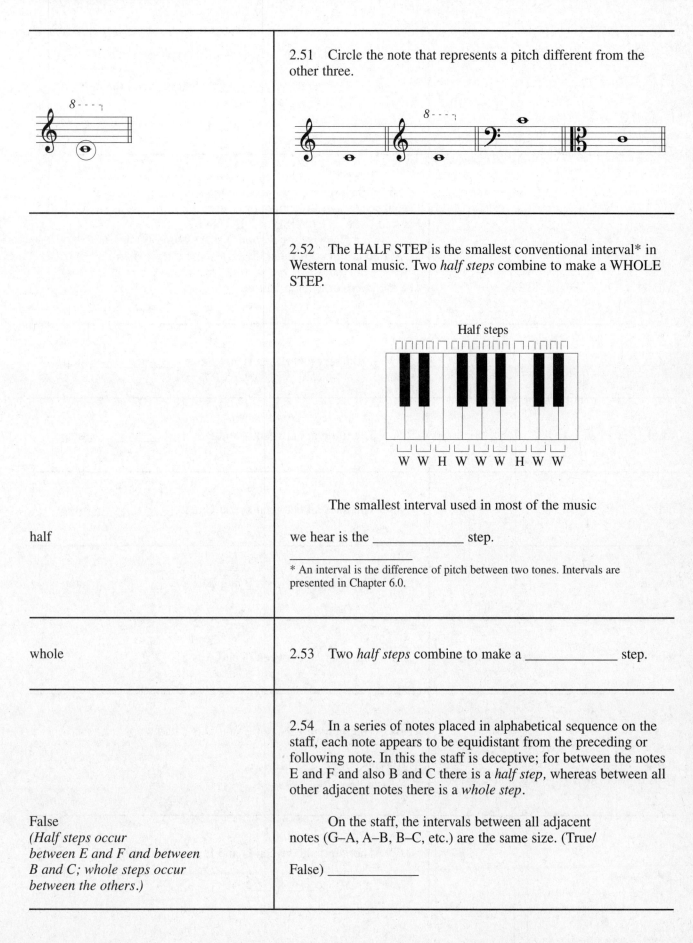

2.51   Circle the note that represents a pitch different from the other three.

2.52   The HALF STEP is the smallest conventional interval* in Western tonal music. Two *half steps* combine to make a WHOLE STEP.

Half steps

W W H W W W H W W

The smallest interval used in most of the music

half   we hear is the _____ step.

* An interval is the difference of pitch between two tones. Intervals are presented in Chapter 6.0.

whole   2.53   Two *half steps* combine to make a _____ step.

False   2.54   In a series of notes placed in alphabetical sequence on the
(Half steps occur   staff, each note appears to be equidistant from the preceding or
between E and F and between   following note. In this the staff is deceptive; for between the notes
B and C; whole steps occur   E and F and also B and C there is a *half step,* whereas between all
between the others.)   other adjacent notes there is a *whole step.*

On the staff, the intervals between all adjacent
notes (G–A, A–B, B–C, etc.) are the same size. (True/

False) _____

E (and) F B (and) C	2.55 On the staff, half steps occur between the notes _____ and _____ and between the notes _____ and _____.
whole	2.56 When notes are placed on the staff in alphabetical sequence (either ascending or descending), the succession is said to be STEPWISE or DIATONIC. In a _stepwise_ (or _diatonic_) succession of notes (with no accidentals [alterations]), some intervals will be half steps and some will be _____ steps.
half	2.57 The interval between E and F is a _____ step.
whole	2.58 The interval between A and B is a _____ step.
half	2.59 The interval between B and C is a _____ step.
whole	2.60 The interval between F and G is a _____ step.
whole	2.61 The interval between G and A is a _____ step.
False _(It is a whole step.)_	2.62 The interval between C and D is a half step. (True/False) _____
True	2.63 The interval between D and E is a whole step. (True/False) _____

stepwise (or diatonic)	2.64 When a succession of notes proceeds *alphabetically* (either ascending or descending), the movement is said to be _____.
Yes *(All are whole steps.)*	2.65 Are all the intervals below the same size? _____
	2.66 Indicate where the *half steps* occur. *(Use the sign ⌒ between the proper notes.)*
	2.67 Indicate where the *half steps* occur. *(Use the sign ⌒ between the proper notes.)*
	2.68 Indicate where the *half steps* occur. *(Use the sign ⌒ between the proper notes.)*
	2.69 Indicate where the *half steps* occur. *(Use the sign ⌒ between the proper notes.)*

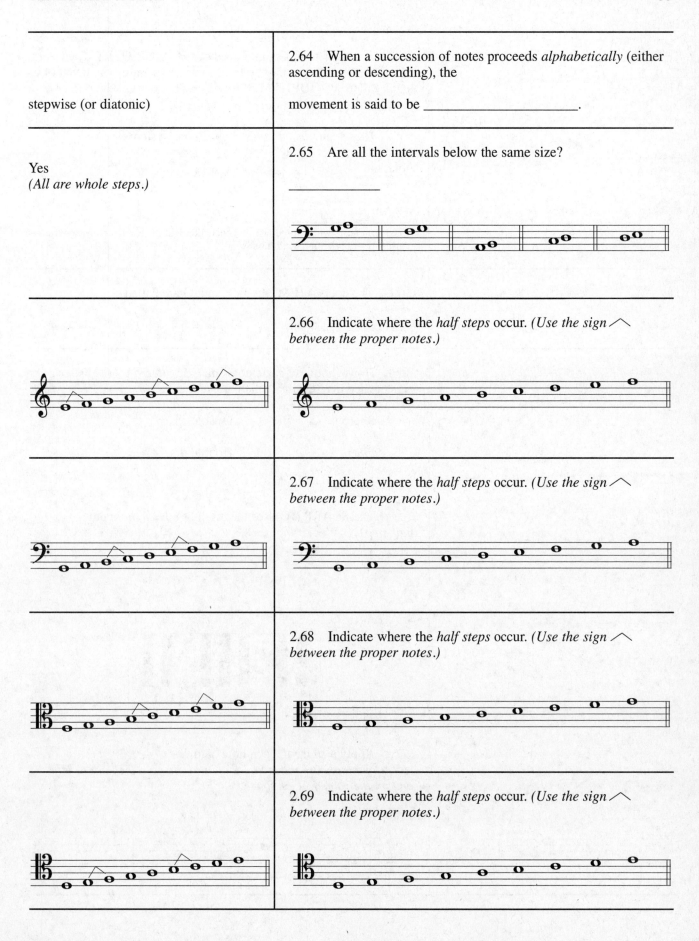

2.70   All notes to this point have been BASIC NOTES. The term *basic** is used in this book to refer to notes that are not affected by signs called ACCIDENTALS. *Basic notes* occur as white notes on the piano keyboard.

How many *basic notes* occur in our system of

notation? _____

Seven
(These are A, B, C, D, E, F, and G.)

_____
* The term *basic* will be used later in connection with scales, intervals, and triads consisting of basic (unaltered) notes.

2.71   The notes A, B, C, D, E, F, and G are called

_____ notes.

basic

2.72   However, these basic notes may be *altered* by the use of signs called *accidentals,* which are shown below.

Sharp	♯	Double sharp	𝄪
Flat	♭	Double flat	♭♭
Natural	♮		

The SHARP (♯) raises the pitch of a *basic note* **one half step.**

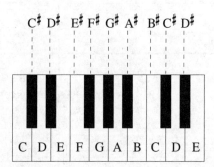

Apply a *sharp* to each note below.
(All accidentals are placed to the left of the note they are to affect and on the same line or space.)

2.73   The DOUBLE SHARP (✕) raises a *basic note* **two** *half steps*.

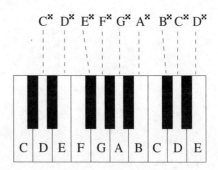

Apply a *double sharp* to each note.

2.74   The FLAT (♭) lowers the pitch of a *basic note* **one** *half step*.

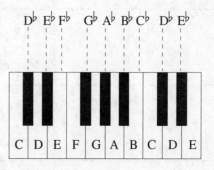

Apply a *flat* to each note.

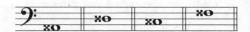

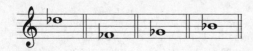

2.75   The DOUBLE FLAT (𝄫) lowers the pitch of a *basic note* **two** *half steps*.

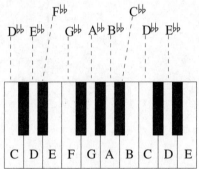

Apply a *double flat* to each note.

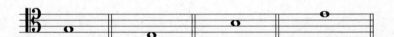

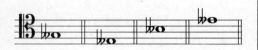

2.76   The NATURAL (♮) cancels a previous accidental. (The result is a basic note.)
      Apply a *natural* to the *second* note in each case.

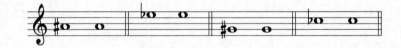

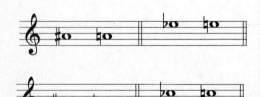

2.77   The *sharp* (♯) raises the pitch of a basic note

by the interval of a _____ step.

half

2.78   The *flat* (♭) lowers the pitch of a basic note by

the interval of a _____ step.

half

2.79   The *natural* (♮) has no effect upon a basic note unless the note previously has been affected by another accidental or by a sharp or a flat in the key signature.*

(True/False) _____

True

---

* The key signature consists of a group of sharps and flats placed immediately after the clef sign on each line of music. For instance, a B♭ in the key signature causes all Bs in the composition to be lowered to B♭. Key signatures are studied in detail in Chapter 10.0.

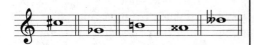

2.80   Notes affected by accidentals are called A-*flat*, D-*sharp*, D-*double flat*, G-*sharp*, E-*natural*, and so on.
     Write the notes as directed. **Remember: The accidental is placed to the *left* of the note it is to affect.**

(In all answers such as this, the note may be written an octave higher or lower than shown.)

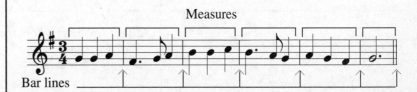

2.81   Vertical lines drawn through the five lines of the staff are called BAR LINES. These lines divide the music into MEASURES.

Accidentals remain in effect throughout the *measure* in which they occur, but they are cancelled by a *bar line*.

If an accidental is to be cancelled *within* a

The natural (♮)

measure, what sign is used? _____

2.82   The TIE is a curved line that connects two notes of the same pitch. It is used to prolong the duration of a note.

When a note that has been affected by an accidental is *tied* across a bar line, the accidental remains in effect for the duration of the *tied* note.

Accidentals remain in effect during the measure in which they occur or when the altered note is

_____ across a bar line.

tied

Note: A curved line, similar to the tie and called a SLUR, is also used in musical notation to indicate phrasing or performance technique. (*See Bibliography, Musical Notation*, p. 381.)

2.83   Accidentals other than the sharps or flats of the key signature are cancelled automatically by

bar

the _____ line.

2.84   An altered note may be extended into the next

tie

measure by means of the _____.

2.85   If a *double sharp* is to be converted later in the same measure to a sharp, the desired accidental is then applied.*

This practice also applies to the *double flat*.

If a natural plus a sharp appears before a note, which accidental actually applies? (The first/The

The second

second) _____

* Older printed music may differ with this practice in that a natural sign may be used to cancel a double sharp, with the desired accidental (sharp signs only, not flats) then applied.

2.86   Although some composers and arrangers are not consistent, accidentals are most commonly interpreted as affecting only notes on the particular line or space on which they are written, not notes in other octaves.

(1)   (2)   (3)   (4)   (5)

Since no sharp appears on the fourth line in the example above, the third note should be played as a D-*natural*.

G-natural

What is the pitch of the fifth note? _____

2.87   Write the name of each note. *(Use the proper accidental sign in responding.)*

E♭, C♯, G♮, B♭♭, D✕

___   ___   ___   ___   ___

2.88   When accidentals are applied so that two or more basic notes represent the same pitch, these notes are said to be ENHARMONIC (or enharmonically related). *Enharmonic* notes are written differently but have the

pitch

same _____.

2.89 Examples of *enharmonic* notes are shown below.

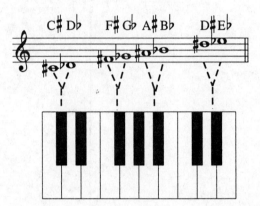

Two basic notes a whole step apart can be made *enharmonic* by applying a flat to the upper note and a

sharp

_____ to the lower note.

2.90 Other examples of *enharmonic* notes are shown below.

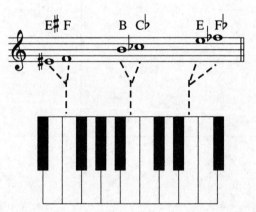

Two basic notes separated by a half step can be made *enharmonic* either by raising the lower note a half step

lowering

or by _____ the upper note a half step.

2.91   Still other examples of enharmonic notes are shown below.

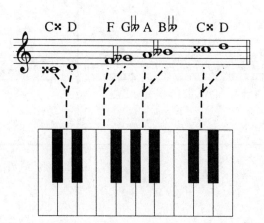

      Write the two accidentals that are capable of altering the pitch of a tone by the interval of a whole

step. _____ _____

x 𝄫

2.92   Three basic notes can be made enharmonically related, as written below.

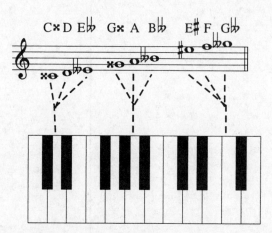

      Notes that sound the same but are written

differently are said to be _____.

enharmonic

2.93 Write an *enharmonic* equivalent for each note.

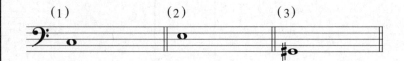

B♯ D♭♭   D𝄪 F♭   A♭

2.94 Write an *enharmonic* equivalent for each note.

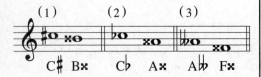

C♯ B𝄪   C♭ A𝄪   A♭♭ F𝄪

2.95 Half steps occur between the notes E and F and the notes B and C. By the use of accidentals, half steps can be written between other notes as well.

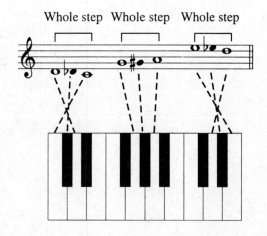

Whole step Whole step Whole step

Successions of notes moving exclusively in half steps are said to be CHROMATIC. A *chromatic* succession of

half   notes moves entirely in _____ steps.

2.96   There is a difference between DIATONIC and
CHROMATIC half steps.
      A *diatonic* half step uses **two** basic notes (notes appearing
on consecutive lines and spaces).
      A *chromatic* half step uses only **one** basic note (notes
appearing on the same line or space).

DIATONIC HALF STEPS   CHROMATIC HALF STEPS

      Is the interval D up to D-sharp a *diatonic* or a

chromatic half step? _____

chromatic

2.97   Is the interval D up to E-flat a *diatonic* or a

chromatic half step? _____

diatonic

2.98   Write a *diatonic* half step above F.

2.99   Write a *chromatic* half step above F.

2.100 Are *diatonic* and *chromatic* half steps the

same size? _____

Yes
(They are all half steps.)

2.101 Below is an example of a CHROMATIC SCALE.*

The notation of *chromatic scales* may vary according to the keys in which they occur. The simplest notation, however, results if sharps are used for notes inflected upward and flats are used for notes inflected downward. Observe in the example above that E and B are the only basic notes that are unaffected by accidentals. This is because the intervals between E and F and between B and

half

C are _____ steps.

_____
* A scale consists of the tones contained in one octave arranged in consecutive series. Scales are studied in detail in Chapters 7.0, 8.0, and 9.0.

2.102 Below is another example of a *chromatic scale*.

Flats are usually used for notes inflected downward. Observe that F and C are the only basic notes unaffected by accidentals. This is because there is a

B (and) C

half step between the notes _____ and _____

E (and) F

and the notes _____ and _____.

2.103 Write a *chromatic scale* ascending from C to C.
(*Use only sharps.*)

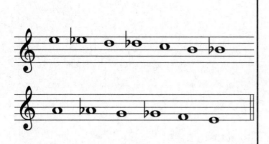

2.104 Write a *chromatic scale* descending from E to E. *(Use only flats.)*

---

chromatic

2.105 A scale consisting entirely of half steps is

called a _____ scale.

Expository Frame

2.106 Sometimes it is necessary to refer to a note in a specific octave. For this purpose, the various octaves are given special designations. The example below shows the octaves upward from *middle C*. **Note the use of lowercase letters.**

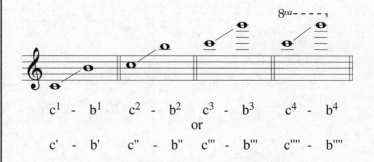

c^1 - b^1 c^2 - b^2 c^3 - b^3 c^4 - b^4
or
c' - b'   c" - b"   c'" - b'"   c'"' - b'"'

All the notes from *middle C* up through the next B are included in the ONE-LINE OCTAVE. For higher octaves, the terms TWO-LINE OCTAVE, THREE-LINE OCTAVE, and FOUR-LINE OCTAVE are used. You may refer to a note such as g^2 as either "two-line g" or "g two," or use a numbered or MIDI designation suitable for a particular performance context.*

(No response required.)

---

* Unfortunately, octave designations are not standardized; so be alert to the terms and symbols used by other writers, as well as to designations developed in musical computer applications such as MIDI (Musical Instrument Digital Interface). (*See Appendix A*, Music Theory Summary, The Notation of Pitch, pp. 353–354, for several complete octave charts).

2.107 Indicate the octave into which each note falls. *(Use the terms one-line, two-line, etc.)*

(1) two-line

(2) three-line

(3) one-line

(1) _____ octave

(2) _____ octave

(3) _____ octave

2.108 Write the notes as indicated. *(Use the ottava sign to avoid excessive ledger lines.)*

a³   b♭¹   f♯²

2.109 Continue as in the preceding frame.

c♯⁴   g♯²   d¹

2.110 The one-line octave begins on middle C.

True

(True/False) _____

2.111 The first two octaves below middle C are shown below.

b - c   B - C

The first octave below middle C is called the SMALL OCTAVE, and lowercase letters are used; the second is called the GREAT OCTAVE, and capital letters are used.

two

The note *great A* is _____ octaves below *a¹*.

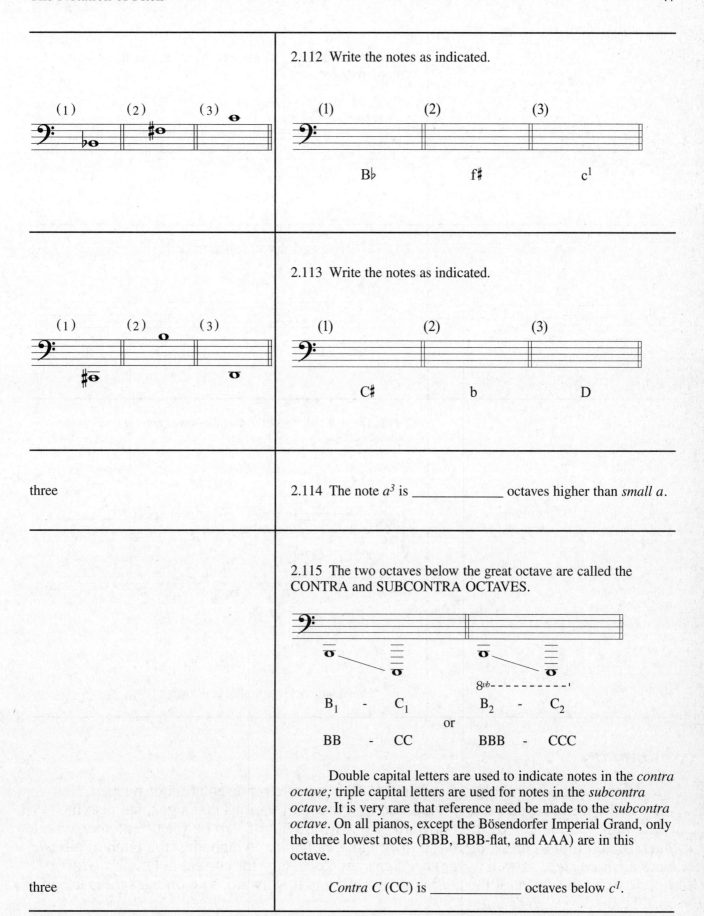

2.112 Write the notes as indicated.

(1)   (2)   (3)

B♭   f♯   c¹

2.113 Write the notes as indicated.

(1)   (2)   (3)

C♯   b   D

three

2.114 The note *a³* is _____ octaves higher than *small a*.

2.115 The two octaves below the great octave are called the CONTRA and SUBCONTRA OCTAVES.

B₁ - C₁   B₂ - C₂
or
BB - CC   BBB - CCC

Double capital letters are used to indicate notes in the *contra octave;* triple capital letters are used for notes in the *subcontra octave*. It is very rare that reference need be made to the *subcontra octave*. On all pianos, except the Bösendorfer Imperial Grand, only the three lowest notes (BBB, BBB-flat, and AAA) are in this octave.

three

Contra C (CC) is _____ octaves below *c¹*.

2.116 Write the notes as indicated. *(Use the ottava sign to avoid excessive ledger lines.)*

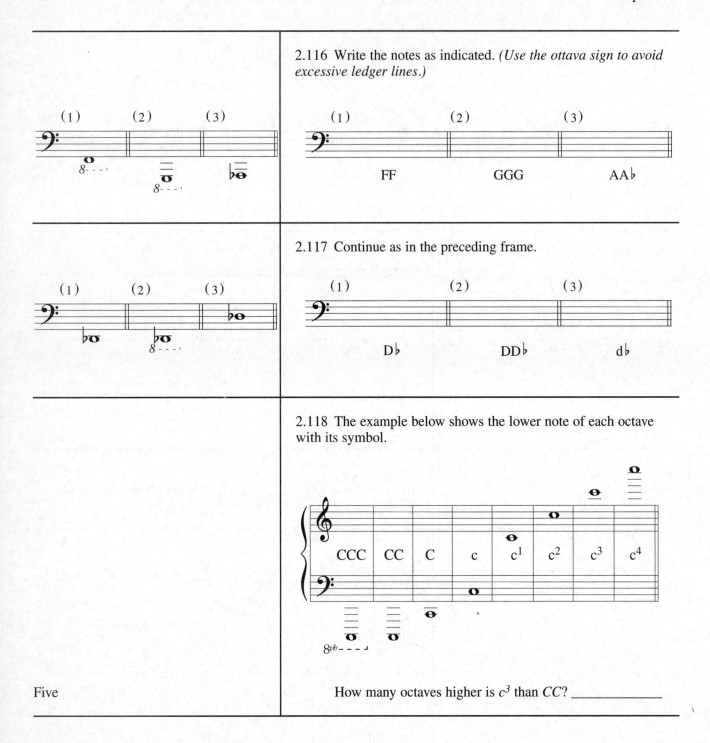

2.117 Continue as in the preceding frame.

2.118 The example below shows the lower note of each octave with its symbol.

Five

How many octaves higher is c^3 than CC? _____

Summary

Many special symbols are required for the specific representation of pitches. Not only is the meaning of the *staff* modified by the use of various *clef* signs, but also the *basic notes* are inflected either upward or downward a *half step* by the use of *sharps* and *flats*. In addition to these, *double sharps* and *double flats,* which alter the pitch of a *basic note* a *whole step,* as well as *natural* signs, are necessary for correct notation. *Ledger lines* extend the range of the *staff* both upward and downward. The *ottava* sign is used to avoid excessive *ledger lines*.

Mastery Frames

	2–1 Indicate the proper name for each clef sign.

(1) Treble   (frame 2.7)

(2) Bass   (2.11)

(3) Alto   (2.18–2.20)

(4) Tenor   (2.18–2.20)

2–2   Identify each note.

E   F   C   A

(2.6–2.10)

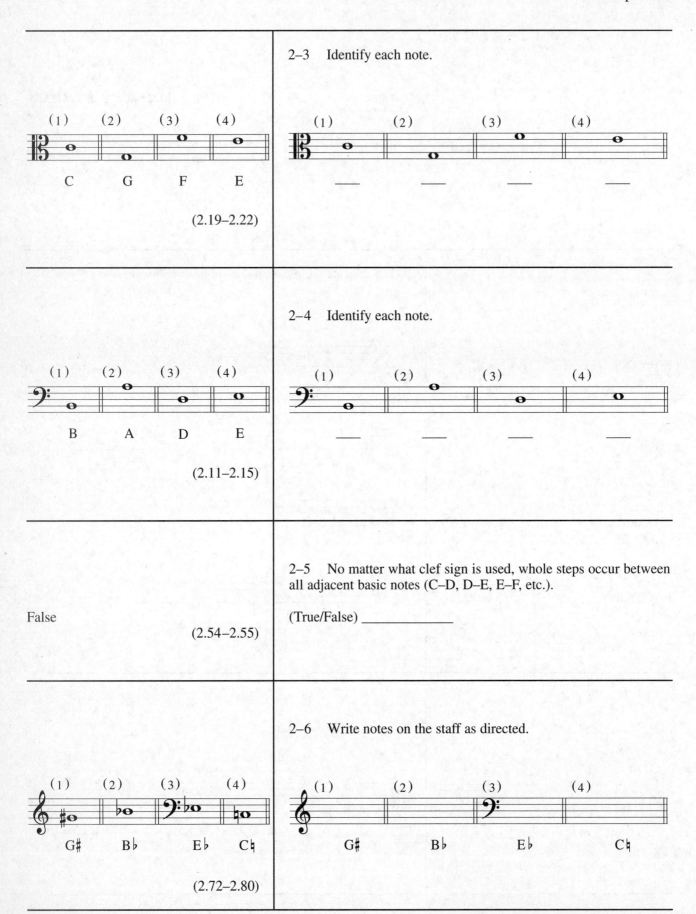

(1)   (2)   (3)   (4)

C   G   F   E

(2.19–2.22)

2–3   Identify each note.

(1)   (2)   (3)   (4)

___   ___   ___   ___

(1)   (2)   (3)   (4)

B   A   D   E

(2.11–2.15)

2–4   Identify each note.

(1)   (2)   (3)   (4)

___   ___   ___   ___

False

(2.54–2.55)

2–5   No matter what clef sign is used, whole steps occur between all adjacent basic notes (C–D, D–E, E–F, etc.).

(True/False) _____

2–6   Write notes on the staff as directed.

(1)   (2)   (3)   (4)

G♯   B♭   E♭   C♮

(2.72–2.80)

(1)   (2)   (3)   (4)

G♯   B♭   E♭   C♮

(1) *(incorrect)*   (2.73)

(2) ✔   (2.79)

(3) ✔   (2.74)

(4) *(incorrect)*

                                     (2.86)

2–7   Check the correct statements.

(1)   A double sharp lowers the pitch of a basic note

      by a whole step. _____

(2)   The natural always produces a basic note.

      _____

(3)   A flat lowers a basic note by a half step.

      _____

(4)   An accidental within a measure affects all such

      notes regardless of the octave. _____

False *(The notes in (2) are
not enharmonic.)*

                                     (2.88–2.94)

2–8   Enharmonic equivalents are shown in each

example. (True/False) _____

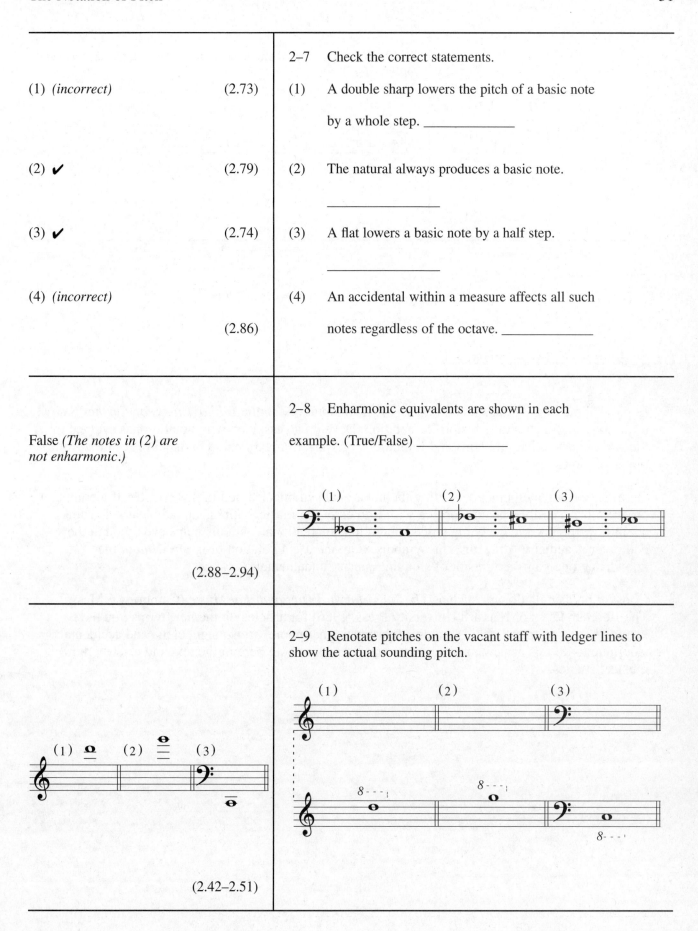

                                     (2.42–2.51)

2–9   Renotate pitches on the vacant staff with ledger lines to
show the actual sounding pitch.

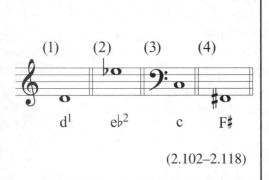

(2.102–2.118)

2–10   Write the precise pitches that are indicated. *(Do not use the ottava sign.)*

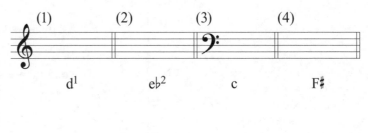

Supplementary Activities

1.   Explore some of the books listed under "Musical Notation" in the *Bibliography for Further Study* to discover more about the history of notation. Develop an essay on why notation has evolved in the way it has—what problems and limitations of Western notational systems have resulted from this evolution?

2.   On manuscript paper, practice writing the notational symbols learned in this chapter. If a computer program is accessible, begin working with it to enter the music symbols already learned. Think about how the knowledge being gained about music notational symbols helps even though the computer is actually "drawing" the symbols. Can one use a notation program *without* the knowledge one gains as a result of studying music fundamentals?

3.   Consult a music dictionary such as *The New Harvard Dictionary of Music* (Cambridge, Mass.: The Belknap Press of Harvard University Press, 1986) for articles on the new terms you have learned in this chapter, such as diatonic, chromatic, harmonic, *ottava* sign, clefs, and accidentals. Continue to do this as new musical terms are discovered both here in the text and elsewhere in musical studies.

Supplementary Assignments

ASSIGNMENT 2–1   Name: _____

1. The lines and spaces of the staff are numbered with the (highest/lowest) _____

   in each case being given the number 1.

2. Name the specific note that each clef identifies.

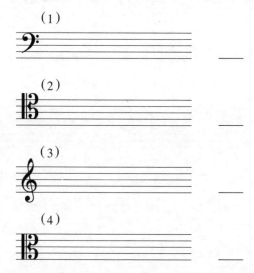

(1)

___

(2)

___

(3)

___

(4)

___

3. Name the notes on the lines and spaces of the treble clef.

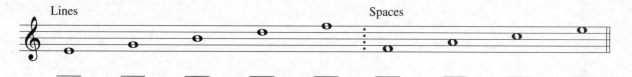

4. Name the notes on the lines and spaces of the bass clef.

5. Name the notes on the lines and spaces of the tenor clef.

6. Name the notes on the lines and spaces of the alto clef.

7. Notate middle C on each clef.

(1)   (2)   (3)   (4)

8. Renotate the notes on the treble clef so they will sound the same (ledger lines are needed in some cases).

9. Renotate the notes an octave higher. Do not use the *ottava* sign.

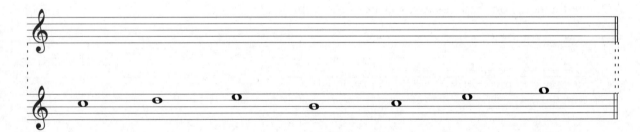

10. Use the *ottava* sign to indicate that the notes are to sound one octave higher.

11. Use the *ottava* sign to indicate that the notes are to sound one octave lower.

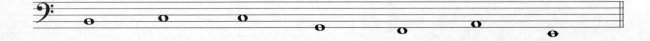

ASSIGNMENT 2–2   Name: _____

1.   Use the sign ⌃ to show where half steps occur in each example.

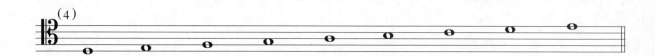

2.   Draw lines to connect each accidental with the proper explanation.

a. ♯   • Cancels a previous accidental
b. ♭   • Raises a basic note a whole step
c. ♮   • Lowers a basic note a whole step
d. ♭♭   • Raises a basic note a half step
e. ×   • Lowers a basic note a half step

3.   Notate an enharmonic equivalent for each note.

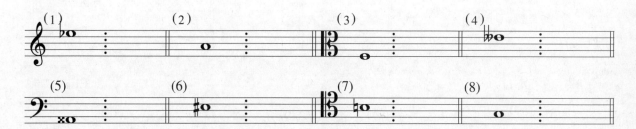

4.   Notate a *chromatic* half step above each note.

5.   Notate a *diatonic* half step below each note.

6.   Notate chromatic scales as indicated.

7.   Notate notes in designated octaves on the grand staff as directed.

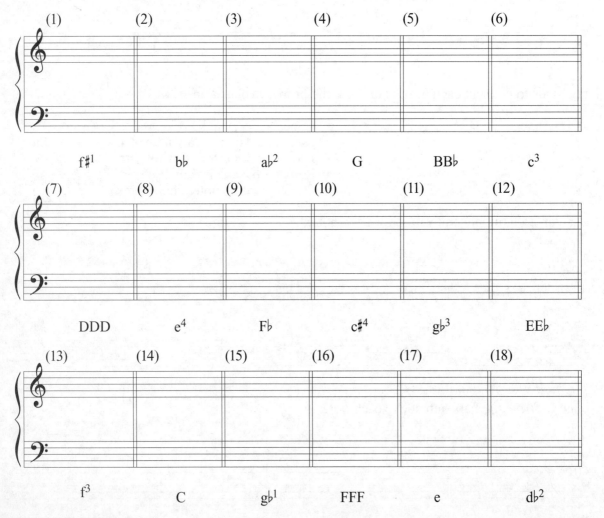

Ear-Training Activities

1. Notes written on the staff in alphabetical sequence (A–G) produce a series of half or whole steps. It is essential that the difference between these two intervals be recognized. The staff produces two half steps and five whole steps. The clef sign determines where the half steps occur.

Sing the notes below using each of the clefs indicated in turn. *(Check pitches at a keyboard.)*

2. Sing the following exercises noting the differences between half and whole steps.

(Sing with *la*.)

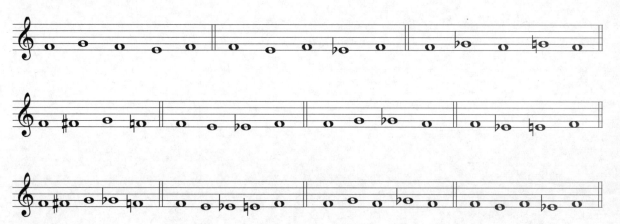

The preceding exercises may be sung on any pitch provided the half- and whole-step relationships are the same.

3. Sing chromatic intervals as in the following:

4. Sing, whistle, or "think" half and whole steps in various, invented patterns.

5. Either by yourself or with a partner, play short half- and whole-step patterns on a keyboard or other instrument and then sing them back to yourself or to your partner. (Use patterns shown in exercises 2 and 3 on the preceding page as models, but also invent your own.) As a further step, try to write the notes down. At this point, make sure half or whole steps are specifically and correctly identified, irregardless of specific pitch name. Accuracy in identifying the half- and whole-step patterns is the important thing. (If in a class, an instructor may do these kinds of exercises as a group.)

6. Begin working with one of the several ear-training or sight-singing texts or programs listed under ear training/sight singing in *Bibliography for Further Study*. As mentioned earlier, many programs are available via the Internet.

Chapter 3.0
Time Classification

...rt; that is, it takes place over a period of time. In addition to
...l of various patterns of duration that combine and interact to
...n time. The various aspects of the organization of time
...usic called rhythm. The basis for rhythm is the beat—a
...s (periodic repetitions) that divides a period of time into equal
...ration are possible, and such beats are often exploited by
...rs. Most Western music of the eighteenth and nineteenth
...ce" period), however, utilizes regular beats. In this book, the
...to the rhythmic practices of the common practice period found
... of Western art music.

	3.1　In most music, pulsations called BEATS divide time into regular units of duration. *Beats* themselves have little expressive value, but additional interest results if some are stressed more strongly than others. 　　*Beats* may show different degrees of ＿＿＿＿＿＿.
No	3.2　The principle of tension and relaxation is brought into play when *beats* are given different degrees of stress. Does the degree of stress affect the duration of the *beat*? ＿＿＿＿＿
stress	3.3　Patterns of stress are known as METER. *Meter* is the pattern produced by beats of varying degrees of ＿＿＿＿＿.
meter	3.4　The pattern that results from beats of differing degrees of stress is called the ＿＿＿＿＿.

beats

3.5   Stressed beats are called STRONG; unstressed beats are called WEAK. The *meter* results from patterns of

strong and *weak* _____.

3.6   The simplest pattern of stresses possible is an alternation of *strong* and *weak* beats.

STRESS PATTERN: >   U   >   U   >   U
                                                                    (continuing)

BEATS: 1   2   1   2   1   2

> =   a *strong* beat

U =   a *weak* beat

Since each pattern (> U) consists of *two* beats, the term DUPLE METER is used. In a *duple* pattern the beat is organized into a sequence of one strong and one

weak

_____ pulsation.

Tap this pattern and stress each first beat as indicated. Notice your response to this meter.

3.7   The simplest possible pattern of stresses results from an alternation of *strong* and *weak* beats. This pattern is

duple

called _____ meter.

3.8   Another simple pattern results when every third pulse is stressed.

STRESS PATTERNS: **>**   U   U   **>**   U   U

                                                              (continuing)

BEATS: 1   2   3   1   2   3

Since each pattern (**>** U U) consists of *three* beats, the term TRIPLE METER is used. A *strong-weak-weak* succession of pulsations results in an organization known as

_____ meter.

Tap this pattern and stress each first beat as indicated. Compare the effect of this meter with that of the meter discussed in frame 3.6.

triple

3.9   In *triple meter* the beat is organized into a

sequence of one strong and _____ weak beats.

two

3.10   Indicate the patterns of pulsations for *duple* and *triple* meter. (*Use the signs* **>** *and* U.)

Duple meter: _____

Triple meter: _____

Duple: **>** U (etc.)

Triple: **>** U U (etc.)

strong-weak-weak	3.11 *Duple meter* and *triple meter* are the two fundamental patterns produced by beats of varying degrees of stress. *Duple meter* is a succession of strong-weak beats; *triple meter* is a series of _____-_____-_____ beats.
duple	3.12 Other extended patterns result from combinations of duple and triple patterns. QUADRUPLE METER is a combination of two duple patterns in which the first beat is stressed more strongly than the third. 　　　　　┌─────── QUADRUPLE METER ───────┐ 　　┌─── Duple ───┐ ┌─── Duple ───┐ 　　>　　　　U　　　　>　　　　U 　　1　　　　2　　　　3　　　　4 　　　A four-beat pattern results from a combination of two _____ patterns.
The first	3.13 In *quadruple meter* both the first and the third beats are strong. Which, however, is the stronger? _____
quadruple	3.14 A combination of two duple patterns results in _____ meter.
2 (and) 4	3.15 Which are the weak beats in quadruple meter? _____ and _____.
2 (and) 3	3.16 Which are the weak beats in triple meter? _____ and _____.

3.17   A five-beat pattern is called QUINTUPLE METER. This results from a combination of a *duple* and a *triple* pattern.

```
┌─────────────────────── QUINTUPLE METER ───────────────────────┐
┌──────── Duple ────────┐  ┌──────────── Triple ────────────────┐
>           U           >           U           U
1           2           3           4           5
```

or

```
┌─────────────────────── QUINTUPLE METER ───────────────────────┐
┌──────────── Triple ────────────┐  ┌──────── Duple ────────┐
>           U           U           >           U
1           2           3           4           5
```

Either the duple or the triple pattern may come first, but in either case the first stressed beat (1) is the strongest.

A five-beat pattern results when a duple and

triple

a _____ pattern are combined.

3.18   A pattern of **> U > U U** or **> U U > U** is

quintuple

called _____ meter.

3.19   There are three strong beats in quintuple

False
(There are two strong beats.)

meter. (True/False) _____

3.20   How many weak beats occur in *quintuple meter*?

Three

_____

3.21   *Quintuple meter* is a combination of a

duple

triple pattern and a _____ pattern.

> U > U U or
> U U > U

3.22 Indicate the pattern of beats known as quintuple meter. *(Use the signs > and U.)*

_____

3.23 The process of combining duple and triple stress patterns can be carried on to include six-beat patterns, seven-beat patterns,* and so forth; but in actual musical experiences, the ear tends to reject the larger patterns and focus instead on smaller, repeated organizations. Thus a six-beat pattern would probably be heard as a combination of two three-beat patterns, and a seven-beat pattern as a combination of a four-beat and a three-beat pattern (or the reverse).

(1) duple

(2) triple
(any order)

What are the two basic meters that are

combined to produce more complex ones? (1)_____;

and (2)_____.

_____

* Although not very common, musical situations involving these patterns may be found, in which case the terms SEXTUPLE and SEPTUPLE are appropriate.

---

quadruple

3.24 The stress pattern (> U > U) is called

_____ meter.

---

duple

3.25 The stress pattern (> U) is called

_____ meter.

---

triple

3.26 The stress pattern (> U U) is called

_____   meter.

beats	3.27 The terms *duple, triple, quadruple,* and *quintuple* refer to the number of _____ in each stress pattern.
Three	3.28 Each stress pattern constitutes a MEASURE. A *measure* in triple meter consists of how many beats? _____
beats	3.29 *Measures* vary in length according to the number of _____ in each stress pattern.
subdivided	3.30 The rhythmic interest of a composition would be slight indeed if the duration of all tones should coincide with the beat. Actually, a single beat may contain two, three, four, five, or more tones. Usually, beats are *divided* normally into two or three parts, or *subdivided* normally into four or six parts.* The beat itself is the most elementary organization of time possible. Establishing a meter through patterns of stress increases the musical value of the beat. A higher level of rhythmic complexity results from dividing the beat into two or three equal parts. Still greater rhythmic interest is obtained if the beat is _____ into four or six parts.† ——————————— * Irregular groups of notes are presented in Chapter 4.0, frames 4.60–4.64. † One tends to hear smaller groups of twos or threes first, but it is also possible to perceive larger successions of the smaller groups, depending on stress patterns emphasized by the composer. In this way rhythm and rhythmic patterns become multidimensional. This concept may suggest further study later on in music studies.

3.31   Concentration will now be on two basic types of rhythmic division that are determined by how beats are normally divided.

If beats are divided consistently into *two* equal parts, the term SIMPLE TIME is used; if beats are divided consistently into *three* equal parts, the term COMPOUND TIME is used.

The terms *simple time* and *compound time* refer

beats   to the manner in which _____ are divided.

3.32   In *simple time* beats are divided normally

Two   into how many equal parts? _____

3.33   If beats are divided consistently into *three* equal

compound   parts, the term _____ time is used.

---

two (or)   3.34   Beats may be divided into either _____ or

three   _____ equal parts.

3.35   The terms *duple, triple, quadruple,* and *quintuple* refer to the number of beats per measure, whereas the terms *simple* and *compound* refer to the manner in which beats

divided   normally are _____.

3.36   A TIME CLASSIFICATION identifies the organization of the meter and indicates the *normal division of the beat.*

In *duple meter,* the stress pattern consists of two beats (**>** U). If each beat is divided into *two* equal parts, the time classification is DUPLE-SIMPLE.

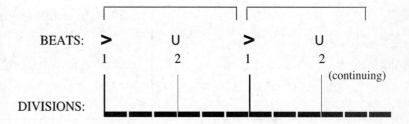

The term *duple-simple* means that there are *two* beats per measure and each *beat* is divided into

two

_____ equal parts.

3.37   If the beats in duple meter are divided into *three* equal parts, the time classification is DUPLE-COMPOUND.

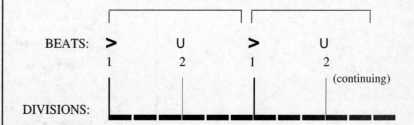

The term *duple-compound* means that there are *two* beats per measure and each *beat* is divided

three

into _____ equal parts.

two

3.38   The term *simple time* means that beats are

normally divided into _____ equal parts.

---

three

3.39   The term *compound time* means that beats are

normally divided into _____ equal parts.

3.40   Music in simple time affects us quite differently than does music in compound time.

Sing the song *Yankee Doodle* as notated below.

Oh,   Yan - kee   Doo - dle came to   town   A -

rid - ing   on   a   po - ny,   He

stuck   a   feath - er   in   his   hat   And

called   it   mac - a   -   ro   -   ni.

Since the beats are divided consistently into *two* equal parts,

simple

this is an example of duple- _____ time.

3.41 Sing the song *Three Blind Mice* as notated below. **Pay careful attention to the relative *lengths* of the dashes and how beats are divided.**

> \>   U   \>   U

Three   blind   mice. _____

> \>   U   \>   U

Three   blind   mice. _____

> \>   U   \>   U

See   how   they   run. _____

> \>   U   \>   U

See   how   they   run. _____   They

> \>   U   \>   U

all   ran   af - ter   the   farm - er's   wife,   She

> \>   U   \>   U

cut off their tails with a   carv - ing   knife,   Did

> \>   U   \>   U

ev - er   you   see   such   a   sight in   your   life   As

> \>   U   \>   U

Three   blind   mice? _____

compound

        This song is an example of duple- _____ time, with the beats ultimately divided into *three* equal parts.

3.42   Composers often use simple time to express musical ideas that are "strong," "straightforward," or "positive." Compound time is often used for ideas of a more "flowing" or "swaying" nature. Do the songs in frames 3.40 and 3.41 demonstrate

(your opinion)

these characteristics? _____

3.43   Do simple and compound time need *always* give rise to emotional responses such as

(your opinion)

these? _____

3.44   Time classifications are interpreted as follows: The *first* part of the classification refers to the *number* of beats per measure; the *second* part indicates the *manner* in which beats are normally divided.

   Thus the time classification *duple-simple* means that there are *two* beats per measure and the *normal division* of the beat is into *two* equal parts.

   Time classifications indicate not only the *number* of *beats* per measure but also the *normal division* of

beat

the _____.

3.45   Duple-simple and duple-compound time both have *two* beats per measure; but in duple-*simple* time the beat is divided into *two* equal parts, whereas in duple-*compound* time the *beat* is divided into

three

_____ equal parts.

The number of beats per measure	3.46 What does the *first* part of a time classification indicate? _____
The normal division of the beat	3.47 What does the *second* part of a time classification indicate? _____
two	3.48 *Triple-simple* indicates: (1) *three* beats per measure; and (2) the *division* of each beat into _____ equal parts.
four	3.49 *Quadruple-compound* indicates: (1) _____ beats per measure; and (2) the *division* of each beat into *three* equal parts.
three	3.50 *Triple-compound* indicates: (1) *three* beats per measure; and (2) the *division* of each beat into _____ equal parts.
two	3.51 *Quadruple-simple* indicates: (1) *four* beats per measure; and (2) the *division* of each beat into _____ equal parts.
five	3.52 *Quintuple-simple* indicates: (1) _____ beats per measure; and (2) the *division* of each beat into *two* equal parts.

	3.53 *Duple-compound* indicates:
	(1) *two* beats per measure; and
three	(2) the *division* of each beat into _____ equal parts.
	3.54 *Duple-simple* indicates:
	(1) *two* beats per measure; and
two	(2) the *division* of each beat into _____ equal parts.
	3.55 *Quintuple-compound* indicates:
	(1) *five* beats per measure; and
three	(2) the *division* of each beat into _____ equal parts.
	3.56 If there are *two* beats per measure and each beat is divided into *two* equal parts, the time
duple-simple	classification is _____-_____.
	3.57 If there are *three* beats per measure and each beat is divided into *two* equal parts, the time
triple-simple	classification is _____-_____.
	3.58 If there are *four* beats per measure and each beat is divided into *three* equal parts, the time
quadruple-compound	classification is _____-_____.

quintuple-simple

3.59   If there are *five* beats per measure and each beat is divided into *two* equal parts, the time

classification is _____-_____.

---

quintuple-compound

3.60   If there are *five* beats per measure and each beat is divided into *three* equal parts, the time

classification is _____-_____.

---

quadruple-simple

3.61   If there are *four* beats per measure and each beat is divided into *two* equal parts, the time

classification is _____-_____.

---

triple-compound

3.62   If there are *three* beats per measure and each beat is divided into *three* equal parts, the time

classification is _____-_____.

---

duple-compound

3.63   If there are *two* beats per measure and each beat is divided into *three* equal parts, the time

classification is _____-_____.

True

3.64   The terms *duple*, *triple*, *quadruple*, and *quintuple* refer to the number of beats per measure.

(True/False) _____

---

how each beat
is divided

3.65   To what do the terms *simple* and *compound*

refer? _____

beat	3.66 The regularly recurring pulse of music is called the _____.
first	3.67 The number of beats per measure is expressed by the (first/second) _____ part of the time classification.
simple (and) compound	3.68 The beat can be divided into *two* or *three* equal parts. This *division* is expressed by the terms _____ and _____.

3.69   The natural division of the beat in *simple* time is into *two* equal parts. The division of the beat into *three* equal parts in simple time is called a BORROWED DIVISION (or *triplet*).

   Tap (or say with the syllable* ta) *the divisions expressed in the line notation below.

SIMPLE TIME

	>	U
BEAT:	1	2
DIVISION:	▬ ▬	▬ ▬
BORROWED DIVISION:	▬ ▬ ▬	▬ ▬ ▬

   The *borrowed division* in *simple* time is sometimes

triplet	called a _____.
borrowed	3.70 *"Triplet"* is another name for a _____ division.

3.71   The natural division of the beat in *compound* time is into *three* equal parts. The division of the beat into *two* equal parts in *compound* time is called a BORROWED DIVISION (or *duplet*).

Tap (or say with the syllable ta) the divisions expressed in the line notation below.

COMPOUND TIME

		>		U	
BEAT:		1		2	

DIVISION:

BORROWED DIVISION:

The *borrowed division* in *compound* time is

two   a division of the beat into _____ equal parts.

3.72   The term *borrowed division* refers to the use of a division in *simple* time that is normal in *compound* time or vice versa. The division is literally "borrowed" from one for use in the other.

The borrowed division in *simple* time is a

three   division of the beat into _____ equal parts.

3.73   Is the division of the beat into *two* equal parts

Yes   a natural division in *simple* time? _____

3.74   Is the division of the beat into *two* equal parts

No
*(This is a borrowed
division or duplet.)*   a natural division in *compound* time? _____

3.75   Is the division of the beat into *three* equal parts

No
*(This is a borrowed
division or triplet.)*   a natural division in *simple* time? _____

simple	3.76 In *simple time* the beat *sub*divides into *four* equal parts. Four is the normal subdivision of the beat in _____ time.
compound	3.77 In *compound time* the beat *sub*divides into *six* equal parts. Six is the normal subdivision of the beat in _____ time.
Four	3.78 What is the natural subdivision of the beat in simple time? _____
Six	3.79 What is the natural subdivision of the beat in compound time? _____
False *(The term* compound time *refers to the division of the beat into three equal parts, not to the number of beats per measure.)*	3.80 The term *compound time* means that there are three beats per measure. (True/False) _____
True	3.81 The term *duple* refers to a meter that has two beats per measure. (True/False) _____

2	3.82 What is the natural division of the beat in simple time? (2, 3, 4, 6) _____
3	3.83 What is the natural division of the beat in compound time? (2, 3, 4, 6) _____
4	3.84 What is the natural subdivision of the beat in simple time? (2, 3, 4, 6) _____
6	3.85 What is the natural subdivision of the beat in compound time? (2, 3, 4, 6) _____
3	3.86 In simple time a borrowed division divides the beat into how many parts? (2, 3, 4, 6) _____
2	3.87 In compound time a borrowed division divides the beat into how many parts? (2, 3, 4, 6) _____
True	3.88 The triplet is the same as a borrowed division in simple time. (True/False) _____
True	3.89 The duplet is the same as a borrowed division in compound time. (True/False) _____

Summary

Time is organized on various levels of complexity. The simplest is the series of pulsations called the *beat*. Next is *meter,* which results from *patterns of stress* imposed on the *beat*. The more common meters are *duple, triple, quadruple,* and *quintuple,* depending on the number of beats between each primary stress. The next level of rhythmic organization is the result of dividing beats into either *two* or *three* parts. The term *simple time* refers to the *division* of the *beat* into *two* equal parts; the term *compound time* refers to the *division* of the *beat* into *three* equal parts. *Borrowed divisions* occur when the *normal division* in *compound* time is used in *simple* time or vice versa. Beats *subdivide* normally into *four* parts in *simple* time and *six* parts in *compound* time.

Mastery Frames

beat (frame 3.1)	3–1 The pulse that divides time into equal durations is called the _____.
True (3.3–3.5)	3–2 *Meter* is the term that refers to patterns of stress applied to beats. (True/False) _____
duple (3.6–3.7)	3–3 When the first of each group of two beats is stressed, the result is _____ meter.
triple (3.8–3.11)	3–4 When the first of each group of three beats is stressed, the result is _____ meter.
divided (3.31–3.35)	3–5 The terms *simple* and *compound* refer to how beats are normally _____.
(1) 2 (2) 3 (3.31–3.35)	3–6 Indicate the number of divisions in each case. (1) Simple time _____ (2) Compound time _____
two (3.36)	3–7 The time classification duple-simple means that there are _____ beats per measure, and the beat is normally divided into two equal parts.

	Beats	Divisions
(1)	3	3
(2)	4	2
(3)	5	3

(3.44–3.68)

3–8   Supply the missing information.

Time Classification	Beats per Measure	Number of Divisions
(1) Triple-compound	_____	_____
(2) Quadruple-simple	_____	_____
(3) Quintuple-compound	_____	_____

---

compound

(3.69–3.70)

3–9   The triplet is a division of the beat that is borrowed

from (simple/compound) _____ time.

True

(3.69–3.75)

3–10   Borrowed divisions occur in both simple and

compound meters. (True/False) _____

Supplementary Activities

1. Utilizing other melodies or "tunes" that are known, try to create other "beat" or rhythmic scores (see frames 3.40–3.41) to determine whether they are in simple or compound time. Any time a piece of music is heard, practice determining whether it is in simple or compound time.

2. Consult *The New Harvard Dictionary of Music* for articles on meter, duration, compound meter (time), time signatures, and so on, to obtain more information on the topics covered in this chapter.

3. Find a text or a poem and practice setting it rhythmically in either simple or compound time or both; do it in a format similar to that in frames 3.40–3.41.

Supplementary Assignments

ASSIGNMENT 3–1   Name: _____

1. Use the signs > and ∪ to indicate the stress patterns indicated below. *(Sufficient beats are marked off to show recurring patterns.)*

   a. Duple |__|__|__|__|__|__|__|__|__|__|__|__|__|__|__|

   b. Triple |__|__|__|__|__|__|__|__|__|__|__|__|__|__|__|

   c. Quadruple |__|__|__|__|__|__|__|__|__|__|__|__|__|__|__|

   d. Quintuple |__|__|__|__|__|__|__|__|__|__|__|__|__|__|__|

2. Triple meter has _____ beats per measure.

3. How many strong beats are contained in one measure of quadruple meter? _____

   _____

4. In simple time the beat is normally divided into _____ equal parts.

5. In compound time the beat is normally divided into _____ equal parts.

6. The first example (a) of the time classifications that follows indicates that there are _____

   beats per measure; the second part indicates that the beat is normally divided into _____ equal parts.

7. Provide the appropriate time classification in each case.

	Beats per Measure	Number of Divisions	Time Classification
a.	2	2	_____-_____
b.	2	3	_____-_____
c.	3	2	_____-_____
d.	3	3	_____-_____
e.	4	2	_____-_____
f.	4	3	_____-_____
g.	5	2	_____-_____
h.	5	3	_____-_____

8. Borrowed divisions in simple time are called _____.

9. Borrowed divisions in compound time are called _____.

10. In simple time the beat normally subdivides into _____ parts.

11. In compound time the beat normally subdivides into _____ parts.

ASSIGNMENT 3–2   Name: _____

Scan and sing the following songs and determine whether they are in simple or compound time.
(Pay careful attention to the relative *lengths* of the dashes and how beats are divided.)

Row, Row, Row Your Boat

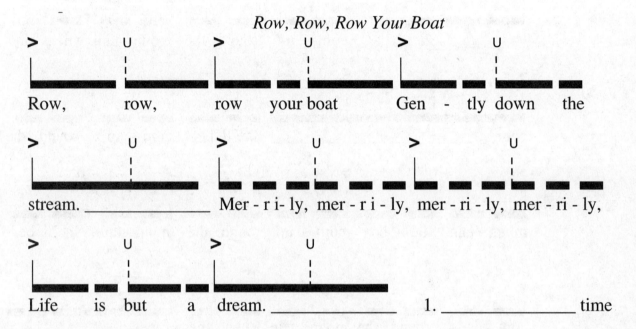

Skip to My Lou

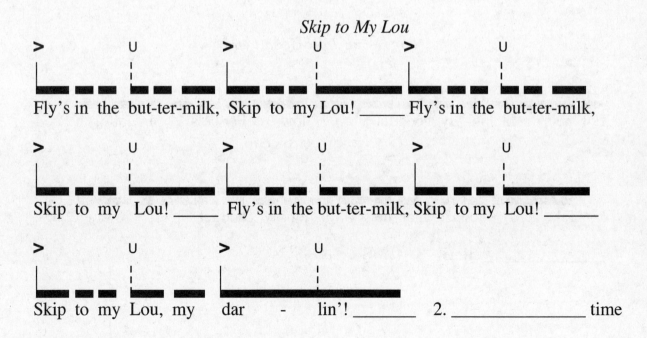

She'll Be Comin' 'Round the Mountain

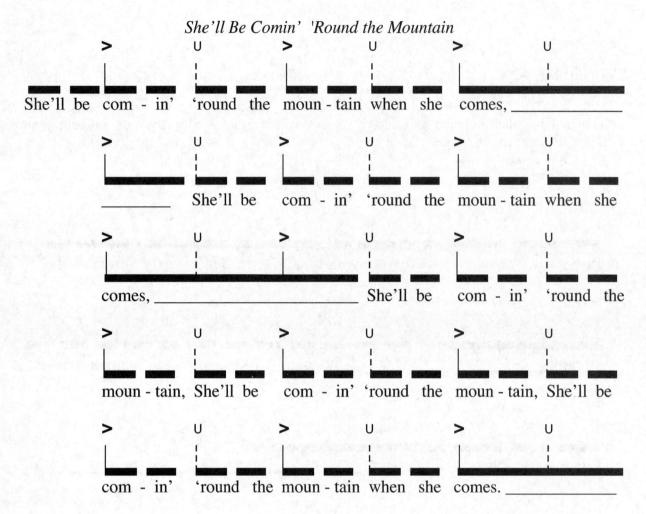

3. _____ time

For He's a Jolly Good Fellow

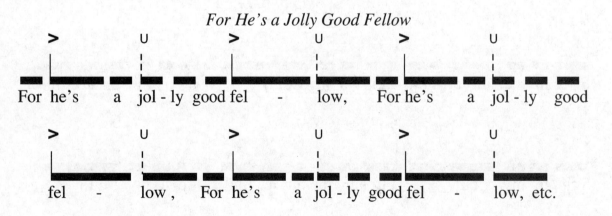

4. _____ time

Ear-Training Activities

Musicians must develop a keen sense of time passing and the various ways time is organized for musical purposes. There are three basic levels of rhythmic organization: (1) the beat, (2) meter, and (3) the division and subdivision of the beat.

The rhythm of most common practice music is based on beats of equal duration; the ability to maintain a steady beat is fundamental to effective performance. Perhaps the best and most accessible resource available to help you develop a feeling for a steady beat is the naturally regular gait of normal walking. Walking also serves as an ideal background for thinking or humming rhythmic patterns.

1. While walking (or marking time), form a mental image that suggests steady movement of a point through space. Then imagine that your steps mark off segments of the line created by the moving point. Create your own image, but the mental association of time and space is useful within many musical contexts, tonal as well as rhythmic.

2. Experience the various meters by thinking, clapping, or humming accents as in the following:

    a. duple meter
    ```
         >    U  |  >    U
       ( 1    2  |  1    2 )
    ```

    b. triple meter
    ```
         >    U    U  |  >    U    U
       ( 1    2    3  |  1    2    3 )
    ```

    c. quadruple meter
    ```
         >    U    >    U  |  >    U    >    U
       ( 1    2    3    4  |  1    2    3    4 )
    ```

    d. quintuple meter
    ```
         >    U    U    >    U  or  >    U    >    U    U
       ( 1    2    3    4    5       1    2    3    4    5 )
    ```

3. By thinking, saying "ta," clapping, or any other means, divide beats into two or three equal parts to produce simple or compound time as in the following:

    a. duple-simple

    b. duple-compound

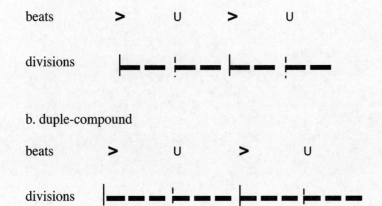

4. Sing songs such as those in frames 3.40 and 3.41 and in assignment 3–2 in the text, focusing attention on the rhythmic structure.

5. Practice improvising a rhythm, or a complete melody, by selecting either simple or compound time and then improvising within that time selection. Once that has been mastered then try moving between simple and compound time within the same improvisation; or, try resetting the improvisation in the opposite time selection, *e.g.* simple into compound and vice versa.

6. If melodies have been found to analyze for time classification or a poem/text has been set rhythmically (as per the Supplementary Activities on page 80), then move to the next step of performing them while physically responding to them (tapping, clapping, *et cetera*) as this is done. Any mental associations that can be made along with this activity are also helpful in strengthening one's abilities in this area of musical study.

7. Continue with any other musical activities that involve performing from music or improvisationally along with which the knowledge of time classification can be applied simultaneously or after the fact.

Chapter 4.0
Note and Rest Values

The symbols used to represent tones are called *notes*. Chapter 2.0 demonstrated that the pitch of tones is indicated by placing notes on the staff. Notes also indicate relative duration. The rhythmic element of music is often complex, but, fortunately, there are only a few basic types of notes. Also, notes bear a simple relationship to one another; each represents a duration twice as long as the next-smaller note. For each type of note there is a corresponding symbol called a *rest,* which indicates an equivalent duration of silence.

4.1   The types of notes that are used to indicate the relative duration of tones are shown below.

	double whole note (or *breve*)*		sixteenth note
	whole note		thirty-second note
	half note		sixty-fourth note*
	quarter note		128th note*
	eighth note		

Write several whole notes on various lines and spaces.

* The double whole note, the sixty-fourth note, and the 128th note are used so rarely that they need not be stressed here. For the remainder of this book, these notes will not be used.

4.2   Observe the name given to each part of the note.

QUARTER NOTE   EIGHTH NOTE

Head →   ← Stem   ← Flag

The eighth note consists of three parts: the flag,

the stem, and the _____.

The 20th and 21st Centuries have brought many innovations to musical notation to accommodate special performance techniques. Note heads have especially undergone many transformations as have concepts to represent durations of notes. Please see Musical Notation in the *Bibliography for Further Study* and books by Read and Stone.

head

4.3   Stems are one octave in length. They are placed on the *right* side of the head and extend upward if the note is *below* the third (middle) line of the staff.

If the note is *below* the third line of the staff, the

stem is placed on the _____ side of the head.

right

4.4   If the note is *above* the third line of the staff, the stem is placed on the *left* side of the head and extends downward.

Stems are placed on the left side of the head and

extend downward if the note is *above* the _____ line of the staff.

third (or middle)

4.5   If the note is *on* the third (middle) line of the staff, the stem may extend either upward or downward.* If the stem extends downward, it is placed on the *left* side of the head; if it extends upward, it is placed on the *right* side of the head.

All stems that extend downward are placed on the left side of the head. All stems that extend

upward are placed on the _____ side of the head.

right

---

* Most printed music shows a preference for the downward stem when notes are on the third line.

4.6 The flag appears on the right side of the stem in all cases.

Add a stem and one flag to each note head.

4.7 Add a stem and two flags to each note head.

sixteenth

4.8 The notes in the preceding frame are (half/quarter/

eighth/sixteenth) _____ notes.

4.9 Circle the notes that are *not* correctly written.

Notes you write should look like this:

4.10 Write several half notes on various lines and spaces.
(Observe correct placement of stems.)

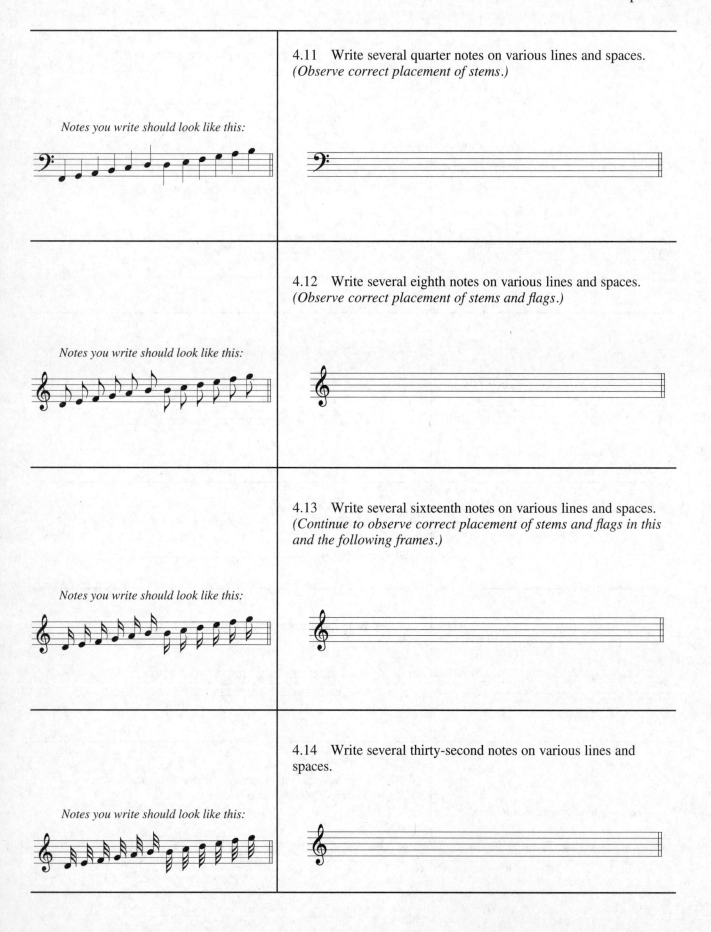

4.11 Write several quarter notes on various lines and spaces. *(Observe correct placement of stems.)*

Notes you write should look like this:

4.12 Write several eighth notes on various lines and spaces. *(Observe correct placement of stems and flags.)*

Notes you write should look like this:

4.13 Write several sixteenth notes on various lines and spaces. *(Continue to observe correct placement of stems and flags in this and the following frames.)*

Notes you write should look like this:

4.14 Write several thirty-second notes on various lines and spaces.

Notes you write should look like this:

4.15   Instead of a separate flag for each note, BEAMS are often used to join several notes together.

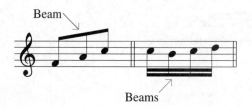

Beams generally connect notes that are to sound within the same metrical unit (the beat or measure).

Beams take the place of _____.

Note: Examples here are *not* to be interpreted within any meter. They are meant to show some generalized situations of how to handle beaming. The examples are *not* meant to be all-inclusive.

flags

4.16   The use of beams often causes one or more of the stems to be placed differently than would be the case if a flag were used. If most of the notes are above the third (middle) line of the staff, stems extend *downward;* if most of the notes are below the third line, the stems extend *upward.*

Note that beams are always *straight* lines.

Connect the notes in each group with beams as directed.

(1)

(2)

(1) EIGHTH NOTES

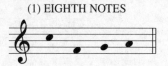

(2) SIXTEENTH NOTES

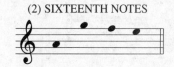

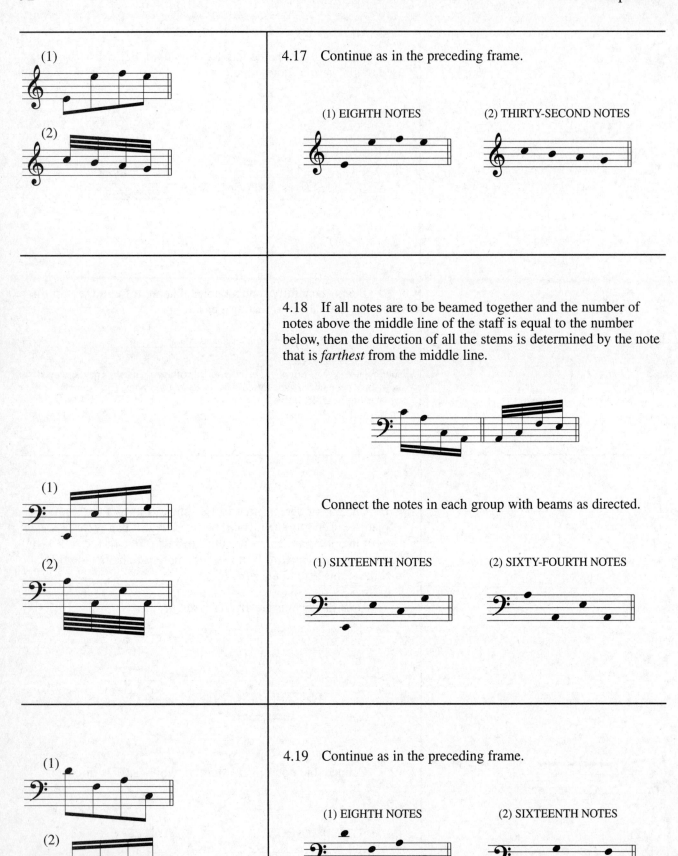

(1)

(2)

4.17 Continue as in the preceding frame.

(1) EIGHTH NOTES   (2) THIRTY-SECOND NOTES

4.18 If all notes are to be beamed together and the number of notes above the middle line of the staff is equal to the number below, then the direction of all the stems is determined by the note that is *farthest* from the middle line.

Connect the notes in each group with beams as directed.

(1) SIXTEENTH NOTES   (2) SIXTY-FOURTH NOTES

(1)

(2)

4.19 Continue as in the preceding frame.

(1) EIGHTH NOTES   (2) SIXTEENTH NOTES

(1)

(2)

4.20   Notes do not, in themselves, indicate duration precisely, but their values are related in the manner indicated by the name of each note.

A whole note = 2 half notes.

A whole note = 4 quarter notes.

A whole note = 8 eighth notes.
   (etc.)

A whole note equals how many sixteenth notes?

16   _____

4.21   Whereas two quarter notes equal one half note,

four   it requires _____ eighth notes to equal one half note.

4.22   A quarter note equals how many eighth notes?

2   _____

4.23   A quarter note equals how many sixteenth notes?

4   _____

4.24   An eighth note equals how many sixteenth notes?

2   _____

4.25   Supply the answer in each case.

(1) 2   (1) A 𝅝 note = _____ 𝅗𝅥 notes.

(2) 2   (2) A 𝅗𝅥 note = _____ 𝅘𝅥 notes.

(3) 2   (3) A 𝅘𝅥 note = _____ 𝅘𝅥𝅮 notes.

(1) 4

(2) 8

(3) 8

4.26 Continue as in the preceding frame.

(1) A o note = _____ ♩ notes.

(2) A ♩ note = _____ ♪ notes.

(3) A ♩ note = _____ ♫ notes.

---

(1) 2

(2) 2

(3) 4

4.27 Continue as in the preceding frame.

(1) An ♪ note = _____ ♫ notes.

(2) A ♫ note = _____ ♬ notes.

(3) A ♩ note = _____ ♪ notes.

---

(1) 4

(2) 4

(3) 1

4.28 Continue as in the preceding frame.

(1) An ♪ note = _____ ♬ notes.

(2) A ♩ note = _____ ♬ notes.

(3) A ♩ note = _____ ♩ notes.

4.29   RESTS are symbols that represent periods of silence. There is a rest sign that corresponds to each of the basic note values.

double whole rest*

whole rest

half rest

quarter rest

eighth rest

sixteenth rest

thirty-second rest

sixty-fourth rest*

128th rest*

Care must be taken not to confuse the whole rest with the half rest. The whole rest hangs from the fourth line of the staff. Write several whole rests.

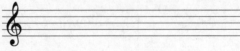

 (etc.)

* The double whole, sixty-fourth, and 128th rests are rarely used. They will not appear in the remainder of this book.

Expository Frame

4.30   There is now a general tradition to use the whole rest "to represent an *entire* measure of rest, [and] it must not ordinarily be employed for *less* than a measure."*
Although there might be exceptions to this in a $\frac{4}{2}$, an $\frac{8}{4}$, or even a rare $\frac{3}{1}$ or $\frac{2}{1}$ meter, "a whole rest must not be used to indicate a fractional portion of a measure."*

(*No response required.*)

* Gardner Read, *Music Notation*, p. 98

(etc.)

4.31 The half rest sits on the third line of the staff. Write several half rests.

(etc.)

4.32 Write several quarter rests.

(etc.)

4.33 Write several eighth rests.

(etc.)

4.34 Write several sixteenth rests.

(etc.)

4.35 Write several thirty-second rests.

4.36   Rests are related to one another in the same way as notes.

   A whole rest = 2 half rests.

   A whole rest = 4 quarter rests.

   A whole rest = 8 eighth rests.

   A whole rest equals how many thirty-second

32   rests?_____

4.37   Supply the answer in each case.

(1) 4   (1) A ⌐ rest = _____ ⌇ rests.

(2) 2   (2) A ⌐ rest = _____ ⌇ rests.

(3) 4   (3) A ⌐ rest = _____ ⌐ rests.

4.38   Supply the answer in each case.

(1) 2   (1) An ⌐ rest = _____ ⌐ rests.

(2) 2   (2) A ⌐ rest = _____ ⌐ rests.

(3) 4   (3) An ⌐ rest = _____ ⌐ rests.

4.39   Supply the answer in each case.

(1) 8   (1) A ⌐ rest = _____ ⌐ rests.

(2) 4   (2) A ⌇ rest = _____ ⌐ rests.

(3) 1   (3) An ⌐ rest = _____ ⌐ rests.

4.40   A DOT may be added to both notes and rests.*

$\mathbf{o}\cdot$, $\downarrow\cdot$, $\downarrow\cdot$, $\flat\cdot$,   etc.

$-\cdot$, $-\cdot$, $\xi\cdot$, $\gamma\cdot$,   etc.

The dot increases the value of a note or a rest by one-half of its original value.

$\downarrow\cdot$ = $\downarrow\smile\downarrow$† $-\cdot$ = $-$ + ξ

$\downarrow\cdot$ = $\downarrow\smile\flat$† $\xi\cdot$ = ξ + γ

The duration of a dotted note is (longer/shorter)

longer

_____ than that of the same note without the dot.

* Printed music issued by some publishers reveals a tendency not to dot rests but, rather, to write separate rests to represent the value desired ($\xi\gamma$ instead of $\xi\cdot$, $\gamma\gamma$ instead of $\gamma\cdot$, etc.). However, it is correct to dot rests if you wish. Many examples of dotted rests can be found in published music.

† A reminder: the curved line connecting the two notes is a *tie* that expresses the longer duration. (*See* fr. 2.82, 5.56.)

4.41   Complete each problem as in the preceding frame.

(1) $\mathbf{o}\smile\downarrow$

(1) $\mathbf{o}\cdot$ = __ __.
        $(\smile)$

(2) $\flat\smile\flat$

(2) $\flat\cdot$ = __ __.
        $(\smile)$

(3) $\flat\smile\flat$

(3) $\flat\cdot$ = __ __.
        $(\smile)$

4.42   Rewrite using dots.

(1) $\downarrow\cdot$

(1) $\downarrow\smile\downarrow$ = ____.

(2) $\flat\cdot$

(2) $\flat\smile\flat$ = ____.

(3) $\mathbf{o}\cdot$

(3) $\mathbf{o}\smile\downarrow$ = ____.

(1) 𝄼 + 𝄼

(2) 𝄿 + 𝄿

(3) 𝄾 + 𝄾

4.43   Complete each problem. *(Refer to frame 4.40.)*

(1) 𝄼· = _____ + _____.

(2) 𝄿· = _____ + _____.

(3) 𝄾· = _____ + _____.

---

(1) 𝄿·

(2) 𝄼·

(3) 𝄼·

4.44   Rewrite using dots.

(1) 𝄿 + 𝄿 = _____.

(2) 𝄽 + 𝄿 = _____.

(3) 𝄼 + 𝄽 = _____.

4.45   An additional dot may be applied to a dotted note or rest.

♩.. , ♩.. , ♪.. , etc.

𝄼·· , 𝄽·· , 𝄿·· , etc.

The second dot increases the value of the note or rest by one-half of the value represented by the first dot.

♩.. = ♩ _ ♩ _ ♪

𝄼·· = 𝄼 + 𝄽 + 𝄿

Each successive dot increases the value of the

note by (1/8, 1/4, 1/2) _____ the value of the preceding dot.

4.46 Complete each problem as in the preceding frame.

(1) 𝄽 + 𝄾 + 𝄿

(1) 𝄽·· = _____ + _____ + _____ .

(2) 𝄾 + 𝄿 + 𝄿

(2) 𝄾·· = _____ + _____ + _____ .

(3) ⁻ + 𝄽 + 𝄾

(3) ⁻·· = _____ + _____ + _____ .

4.47 Complete each problem.

(1) ♩ ♪ ♬ (1) ♩·· = ___ ___ ___ .
                    (◡) (◡)

(2) ♪ ♬ ♬ (2) ♪·· = ___ ___ ___ .
                    (◡) (◡)

(3) ♩ ♩ ♪ (3) ♩·· = ___ ___ ___ .
                    (◡) (◡)

4.48 An undotted note divides naturally into *two* equal parts.

𝅝 = 𝅗𝅥 𝅗𝅥

𝅗𝅥 = ♩ ♩

♩ = ♫

Show the natural division of an eighth note.

♫

♪ = _____

4.49 A dotted note, representing half again as long a duration as the same note without a dot, divides naturally into *three* equal parts.

♩. = ♩ ♩ ♩

♩. = ♫♫

♪. = ♫♫

Show the natural division of a dotted sixteenth note.

♪. = _____

4.50 Show (with notes) the division of each note below.

(1) ♩ divides into _____.

(2) ♩ divides into _____.

4.51 Continue as in the preceding frame.

(1) ♩. divides into _____.

(2) ♩. divides into _____.

4.52 Continue as in the preceding frame.

(1) 𝅝 divides into _____.

(2) ♪. divides into _____.

4.53 Continue as in the preceding frame.

(1) ♩ divides into _____.

(2) ♩. divides into _____.

4.54 Continue as in the preceding frame.

(1) ♪ divides into _____.

(2) ♩. divides into _____.

---

(1) ♫

(2) ♪♫

4.55 As notes can be divided so they can be "divided" yet again into a *subdivision*. An undotted note subdivides naturally into *four* equal parts.

𝅗𝅥 subdivides into ♫♫

♩ subdivides into ♫♫

♪ subdivides into ♫♫

The normal subdivision of an undotted note is

into _____ equal parts.

---

four

4.56 Show how each note naturally subdivides.

(1) ♩ subdivides into _____.

(2) ♪ subdivides into _____.

---

(1) ♫♫

(2) ♫♫

4.57 A dotted note subdivides naturally into *six* equal parts.

𝅗𝅥. subdivides into ♫♫♫

♩. subdivides into ♫♫♫

♪. subdivides into ♫♫♫

The normal subdivision of a dotted note is into

_____ equal parts.

---

six

4.58 Show how each note naturally subdivides.

(1) ♩. subdivides into _____.

(2) ♩. subdivides into _____.

(1) ♫♫♫

(2) ♫♫♫

4.59 Show how each note naturally subdivides.

(1) ♩ subdivides into _____.

(2) ♪. subdivides into _____.

4.60 By use of the proper indication, notes may be subdivided into four, five, six, seven, or more parts.

FOUR	FIVE	SIX	SEVEN

Subdivision of an undotted note into five, six, or seven parts, or the subdivision of a dotted note into four, five, or seven parts results in IRREGULAR GROUPS.* Such groups are not the result of a natural division or subdivision and thus may be regarded as "artificial." As shown above, a number is used to indicate how many notes are included in the group, and a number *must be used* for this artificial indication to be clear to the performer.

Is six a natural subdivision of an undotted note?

_____

No
(An undotted note subdivides naturally into four equal parts.)

_____

* The terms "tuplet," "foreign," and "mixed" groups are also used.

Expository Frame

4.61   There is a lack of standardization regarding the note
values used to indicate irregular groups.* A simple and practical
principle to follow is to use the note value of the division until
the subdivision is reached, and to continue to use the value of
the subdivision until the natural division of the subdivision is
reached.

(No response required.)

---

* For further information regarding the notation of irregular divisions, see Gardner
Read, "Some Problems of Rhythmic Notation," *Journal of Music Theory,* 9/1
(1965), pp. 153–62; or Gardner Read, *Music Notation,* Chapter 11: "Barlines and
Rhythms," pp. 182–222.

(1) (2)	4.62 Supply the correct notation. (1) A ♩ note subdivided into five parts is notated _____ . (2) A ♩ note subdivided into seven parts is notated _____ .
(1) (2)	4.63 Continue as in the preceding frame. (1) An ♪ note subdivided into five parts is notated _____ . (2) A ♩. note subdivided into seven parts is notated _____ .
(1) (2)	4.64 Continue as in the preceding frame. (1) A ♩. note subdivided into four parts is notated _____ . (2) A ♪. note subdivided into five parts is notated _____ .
Three	4.65 The note that represents the duration of the beat is called the UNIT. How many *units* are there in one measure of triple meter? _____
Two	4.66 How many *units* are there in one measure of duple meter? _____
Four	4.67 How many *units* are there in one measure of quadruple meter? _____

4.68   The unit in simple time is always an undotted note, since this type of note divides naturally into *two* equal parts. Any note may be the unit, but the most usual values are the half note, the quarter note, and the eighth note.

       The unit is always an undotted note in _____ time.

simple

4.69   The unit in compound time is always a dotted note, since this type of note divides naturally into *three* equal parts. The most common units in compound time are the dotted half note, the dotted quarter note, and the dotted eighth note.

       The dotted note divides naturally into _____ equal parts.

three

4.70   The note that represents the duration of the beat is called the _____.

unit

4.71   The undotted note divides naturally into _____ equal parts.

two

4.72   The unit is always a dotted note in _____ time.

compound

4.73   Which of the notes below could represent the beat in simple time? _____

(2) ♩

(4) ♪

       (1) ♩. (2) ♩ (3) ♪. (4) ♪

(1) 𝅗𝅥.

(3) ♪.

(4) 𝅗𝅥.

4.74 Which of the notes below could be the unit in compound time? _____

(1) 𝅗𝅥. (2) 𝅝 (3) ♪. (4) 𝅗𝅥.

Division: ♫

Subdivision: ♬♬

4.75 Show the division and the subdivision of the unit.

Unit	Division	Subdivision
♩	_____	_____

Division: ♫

Subdivision: ♬♬

4.76 Continue as in the preceding frame.

Unit	Division	Subdivision
♪	_____	_____

Division: ♩♩♩

Subdivision: ♫♫♫

4.77 Continue as in the preceding frame.

Unit	Division	Subdivision
𝅗𝅥.	_____	_____

Division: ♩♩♩ Subdivision: ♫♫♫	**4.78** Continue as in the preceding frame. *Unit* *Division* *Subdivision* ♩. _____ _____
Division: ♫♩ Subdivision: ♬♬♬	**4.79** Continue as in the preceding frame. *Unit* *Division* *Subdivision* ♪. _____ _____
Division: ♩♩ Subdivision: ♫♫	**4.80** Continue as in the preceding frame. *Unit* *Division* *Subdivision* ♩ _____ _____
(1) ♩ (2) ♩ (3) ♪	**4.81** Indicate the most common units in simple time: (1)____ (2)____ (3)____
(1) ♩. (2) ♩. (3) ♪.	**4.82** Indicate the most common units in compound time: (1)____ (2)____ (3)____

4.83 Notes, in themselves, represent only relative duration. Exact duration can be indicated by establishing the rate of the unit. A sign such as M.M. ♩ = 60* (or simply ♩ = 60) at the beginning of a composition indicates that the quarter note is to progress at the rate of 60 per minute.

With the same indication (♩ = 60), what is the

rate of the eighth note? _____ per minute.

120

_____

* The two M's stand for Mälzel's Metronome. In 1816 Mälzel invented an instrument based upon the principle of the double pendulum that could be set to indicate a given number of beats per minute. Beethoven was one of the first composers to make use of metronome indications in his music. Today there are both mechanical and electronic *metronomes* to instantaneously establish a note rate or *tempo*.

4.84 If the indication is ♩ = 72, what is the rate of

the quarter note? _____ per minute

144

4.85 If the indication is ♩. = 60, what is the rate of

the eighth note? _____ per minute

180

4.86 If the indication is ♩ = 120, what is the rate of

the whole note? _____ per minute

60

4.87 If the indication is ♪. = 96, what is the rate of

the dotted quarter note? _____ per minute

48

4.88   Composers often use Italian (sometimes English, German, or French) terms to indicate the approximate speed and character of their music. Some of the most common terms are listed below.*

Prestissimo	Extremely fast
Presto	Very fast
Allegro	Fast
Allegretto	Fast, but slower than *allegro*
Moderato	Moderate
Andante	Moderately slow
Adagio	Slow
Largo	Extremely slow

Terms such as these do not indicate the precise speed of a composition; precise speed can be determined only by making use of the metronome.

_____
* Consult the *Glossary of Musical Terms*, p. 373, for other tempo and phrasing indications commonly found in music.

(No response required.)

4.89   The basic rhythmic organization of *simple time* is shown below.

UNIT:

DIVISION:

BORROWED DIVISION:

SUBDIVISION:

The note that represents the duration of the beat is called the *unit*. The quarter note is often used as the unit, but we should not think of the quarter note as always "getting the beat." The eighth note and the half note are

simple

also used as units in _____ time.

4.90   The basic rhythmic organization of *compound time* is shown below.

UNIT: 𝅗𝅥.   ♩.   ♪.

DIVISION: ♩ ♩ ♩   ♫♫   ♬♬

BORROWED DIVISION: ♩² ♩   ♫²   ♬²

SUBDIVISION: ♬♬♬   ♬♬♬   ♬♬♬

The unit in compound time is always a(n) (dotted/

undotted) _____ note.

dotted

Summary

Notes and *rests* are the two basic symbols used to notate rhythm. Accurate interpretation of these symbols is necessary for correct performance. Notes represent durations of sound; rests represent durations of silence. For each type of note there is a corresponding rest.

Notes may be either *dotted* or *undotted*. *Dotted notes* divide naturally into *three* equal parts, and *undotted notes* divide naturally into *two* equal parts. In *simple time* the *unit* of the beat is an undotted note; in *compound time* the *unit* of the beat is a dotted note.

The *division* of the beat into *three* equal parts in simple time is a *borrowed division* (or triplet); the *division* of the beat into *two* equal parts in compound time is called a *borrowed division* (or duplet). The normal *subdivision* of the beat in simple time is into four parts; in compound time it is into six equal parts. *Subdivisions* of five, seven, eleven, or more in simple time are called *irregular groups;* in compound time *subdivisions* of four, five, seven, eight, nine, ten, and eleven are also called *irregular groups*.

Mastery Frames

	4–1 Provide the name of each note in the example below.
(1) eighth	
	(1)_____ (4)_____
(2) whole	
	(2)_____ (5)_____
(3) sixteenth	
	(3)_____ (6)_____
(4) quarter	
(5) thirty-second	(1) (2) (3) (4) (5) (6)
(6) half	
(frame 4.1)	

	4–2 Supply the answer in each case.
(1) 2	(1) An eighth note = _____ sixteenth notes.
(2) 4	(2) A whole note = _____ quarter notes.
(3) 2	(3) A quarter note = _____ eighth notes.
(4.20–4.28)	

	4–3 Provide the name of each rest in the example below.
(1) sixteenth	
	(1)_____ (4)_____
(2) quarter	
	(2)_____ (5)_____
(3) half	
	(3)_____ (6)_____
(4) eighth	
(5) whole	(1) (2) (3) (4) (5) (6)
(6) thirty-second	
(4.29)	

(1) 4

(2) 2

(3) 4

(4.36–4.39)

4–4   Supply the answer in each case.

(1) A half rest   = _____ eighth rests.

(2) A sixteenth rest = _____ thirty-second rests.

(3) A quarter rest   = _____ sixteenth rests.

---

(1) 𝅗𝅥⌣♩

(2) 𝅗𝅥⌣♪

(4.40–4.42)

4–5   Show with tied notes the total value of the dotted note in each case.

(1) 𝅗𝅥. = ___ ___.

(2) 𝅗𝅥. = $\dfrac{(\smile)}{(\smile)}$ ___ ___.

---

(1) ♪⌣♪⌣♬

(2) 𝅝⌣𝅗𝅥⌣♩

(4.45–4.47)

4–6   Show with tied notes the total value of the doubly dotted note in each case.

(1) ♪.. = ___ ___ ___.

(2) 𝅝.. = $\dfrac{(\smile)\ (\smile)}{(\smile)\ (\smile)}$ ___ ___ ___.

---

(1) ♫

(2) ♪♫

(4.48–4.54)

4–7   Show how each note normally divides.

(1) ♩ _____.

(2) 𝅗𝅥. _____.

---

(1) ♫♫

(2) ♫♫♫

(4.55–4.59)

4–8   Show how each note normally subdivides.

(1) 𝅗𝅥 _____.

(2) 𝅗𝅥. _____.

(1) 𝅗𝅥 (4) ♪	(4.68–4.73)	4–9 Which of the notes below could be the unit in simple time? _____ (1) 𝅗𝅥 (2) 𝅗𝅥. (3) ♪. (4) ♪
192	(4.83–4.87)	4–10 If the metronome indication is 𝅗𝅥 = 96, how many quarter notes will occur per minute? _____

Supplementary Activities

1. Utilizing the rhythmic materials provided in this chapter, invent short rhythmic patterns to perform. Consider expanding these rhythmic patterns into a short composition (rhythm only); or, upon completion of the next chapter (Time Signatures), try to do the same. A further suggestion is to use hand clapping or "body percussion" as a performing medium. Do the piece with or without a text.

2. Continue exploring topics under the general rubric of "notation" as possibilities for short essays or reports. Many of the notation references listed in the *Bibliography for Further Study* will provide helpful resources, as will *The New Harvard Dictionary of Music*.

Supplementary Assignments

ASSIGNMENT 4–1   Name: _____

1. Draw lines to connect each note with the correct name.

   a. 𝐨   • Quarter note

   b. ♪   • Half note

   c. ♫   • Whole note

   d. ♩   • Sixteenth note

   e. ♩   • Eighth note

2. Draw lines to connect each note with its corresponding rest.

   a. ♬   • 𝄾

   b. ♩   • 𝄾

   c. ♪   • ▬

   d. ♩   • 𝄾

   e. 𝐨   • ▬

3. Draw lines to connect each note with its correct name or corresponding rest.

   a. ♪.   • ▬.

   b. ♩.   • 𝄾.

   c. ♫.   • Dotted half note

   d. 𝐨.   • Dotted eighth note

   e. ♫.   • Dotted thirty-second note

   f. ♩.   • 𝄾.

4. Supply the information required.

    a. A 𝅗𝅥. note = _____ ♪ notes.

    b. An ♪ note = _____ 𝅘𝅥𝅰 notes.

    c. A ♪. note = _____ 𝅘𝅥𝅯 notes.

    d. A 𝅝 note = _____ 𝅗𝅥 notes.

5. Supply the information required.

    a. A 𝄽 rest = _____ 𝄾 rests.

    b. A ▬· rest = _____ ▬ rests.

    c. __ 𝄾 rests = 2 𝄽 rests.

    d. __ 𝄾 rests = 1 ▬· rest.

6. Show with tied notes the value of each note.

    a. 𝅝· = _____

    b. 𝅗𝅥.. = _____

    c. ♪. = _____

    d. 𝅗𝅥.. = _____

7. Supply the information required.

    a. _____ ♪ notes = _____ 𝅘𝅥. notes.

    b. _____ 𝄽 rests are equivalent to _____ 𝅝 note(s).

    c. _____ ♪ notes are equivalent to _____ 𝄽 rest(s).

    d. _____ 𝄽· rests = _____ ▬·· rest(s).

ASSIGNMENT 4–2   Name: _____

1. Write four notes that can serve as the unit of the beat in simple time.

    _____   _____   _____   _____

2. Write four notes that can serve as the unit of the beat in compound time.

    _____   _____   _____   _____

3. Show the normal division and subdivision of each note, as well as the borrowed division.

		Division	*Borrowed Division*	*Subdivision*
a.	♩.	_____	_____	_____
b.	♩	_____	_____	_____
c.	♪	_____	_____	_____
d.	♪.	_____	_____	_____

4. Show the proper notation for the various divisions and subdivisions of the quarter note.

♩

Two parts   _____

Three parts   _____

Four parts   _____

Five parts   _____

Six parts   _____

Seven parts   _____

5. Show the proper notation for the various divisions and subdivisions of the dotted quarter note.

♩.

Two parts   _____

Three parts   _____

Four parts   _____

Five parts   _____

Six parts   _____

Seven parts   _____

6. Indicate the number of notes that would occur per minute in each case with the given metronome indication.

Number per Minute

a. ♩ = 80   o   _____

                                         𝅗𝅥   _____

                                         ♩   _____

                                         ♪   _____

                                         𝅘𝅥𝅯   _____

b. ♩. = 60   o·   _____

                                         𝅗𝅥.   _____

                                         𝅗𝅥.   _____

                                         ♩   _____

                                         ♩.   _____

                                         ♪   _____

Ear-Training Activities for Chapters 4.0 and 5.0

Music, the most abstract of all the arts, is often difficult to approach in a concrete way. Sometimes, mental imagery or analogy can assist in comprehending and effectively interpreting a musical figure or phrase. This is true not only of subtle nuances of phrasing but also of basics such as note values and rhythmic patterns. The notation of music itself causes one to think in this way. Graphically, the time (rhythmic) element of music is represented on a horizontal plane; the sound (pitch) element is represented on a vertical plane.

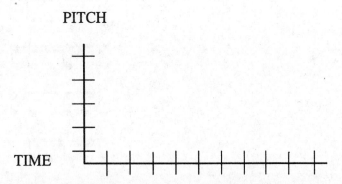

The ability to form musical images mentally varies. Even though few people are endowed with photographic memories for images they have seen, less literal images can also be helpful. Thus, devise mental associations and form images that help you.

Visualize as vividly as possible what music notation looks like. Because printed notes are spaced approximately proportionate to their duration, mental pictures of rhythmic patterns can help to perform figures properly.

1. The basic rhythmic patterns that occur in *simple time* are notated as follows:

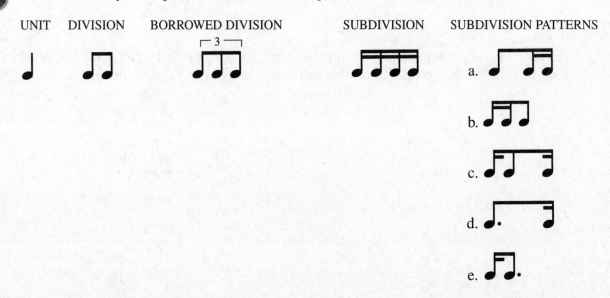

Against a steady beat (supplied by walking or by a metronome), practice each of these patterns separately and in combinations of self invention. Imagine (write out, if necessary) the patterns with the eighth note and the half note as the unit.

It is within the context of these simple exercises that an ability to make mental associations will grow. Do not neglect this type of drill.

2. Apply the methods described in number 1 to the following rhythmic patterns that occur in *compound time*.

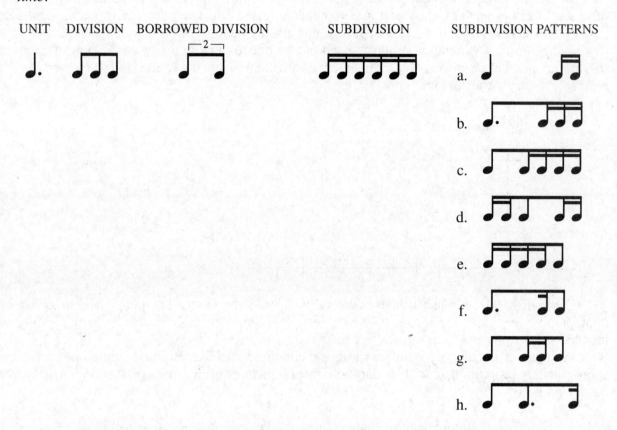

3. Continue with any other musical activities that involve performing from music or improvisationally along with which the knowledge of note and rest values can be applied simultaneously or after the fact.

Chapter 5.0
Time Signatures

Time signatures indicate the metrical organization of a composition. The preceding chapter illustrated that there are two types of meter: simple and compound. In simple time, beats divide naturally into two equal parts; in compound time, beats divide naturally into three equal parts. Time signatures fall into two groups: one to represent simple time, and the second to represent compound time. In this chapter the interpretation of time signatures of each group will be demonstrated.

5.1   The metrical organization of a musical composition is indicated by a TIME SIGNATURE.* A time signature consists of two numbers placed on the staff one above the other at the beginning of the composition. There are two types of time signatures: those that indicate *simple* time, and those that indicate *compound* time.

This is how to distinguish between simple and compound time signatures: *If the upper number is 6, 9, 12, 15, or 18,[†] the time signature represents COMPOUND time. Any number other than these, including the number 3, means that the signature represents SIMPLE time.*

If the upper number of the time signature is 6, 9, 12, 15,

compound

or 18, the signature represents _____ time.

---

* Time signatures are also called meter signatures.

[†] The numbers 15 and 18 are rarely used in music literature.

---

(1) $\dfrac{6}{2}$

(4) $\dfrac{9}{4}$

5.2   Which of the following time signatures indicate *compound* time? _____

(1) $\dfrac{6}{2}$ (2) $\dfrac{5}{4}$ (3) $\dfrac{3}{8}$ (4) $\dfrac{9}{4}$

(2) $\frac{2}{4}$

(3) $\frac{4}{8}$

6, 9, 12, 15, 18

1, 2, 3, 4, 5, 7, 8
(*Others are possible
but not practical.*)

upper number

(1) 3

(2) 4

(3) 5

5.3   Which of the following time signatures indicate *simple* time? _____

(1) $\frac{12}{8}$ (2) $\frac{2}{4}$ (3) $\frac{4}{8}$ (4) $\frac{6}{4}$

5.4   What numbers are found in the upper part of *compound* time signatures?

_____

5.5   Write some of the numbers that could be found in the upper part of *simple* time signatures.

_____

5.6   The upper number of the time signature tells us the number of beats per measure. Whether the meter is *duple, triple, quadruple,* or *quintuple* is shown

by the _____ _____ of the time signature.

5.7   The upper number of *simple* time signatures directly indicates the number of beats per measure.

$\frac{2}{4}$ = 2 beats per measure

Show the number of beats per measure indicated by each of the simple time signatures below.

(1) $\frac{3}{2}$ = _____ beats per measure.

(2) $\frac{4}{4}$ = _____ beats per measure.

(3) $\frac{5}{4}$ = _____ beats per measure.

5.8   The upper number of *compound* time signatures does not directly indicate the number of beats per measure as was the case in simple time. To determine the number of beats per measure, the upper number of compound time signatures must be divisible by three.

$$\frac{6}{4} \div 3 = 2 \text{ beats per measure}$$

Show the number of beats per measure indicated by each of the compound time signatures below.

(1) 3

(1) $\frac{9}{8}$ = _____ beats per measure.

(2) 4

(2) $\frac{12}{8}$ = _____ beats per measure.

(3) 5

(3) $\frac{15}{8}$ = _____ beats per measure.

Note: There are musical examples in which a $\frac{6}{4}$ meter may be notated to imply three beat units—that is, a $\frac{3}{2}$ meter—but it is still classified as compound time because of the 6. Also, time signatures *should not* be written as fractions, because they refer to complete measures, not fractions of themselves.

5.9   The upper number of the time signature directly indicates the number of beats per measure in

simple

_____ time.

5.10   To determine the number of beats per measure in compound time, the upper number of the time signature must be

three

divisible by _____.

Note: (*This assumes the division of the divisible beat unit is three in number.*)

5.11   Show the number of beats per measure indicated by each of the time signatures below. *Determine first whether each is a simple or a compound signature.*

(1) 2

(1) $\frac{2}{8}$ = _____ beats per measure.

(2) 2

(2) $\frac{6}{4}$ = _____ beats per measure.

(3) 4

(3) $\frac{4}{2}$ = _____ beats per measure.

5.12   Continue as in the preceding frame.

(1) 5   (1) $\frac{5}{8}$ = _____ beats per measure.

(2) 3   (2) $\frac{9}{4}$ = _____ beats per measure.

(3) 4   (3) $\frac{12}{16}$ = _____ beats per measure.

5.13   Continue as in the preceding frame.

(1) 3   (1) $\frac{3}{2}$ = _____ beats per measure.

(2) 7   (2) $\frac{7}{8}$ = _____ beats per measure.

(3) 5   (3) $\frac{15}{8}$ = _____ beats per measure.

5.14   What do the members of each pair of time signatures below have in common?

(1) $\frac{2}{4}$ & $\frac{6}{8}$ (2) $\frac{3}{8}$ & $\frac{9}{4}$ (3) $\frac{4}{4}$ & $\frac{12}{8}$

The members of each
pair indicate the same
number of beats   _____
per measure:
(1) two beats
(2) three beats
(3) four beats   _____

5.15   From the upper number of the time signature we deduce the meter (the number of beats per measure). The UNIT is indicated by the lower number, but simple and compound time signatures must be interpreted differently.

The kind of note that represents the beat is deduced

lower   from the (upper/lower) _____ number of the time signature.

(1) ♩

(2) ♪

(3) ♩

5.16 The lower number of *simple* time signatures directly indicates the *unit.**

$\frac{2}{4}$ Unit: = ♩

(The number 4 represents a quarter note.)

Show the *unit* indicated by each of the simple time signatures below.

(1) $\frac{5}{2}$ Unit = _____

(2) $\frac{3}{8}$ Unit = _____

(3) $\frac{4}{4}$ Unit = _____

_____
* The type of note that receives one beat.

(1) ♪

(2) ♪

(3) ♩

5.17 The lower number of *compound* time signatures represents the DIVISION of the *unit.**

$\frac{6}{8}$ Division: = ♪

(The number 8 represents an eighth note.)

Show the *division* indicated by each of the compound time signatures below.

(1) $\frac{12}{16}$ Division = _____

(2) $\frac{6}{8}$ Division = _____

(3) $\frac{9}{4}$ Division = _____

_____
* The type of note that is the *division* of the (beat) unit.

division

5.18 The lower number of *simple* time signatures indicates the *unit*.

The lower number of *compound* time signatures

indicates the _____.

5.19   The *unit* in *compound* time consists of three *divisions*. Thus, three *divisions* combine to make the *unit*.

$$\begin{matrix} 6 \\ 8 \end{matrix} \text{ Division: } = ♪$$

$$♪\_♪\_♪ = ♩. \text{ (the unit)}$$

In compound time a note that is equal in value

unit   to three divisions is called the _____.

5.20   The unit in compound time is equal in value to

divisions   three _____.

5.21   The unit in compound time is always a DOTTED note.*

Show the unit indicated by each of the compound time signatures below.

(1) ♩.   (1) $\begin{matrix} 9 \\ 8 \end{matrix}$ Unit = _____

(2) 𝅗𝅥.   (2) $\begin{matrix} 6 \\ 4 \end{matrix}$ Unit = _____

(3) 𝅝.   (3) $\begin{matrix} 12 \\ 8 \end{matrix}$ Unit = _____

_____

* In a very slow tempo it may be more convenient to assign the beat to the division rather than to the unit. Duple-compound meter, for example, might be counted as a six-beat measure. However, chord changes, rhythmic patterns, phrase structure, and the location of cadences will usually give evidence of the underlying duple organization.

	5.22 Continue as in the preceding frame.
(1) ♩.	(1) $\frac{15}{8}$ Unit = _____
(2) ♪.	(2) $\frac{6}{16}$ Unit = _____
(3) ♩.	(3) $\frac{9}{4}$ Unit = _____

	5.23 In compound time the lower number of the time signature indicates the division. Three divisions combine to make the unit. The unit in compound time is always
dotted	a(n) (dotted/undotted) _____ note.

	5.24 In simple time the lower number of the time signature directly indicates the unit. The unit in simple time is always a(n) (dotted/undotted)
undotted	_____ note.

	5.25 Show the unit indicated by each of the time signatures below. *Determine first whether each is a simple or a compound signature.*
(1) ♩.	(1) $\frac{9}{8}$ Unit = _____
(2) ♩	(2) $\frac{2}{4}$ Unit = _____
(3) ♩.	(3) $\frac{12}{4}$ Unit = _____

5.26   Continue as in the preceding frame.

(1) ♩.

(1) $\frac{15}{8}$ Unit = _____

(2) ♩

(2) $\frac{3}{2}$ Unit = _____

(3) ♪

(3) $\frac{4}{8}$ Unit = _____

5.27   Continue as in the preceding frame.

(1) ♩.

(1) $\frac{9}{4}$ Unit = _____

(2) ♩.

(2) $\frac{12}{8}$ Unit = _____

(3) ♩

(3) $\frac{5}{4}$ Unit = _____

5.28   TIME CLASSIFICATION is expressed by terms such as duple-simple, duple-compound, triple-simple, quadruple-simple, and quintuple-simple.

The first part of the classification refers to the number of beats per measure.

Duple	=	two beats per measure.
Triple	=	three beats per measure.
Quadruple	=	four beats per measure.
Quintuple	=	five beats per measure.

Indicate the *first* part of the time classification for each signature.

(1) triple

(1) $\frac{3}{4}$ _____

(2) triple

(2) $\frac{9}{8}$ _____

(3) duple

(3) $\frac{2}{4}$ _____

(1) duple	5.29 Continue as in the preceding frame. (1) $\frac{6}{8}$ _____
(2) quadruple	(2) $\frac{4}{4}$ _____
(3) quadruple	(3) $\frac{12}{8}$ _____
(1) quintuple	5.30 Continue as in the preceding frame. (1) $\frac{5}{4}$ _____
(2) triple	(2) $\frac{3}{2}$ _____
(3) quintuple	(3) $\frac{15}{8}$ _____
(1) triple	5.31 Continue as in the preceding frame. (1) $\frac{3}{8}$ _____
(2) duple	(2) $\frac{6}{4}$ _____
(3) quadruple	(3) $\frac{4}{8}$ _____
	5.32 The second part of the time classification tells whether the beat is divided into *two* parts (simple time) or *three* parts (compound time). It also tells whether the unit is an undotted or a dotted note. Indicate the *second* part of the time classification for each time signature.
(1) simple	(1) $\frac{2}{4}$ _____
(2) simple	(2) $\frac{3}{8}$ _____
(3) compound	(3) $\frac{9}{8}$ _____

5.33   Continue as in the preceding frame.

(1) compound

(1) $\dfrac{12}{4}$ _____

(2) simple

(2) $\dfrac{5}{8}$ _____

(3) compound

(3) $\dfrac{6}{4}$ _____

5.34   Continue as in the preceding frame.

(1) compound

(1) $\dfrac{15}{8}$ _____

(2) simple

(2) $\dfrac{3}{4}$ _____

(3) simple

(3) $\dfrac{7}{8}$ _____

5.35   The time classification of simple time signatures is interpreted thus:

Time signature: $\begin{cases} \dfrac{3}{4} & = \quad 3 \text{ beats per measure - TRIPLE} \\[2em] \dfrac{3}{4} & = \quad \text{Unit: } \♩ \text{; Div.: } \♫ \text{ - SIMPLE} \end{cases}$

Time classification: TRIPLE-SIMPLE

Supply the time classification for each of the time signatures below.

(1) quadruple-simple

(1) $\dfrac{4}{4}$ _____ - _____

(2) quintuple-simple

(2) $\dfrac{5}{8}$ _____ - _____

(3) duple-simple

(3) $\dfrac{2}{2}$ _____ - _____

5.36 The time classification of compound time signatures is interpreted thus:

Time signature: $\begin{cases} \dfrac{9}{8} \div 3 = 3 \text{ beats per measure - TRIPLE} \\[2mm] \dfrac{9}{8} = \text{Div.: } ♪; \; ♫♪ = ♩. \; \text{(Unit) - COMPOUND} \end{cases}$

Time classification: TRIPLE-COMPOUND

Supply the time classification for each of the time signatures below.

(1) $\dfrac{6}{2}$ _____ - _____

(2) $\dfrac{12}{16}$ _____ - _____

(3) $\dfrac{15}{16}$ _____ - _____

(1) duple-compound

(2) quadruple-compound

(3) quintuple-compound

5.37 Continue as in the preceding frame.

(1) $\dfrac{4}{8}$ _____ - _____

(2) $\dfrac{6}{16}$ _____ - _____

(3) $\dfrac{3}{2}$ _____ - _____

(1) quadruple-simple

(2) duple-compound

(3) triple-simple

5.38 Continue as in the preceding frame.

(1) $\dfrac{9}{4}$ _____ - _____

(2) $\dfrac{4}{2}$ _____ - _____

(3) $\dfrac{12}{8}$ _____ - _____

(1) triple-compound

(2) quadruple-simple

(3) quadruple-compound

5.39   In simple time the upper number directly indicates the number of beats per measure.

Does the upper number in compound time signatures directly indicate the number of beats per measure?

No (*It must be divided by three.*)

_____

5.40   Notice the relation of the upper number of the time signature to the number of beats per measure in compound time:

Upper Number	Beats per Measure	Meter
6	2	duple
9	3	triple
12	4	quadruple
15	5	quintuple

In simple time, duple meter is indicated by the number 2. What is the upper number of the time signature in duple-compound time? _____

6

5.41   Supply three of the possible time signatures for the time classification below.

Triple-simple _____ _____ _____

$\frac{3}{2}$ $\frac{3}{4}$ $\frac{3}{8}$ $\frac{3}{16}$

(*any three*)

5.42   Continue as in the preceding frame.

Duple-compound _____ _____ _____

$\frac{6}{4}$ $\frac{6}{8}$ $\frac{6}{16}$

$\frac{9}{4}$ $\frac{9}{8}$ $\frac{9}{16}$

5.43 Continue as in the preceding frame.

Triple-compound _____ _____ _____

$\frac{2}{2}$ $\frac{2}{4}$ $\frac{2}{8}$ $\frac{2}{16}$

(any three)

5.44 Continue as in the preceding frame.

Duple-simple _____ _____ _____

$\frac{4}{2}$ $\frac{4}{4}$ $\frac{4}{8}$ $\frac{4}{16}$

(any three)

5.45 Continue as in the preceding frame.

Quadruple-simple _____ _____ _____

$\frac{15}{4}$ $\frac{15}{8}$ $\frac{15}{16}$

5.46 Continue as in the preceding frame.

Quintuple-compound _____ _____ _____

$\frac{12}{4}$ $\frac{12}{8}$ $\frac{12}{16}$

5.47 Continue as in the preceding frame.

Quadruple-compound _____ _____ _____

$\frac{5}{2}$ $\frac{5}{4}$ $\frac{5}{8}$ $\frac{5}{16}$

(any three)

5.48 Continue as in the preceding frame.

Quintuple-simple _____ _____ _____

c

5.49 Two time signatures (**c** and **¢**) are vestiges of earlier systems of notation.* The sign **c** stands for the signature $\frac{4}{4}$ (quadruple-simple) and is called COMMON TIME.

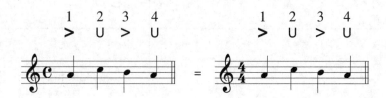

Common time is the same as quadruple-simple.

Write the signature for *common time.* _____

----

* These time signature markings date from the Middle Ages when many notational concepts had religious associations. For an excellent discussion of the evolution of these time signatures *see* Gardner Read, *Music Notation*, pp. 150, 156–157

----

duple-simple

5.50 The signature **¢** is called ALLA BREVE (or "cut time"). This indicates a quick duple-simple meter in which the half note receives the beat. It is the equivalent of $\frac{2}{2}$ time.

The time classification of *alla breve* is _____-

_____.

¢

5.51 Write the signature for *alla breve.* _____

Note: Although the terms *common time* and *alla breve* are essentially the same as the $\frac{4}{4}$ and $\frac{2}{2}$ signatures, they should be properly used only in conjunction with the signature signs **c** and **¢**.

	5.52 How many beats per measure are indicated by the signature **c**?
Four	_____
	5.53 How many beats per measure are indicated by the signature **¢**?
Two	_____
♩	5.54 Write the unit in common time. _____
♩	5.55 Write the unit in alla breve. _____
	5.56 The TIE is a curved line that connects two notes of the same pitch to express a longer duration.

$$\text{♩}\smile\text{♪} = \text{♩.}$$
$$\text{♩.}\smile\text{♩.} = \text{♩.}$$

The duration of one note value can be added to the |
| tie | duration of another by the use of a _____. |

5.57 Ties between units in simple time

Some typical patterns:*

Renotate without ties (as above) the following rhythm:

* Although it is possible to show any arithmetically correct groups of notes and rests within a measure, musicians generally expect notes and rhythms to be consistently grouped in accordance with the time signature, so that the patterns portrayed proceed in a logical and easily perceived way by those reading them.

5.58 Ties between units in compound time

Some typical patterns:

Renotate without ties (as above) the following rhythm:

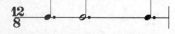

5.59   Ties between divisions in simple time

Some typical patterns:

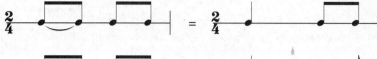

Borrowed division:

Renotate without ties (as above) the following rhythm:
(Note that in rewriting rhythmic patterns, the beat should not be hidden. This and the following exercises should bear that out.)

5.60   Renotate without ties the following rhythm:

5.61   Continue as in the preceding frame.

5.62   Continue as in the preceding frame.

5.63   Ties between divisions in compound time

Some typical patterns:

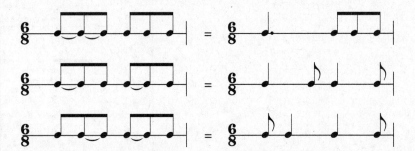

Renotate the rhythm below without ties.

5.64   Renotate the rhythm below without ties.

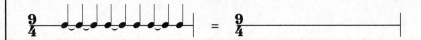

5.65   Continue as in the preceding frame.

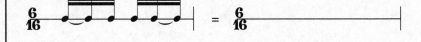

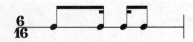

5.66   Continue as in the preceding frame.

5.67   Typical subdivision patterns in simple time

Unit: ♩

Renotate the rhythm below without ties.

5.68   Renotate the rhythm below without ties.

5.69   Continue as in the preceding frame.

5.70   Continue as in the preceding frame.

5.71 Typical subdivision patterns in compound time*

Unit: ♩.

Renotate the rhythm below without ties.

_____

* Subdivision patterns in compound time are so numerous that only the most common are shown.

5.72 Renotate the rhythm below without ties.

5.73 Continue as in the preceding frame.

5.74 Continue as in the preceding frame.

5.75 Continue as in the preceding frame.

5.76 When notes are tied in such a way that the longer values do not coincide with the beat, the result is called SYNCOPATION. *Syncopation* is demonstrated in each case below.

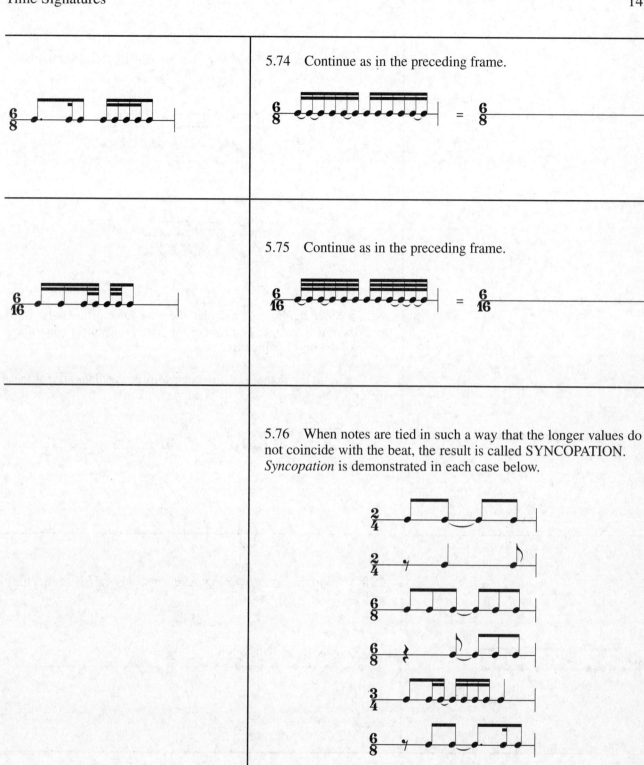

   Syncopation causes accents to be placed more or less counter to the stresses of the meter, which creates the impression that the beat (or pulse) is not where it is expected. One way this is accomplished is through a displacement of the notes by means of

ties

rests or by the use of _____.

5.77   Notes that occur within a beat are usually beamed together.

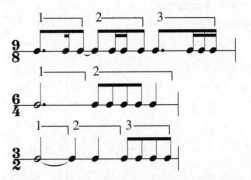

Notice that in each example the total value of the notes in every beat is the same. The sum of the note values must equal the value of the unit in all cases.

Group the notes by using beams instead of flags so that the meter is clearly expressed.

5.78   Group the notes by using beams instead of flags so that the meter is clearly expressed.

5.79   Continue as in the preceding frame.

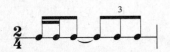

5.80   Continue as in the preceding frame.

5.81   Continue as in the preceding frame.

5.82   Continue as in the preceding frame.

5.83   Continue as in the preceding frame.

(1) $\frac{3}{8}$

(2) $\frac{6}{4}$

to be $\frac{12}{8}$ would need to be:

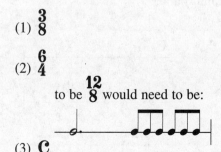

(3) 𝄵

5.84   Each of the examples below is a complete measure. Select the correct time signature from the alternatives supplied.

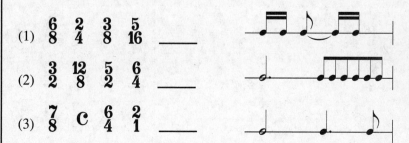

(1) $\frac{6}{8}$ $\frac{2}{4}$ $\frac{3}{8}$ $\frac{5}{16}$ _____

(2) $\frac{3}{2}$ $\frac{12}{8}$ $\frac{5}{2}$ $\frac{6}{4}$ _____

(3) $\frac{7}{8}$ 𝄴 $\frac{6}{4}$ $\frac{2}{1}$ _____

5.85   Continue as in the preceding frame.

(1) $\frac{5}{8}$

(1) $\frac{2}{4}$ $\frac{3}{4}$ $\frac{5}{8}$ $\frac{2}{2}$ _____

(2) $\frac{6}{8}$

(2) $\frac{6}{8}$ $\frac{3}{4}$ $\frac{7}{8}$ $\frac{2}{2}$ _____

(3) $\frac{2}{4}$

(3) $\mathbf{C}$ $\frac{2}{4}$ $\frac{5}{8}$ $\frac{3}{8}$ _____

5.86   Continue as in the preceding frame.

(1) $\frac{12}{8}$

(1) $\frac{4}{4}$ $\frac{2}{2}$ $\frac{6}{4}$ $\frac{12}{8}$ _____

(2) $\frac{4}{4}$

(2) $\frac{4}{4}$ $\frac{3}{2}$ $\frac{7}{8}$ $\frac{5}{4}$ _____

(3) $\frac{3}{8}$

(3) $\mathbf{C}$ $\frac{6}{8}$ $\frac{3}{8}$ $\frac{9}{16}$ _____

5.87   Continue as in the preceding frame.

(1) $\frac{2}{2}$

(1) $\frac{5}{4}$ $\frac{2}{2}$ $\frac{3}{4}$ $\frac{6}{4}$ _____

(2) $\frac{9}{4}$

(2) $\frac{3}{2}$ $\frac{9}{4}$ $\frac{5}{2}$ $\frac{3}{1}$ _____

(3) $\frac{3}{4}$

(3) $\frac{3}{4}$ $\frac{7}{8}$ $\frac{4}{4}$ $\frac{5}{8}$ _____

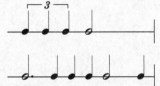

(1) $\frac{5}{4}$

(2) $\frac{3}{2}$

(3) $\frac{6}{16}$

5.88　Continue as in the preceding frame.

(1) $\frac{4}{4}$ $\frac{9}{8}$ $\frac{5}{4}$ $\frac{12}{8}$ _____

(2) $\frac{6}{4}$ $\frac{5}{4}$ $\mathbf{C}$ $\frac{3}{2}$ _____

(3) $\frac{3}{8}$ $\frac{6}{16}$ $\frac{2}{4}$ $\frac{4}{16}$ _____

Summary

Time signatures are interpreted differently, depending on whether they represent *simple* or *compound* time. *The upper number of simple time signatures indicates the number of beats per measure (meter), and the lower number represents the unit. In the case of compound time signatures, however, the upper number must be divided by three to ascertain the number of beats per measure, and since the lower number represents the division rather than the unit, three of the notes represented by this number must be combined to produce the unit.* Notes that occur in a single beat or in some other metric unit, such as the measure, are usually beamed together whenever possible. This is to facilitate the interpretation of rhythmic patterns by making a graphic representation of the pulse.

Mastery Frames

	5–1 Write four numbers that, when they appear in the upper part of a time signature, represent compound time.
6, 9, 12, 15 (frames 5.1–5.4)	_____
	5–2 The upper number of both simple and compound time signatures directly indicates the number of beats
False (5.7–5.8)	per measure. (True/False) _____
	5–3 Show the number of beats per measure in each case.
(1) 2	(1) $\frac{6}{8}$ = _____ beats per measure.
(2) 4	(2) $\frac{4}{4}$ = _____ beats per measure.
(3) 3 (5.7–5.14)	(3) $\frac{3}{8}$ = _____ beats per measure.
	5–4 Continue as in the preceding frame.
(1) 2	(1) $\frac{2}{2}$ = _____ beats per measure.
(2) 3	(2) $\frac{9}{8}$ = _____ beats per measure.
(3) 2 (5.7–5.14)	(3) $\frac{6}{4}$ = _____ beats per measure.
	5–5 The lower number of a simple time signature directly indicates the unit of the beat. (True/False)
True (5.16)	_____

division (5.17)	5–6 The lower number of a compound time signature represents the (unit/division/subdivision)_____ of the beat.
(1) 𝅗𝅥 (2) ♪ (3) 𝅘𝅥 (5.16)	5–7 Write the note that serves as the unit of the beat in each case. (1) $\frac{3}{2}$ Unit = _____ (2) $\frac{4}{8}$ Unit = _____ (3) $\frac{5}{4}$ Unit = _____
(1) 𝅘𝅥. (2) ♪. (3) 𝅗𝅥. (5.17–5.22)	5–8 Write the note that serves as the unit of the beat in each case. (1) $\frac{12}{8}$ Unit = _____ (2) $\frac{6}{16}$ Unit = _____ (3) $\frac{9}{4}$ Unit = _____
(1) 𝄴 (2) 𝄵 (5.49–5.55)	5–9 Write time signatures as directed. (1) Common time _____ (2) Alla breve _____

Supplementary Activities

1. Explore the topic of time in an essay or a short report. Consider the contradictions of "real" time as opposed to "psychological" time—why does an interesting piece of music that may last many minutes not seem long but a boring conversation of only a few minutes seems to take hours or eons of time? What factors can cause our perception of time to change? If it is "musical time" as opposed to other kinds of time—does that make a difference? Does it vary from one person to another?

2. Continue to explore the general types of time and how time is organized through any articles or books that can be found.

3. Continue to create short rhythmic compositions, but now try to attach specific time signatures to them and notate them with the correct note and rest values. Try to do these both with and without a text. Again, hand clapping, "body percussion," or simple vocal syllables may be the easiest to use.

Supplementary Assignments

ASSIGNMENT 5–1   Name: _____

1. Explain the chief difference between simple and compound time.

_____

_____

_____

2. Indicate the type of time signature in each case.

	Simple	*Compound*			*Simple*	*Compound*
6/4	_____	_____		**7/4**	_____	_____
3/2	_____	_____		**15/8**	_____	_____
5/4	_____	_____		**3/4**	_____	_____
2/2	_____	_____		**4/4**	_____	_____
9/8	_____	_____		**12/16**	_____	_____

3. Explain how the number of beats per measure is deduced by referring to the upper number of a time signature in each case.

Simple time signatures: _____

_____

_____

Compound time signatures: _____

_____

_____

4. Explain how the unit of the beat is deduced by referring to the lower number of a time signature in each case.

    Simple time signatures: _____

    _____

    _____

    Compound time signatures: _____

    _____

    _____

5. Provide information regarding the time signatures below.

	Time Classification	*Unit*
𝄴	_____	_____
𝄵	_____	_____

6. Provide information as indicated.

	Beats per Measure	*Unit*
$\frac{12}{8}$	_____	_____
$\frac{3}{2}$	_____	_____
$\frac{6}{16}$	_____	_____
$\frac{5}{8}$	_____	_____
$\frac{9}{4}$	_____	_____

ASSIGNMENT 5–2   Name: _____

1. Explain what is meant by the term *syncopation*. _____

_____

_____

2. Which measures contain an example of *syncopation*? _____

3. Renotate the examples using beams to clarify the meter.

4. Each example below represents one complete measure. Provide an appropriate time signature in each case.

5. Compose short examples demonstrating different time signatures and rhythmic patterns.

Chapter 6.0
Intervals

The musical distance between two tones is called an *interval*. The tones may sound successively or simultaneously. Because intervals are basic building blocks for both melody (linear movement) and harmony (vertical soundings), knowledge about them is essential. Intervals express the relationship between two notes and only two notes. Successful, advanced music study will depend on an ability to write intervals, recognize them aurally, and apply the terminology used to classify them. (While working on this chapter, try to reinforce reading and comprehension by singing the intervals or playing them on a keyboard or instrument; or reference them in Ear Training Activities, p. 191*ff.*)

---

melodic

6.1   Two tones sounding simultaneously produce a HARMONIC interval. A MELODIC interval occurs when two tones are sounded successively.

The interval below is a (harmonic/melodic)

_____ interval.

---

harmonic

6.2   The interval below is a (harmonic/melodic)

_____ interval.

---

difference

6.3   The concern now is to learn the terminology used to classify the difference in pitch between the two tones of an interval. When the difference in pitch is relatively great, the tones sound "far apart" and the interval seems "large." When the difference is relatively little, the tones sound "close together" and the interval seems "small."

Intervals vary in size depending on the _____ in pitch between the two tones that constitute them.

6.4   There are various methods of classifying intervals. In the field of acoustics (the scientific study of sound), for example, intervals are classified mathematically as the ratio between the frequencies of the two tones. But that is a specialized approach seldom used in practical musical terminology. In music theory, intervals are classified numerically from 1 to 8, according to the number of basic notes encompassed by the interval.

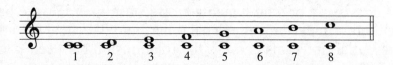

The basic classification of intervals is numerical.*

The numbers _____ to _____ are used to make this classification.

1 (to) 8

---

* Note that it doesn't matter what the interval sounds like, it is how it is written that gives it an interval number.

6.5   The numerical classification of intervals is very easy to determine. Merely count the number of basic notes encompassed by the interval. *Remember: Both the lower and the upper notes are part of the interval.* Call the lower note 1, and count lines and spaces to include the upper note.

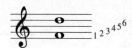

The interval is a 6th.

Indicate the numerical classification of each interval.

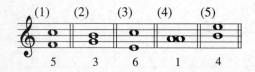

5   3   6   1   4

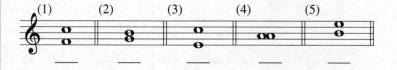

____   ____   ____   ____   ____

6.6   Indicate the numerical classification of each interval.

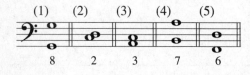

8   2   3   7   6

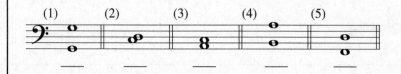

____   ____   ____   ____   ____

octave

6.7   The intervals that have been designated 1 and 8 have special names derived from Latin numerations: 1 = unison,* 8 = octave. It is customary to use ordinal numbers when referring to the remaining intervals.

1 unison	(or prime)
2 second	(2nd)
3 third	(3rd)
4 fourth	(4th)
5 fifth	(5th)
6 sixth	(6th)
7 seventh	(7th)
8 octave	(8th)

An interval that encompasses eight lines and

spaces is called a(n) _____.

---

* The term *prime* is also used.

octave

6.8   Intervals larger than an octave are called COMPOUND INTERVALS.

9th   10th   11th   12th

All *compound intervals* are larger than an

_____.

5th

6.9   Occasionally, it is necessary to refer to *compound intervals* as 9ths, 10ths, 11ths, and so on, but often they are analyzed as simple intervals (within a single octave). The relation of certain *compound intervals* to *simple intervals* is shown below.

Compound: 9th   10th   11th   12th
Simple: 2nd   3rd   4th   5th

If reduced in size by the interval of an octave, a

12th becomes a _____.

3rd

6.10 The example below shows that the interval of a

10th consists of an octave plus a _____.

8ve   10th

_____

Note: Compound intervals are classified the same as their smaller counterparts, so they need not be of further concern in this study.

6.11 Write intervals *above* the notes as directed.

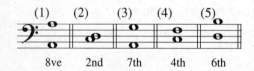

2nd   4th   unis.   3rd   5th

2nd   4th   unis.   3rd   5th

6.12 Write intervals *above* the notes as directed.

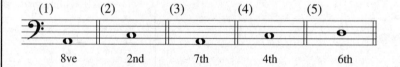

8ve   2nd   7th   4th   6th

8ve   2nd   7th   4th   6th

6.13 Intervals may be written below a note by counting *down* the required number of lines and spaces. To write a 7th below C, for example, call the third space 1, and count down seven lines and spaces.

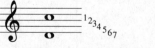

7th

F

What note is a 5th below C? _____

Intervals   159

---

(1) (2) (3) (4) (5)

8ve   6th   3rd   5th   7th

6.14   Write intervals *below* the notes as directed.

(1)   (2)   (3)   (4)   (5)

8ve   6th   3rd   5th   7th

---

(1) (2) (3) (4) (5)

4th   5th   2nd   6th   unis.

6.15   Write intervals *below* the notes as directed.

(1)   (2)   (3)   (4)   (5)

4th   5th   2nd   6th   unis.

6.16   The numerical classification of intervals is not affected by accidentals. The intervals in the example below are all 3rds.

(1)   (2)   (3)   (4)

3rd   3rd   3rd   3rd

numerical

Accidentals do not affect the _____ classification of intervals.

6.17   Accidentals applied to a basic interval make it larger or smaller, yet no amount of alteration changes the basic (numerical) classification. Thus, additional terminology is necessary to distinguish between different types of 3rds, 6ths, and so on. As the first step in learning to use the terms applied to intervals, the intervals can be divided into two groups:

GROUP I	GROUP II
unison	2nd
4th	3rd
5th	6th
octave	7th

The unison, 4th, 5th, and octave constitute one group of intervals. Name the intervals that make up the

2nd, 3rd, 6th, 7th

second group. _____

unison, 4th, 5th, 8ve	6.18 Name the intervals of Group I. _____ _____

d	6.19 The intervals of Group I (unison, 4th, 5th, and 8ve) can be PERFECT, AUGMENTED, and DIMINISHED.* These terms are abbreviated as follows:
	
	        Perfect P
	        Augmented A
	        Diminished d
	
	     A capital P is used to symbolize the term *perfect;* a capital A is used to symbolize the term *augmented.*
	
	     What is the symbol for the term *diminished*? _____
	
	 _____
	 * There is one exception: The unison cannot be diminished (see frame 6.25).

No	6.20 A PERFECT UNISON consists of two tones of the same pitch and notation. Is there any difference in pitch between the two tones that produce a *perfect unison*? _____
	6.21 Write the note that will produce a perfect unison in each case.

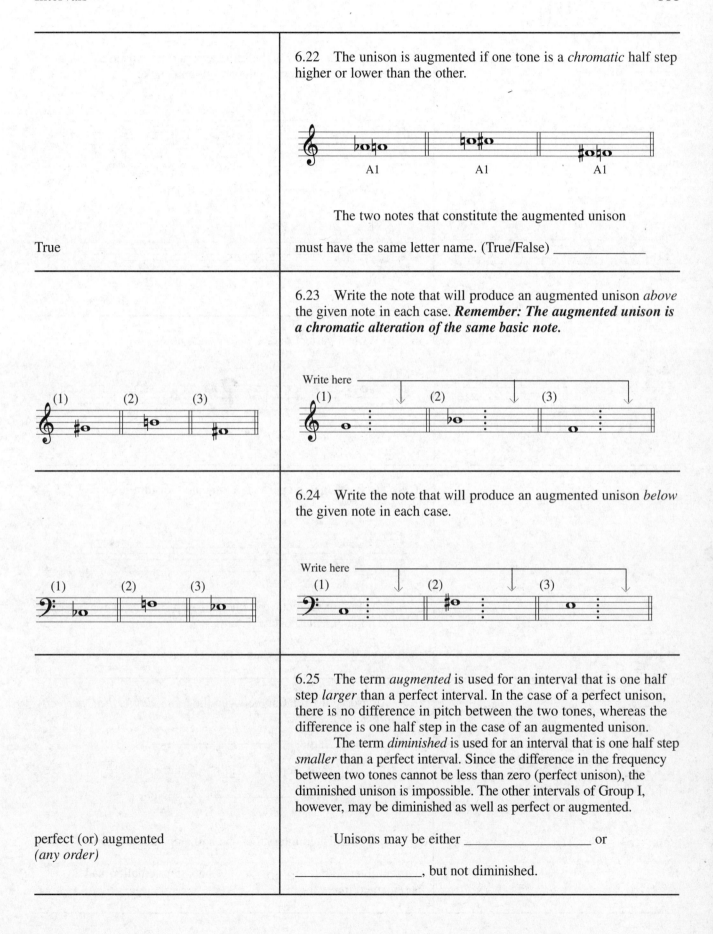

6.22   The unison is augmented if one tone is a *chromatic* half step higher or lower than the other.

A1   A1   A1

The two notes that constitute the augmented unison

True

must have the same letter name. (True/False) _____

6.23   Write the note that will produce an augmented unison *above* the given note in each case. ***Remember: The augmented unison is a chromatic alteration of the same basic note.***

Write here

(1)   (2)   (3)

6.24   Write the note that will produce an augmented unison *below* the given note in each case.

Write here

(1)   (2)   (3)

6.25   The term *augmented* is used for an interval that is one half step *larger* than a perfect interval. In the case of a perfect unison, there is no difference in pitch between the two tones, whereas the difference is one half step in the case of an augmented unison.

The term *diminished* is used for an interval that is one half step *smaller* than a perfect interval. Since the difference in the frequency between two tones cannot be less than zero (perfect unison), the diminished unison is impossible. The other intervals of Group I, however, may be diminished as well as perfect or augmented.

perfect (or) augmented
(any order)

Unisons may be either _____ or

_____, but not diminished.

6.26 A perfect octave is the same as a perfect unison except that one note is displaced by the interval of an octave.

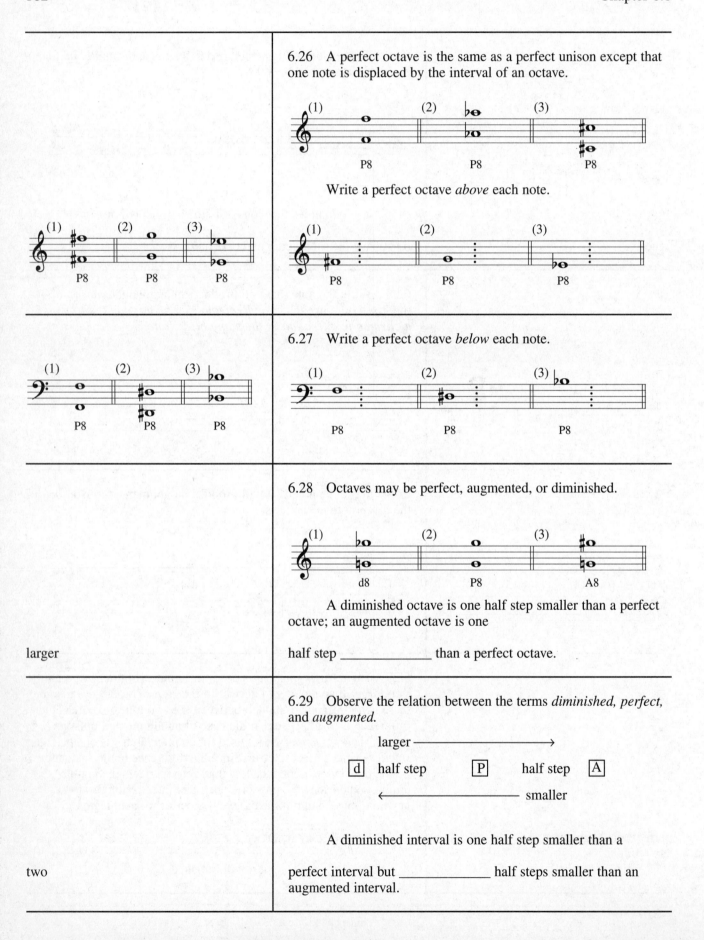

Write a perfect octave *above* each note.

6.27 Write a perfect octave *below* each note.

6.28 Octaves may be perfect, augmented, or diminished.

A diminished octave is one half step smaller than a perfect octave; an augmented octave is one

larger

half step _____ than a perfect octave.

6.29 Observe the relation between the terms *diminished, perfect,* and *augmented.*

larger ——————————→

[d] half step   [P] half step   [A]

←—————————— smaller

A diminished interval is one half step smaller than a

two

perfect interval but _____ half steps smaller than an augmented interval.

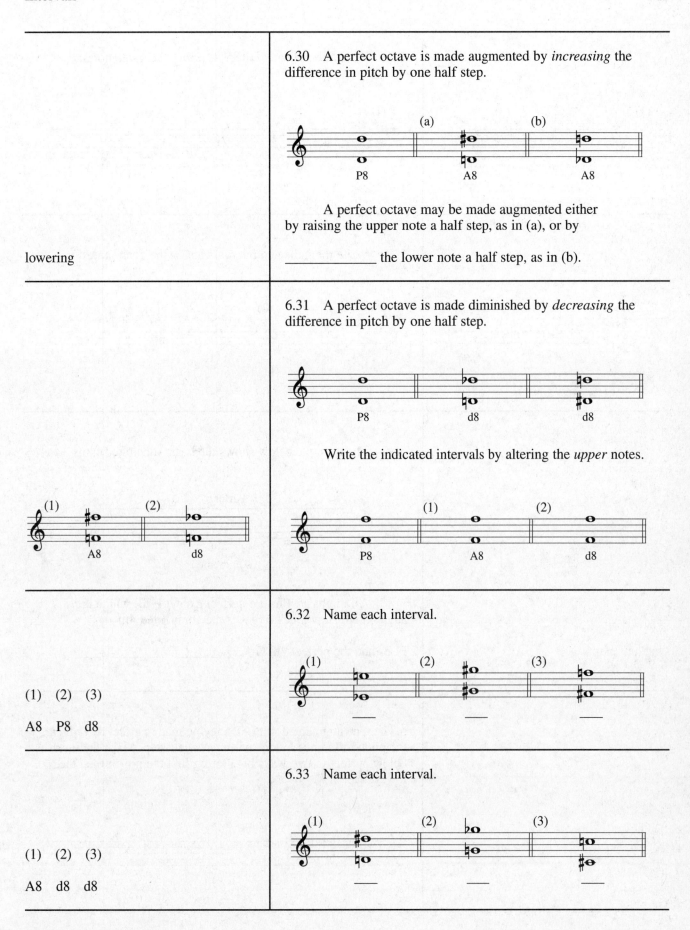

6.30   A perfect octave is made augmented by *increasing* the difference in pitch by one half step.

P8   A8   A8

A perfect octave may be made augmented either by raising the upper note a half step, as in (a), or by

lowering

_____ the lower note a half step, as in (b).

6.31   A perfect octave is made diminished by *decreasing* the difference in pitch by one half step.

P8   d8   d8

Write the indicated intervals by altering the *upper* notes.

(1)   (2)
A8   d8

P8   A8   d8

6.32   Name each interval.

(1)   (2)   (3)

A8   P8   d8

6.33   Name each interval.

(1)   (2)   (3)

A8   d8   d8

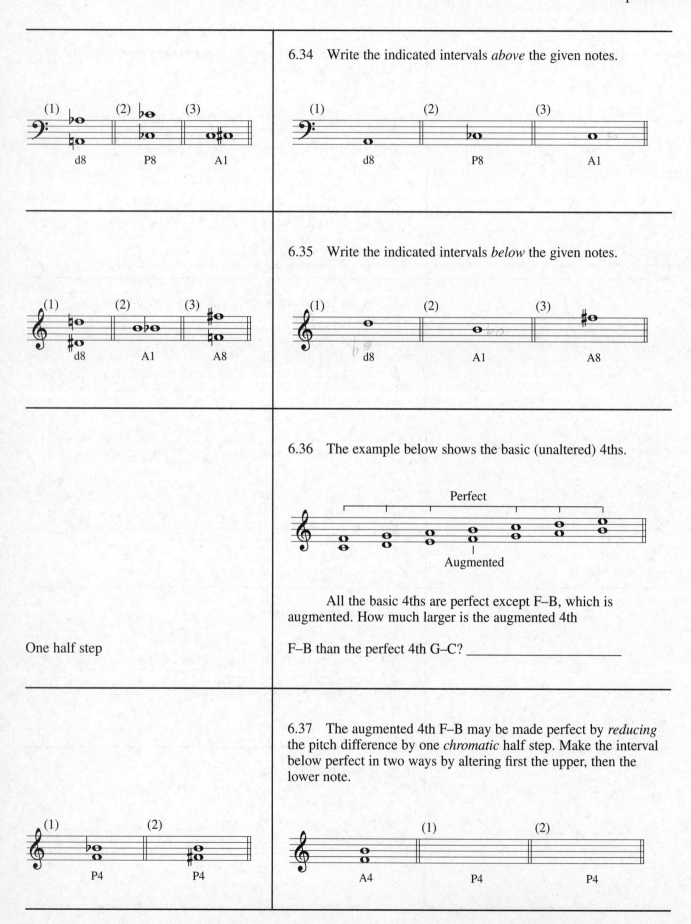

6.34 Write the indicated intervals *above* the given notes.

(1)   (2)   (3)

d8   P8   A1

6.35 Write the indicated intervals *below* the given notes.

(1)   (2)   (3)

d8   A1   A8

6.36 The example below shows the basic (unaltered) 4ths.

Perfect

Augmented

All the basic 4ths are perfect except F–B, which is augmented. How much larger is the augmented 4th

One half step   F–B than the perfect 4th G–C? _____

6.37 The augmented 4th F–B may be made perfect by *reducing* the pitch difference by one *chromatic* half step. Make the interval below perfect in two ways by altering first the upper, then the lower note.

(1)   (2)   (1)   (2)

P4   P4   A4   P4   P4

6.38   If the basic interval is perfect, the same accidental applied to each note will cause no change in quality.

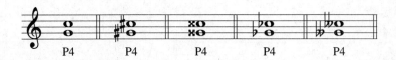

But if the two notes are affected differently, a change of quality will occur.

False
(F–B is an augmented 4th.)

All basic 4ths are perfect. (True/False) _____

6.39   By referring to the quality (perfect or augmented) of the basic interval and taking into account the effect of accidentals (if any), you should be able to analyze any 4th. ***Remember: A perfect interval made a half step smaller is diminished; a perfect interval made a half step larger is augmented.***

Name each interval.

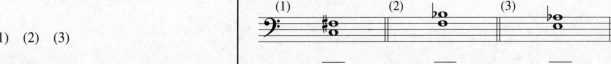

(1)   (2)   (3)

A4   P4   d4

6.40   Name each interval.

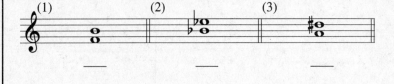

(1)   (2)   (3)

A4   P4   A4

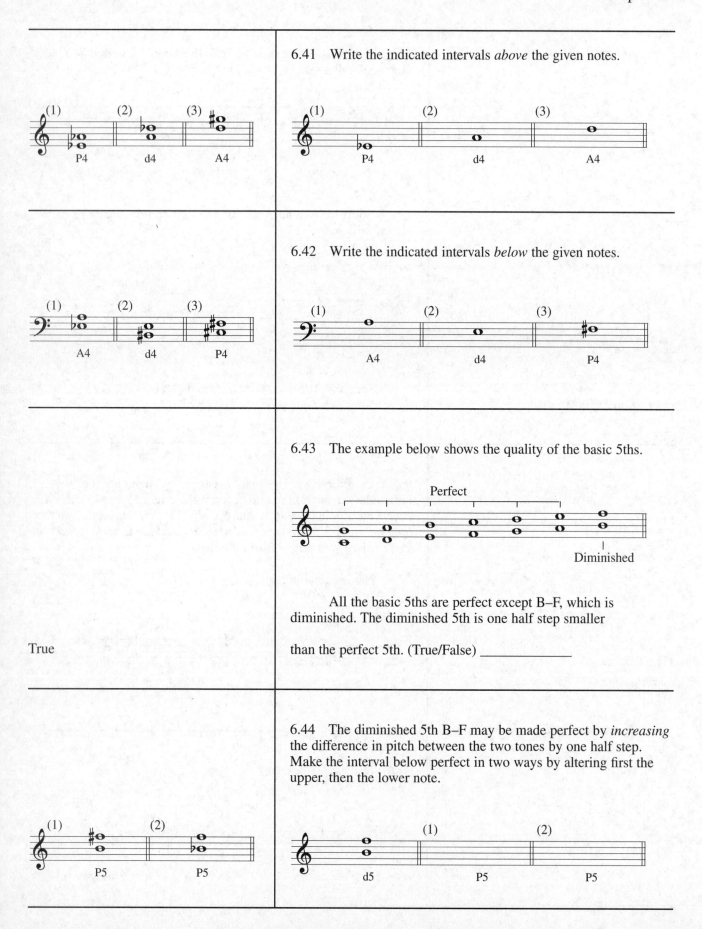

6.41   Write the indicated intervals *above* the given notes.

(1)   (2)   (3)

P4   d4   A4

6.42   Write the indicated intervals *below* the given notes.

(1)   (2)   (3)

A4   d4   P4

6.43   The example below shows the quality of the basic 5ths.

Perfect

Diminished

All the basic 5ths are perfect except B–F, which is diminished. The diminished 5th is one half step smaller

True   than the perfect 5th. (True/False) _____

6.44   The diminished 5th B–F may be made perfect by *increasing* the difference in pitch between the two tones by one half step. Make the interval below perfect in two ways by altering first the upper, then the lower note.

(1)   (2)   (1)   (2)

P5   P5   d5   P5   P5

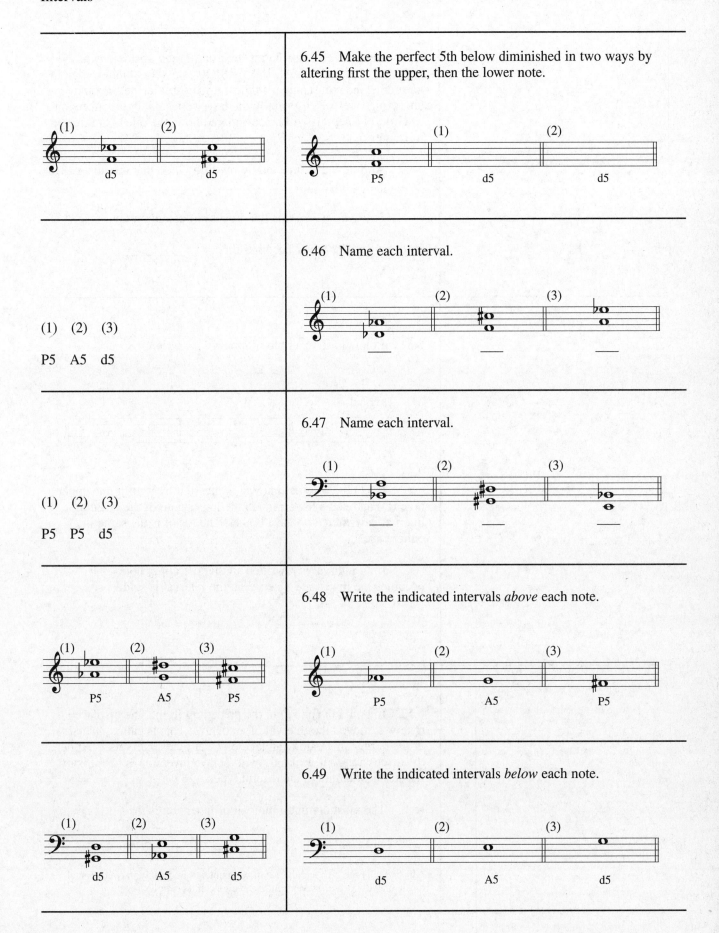

6.45   Make the perfect 5th below diminished in two ways by altering first the upper, then the lower note.

6.46   Name each interval.

6.47   Name each interval.

6.48   Write the indicated intervals *above* each note.

6.49   Write the indicated intervals *below* each note.

(1)   (2)   (3)

P5   A5   d5

(1)   (2)   (3)

P5   P5   d5

6.50   Intervals can also be inverted or "turned upside down." A knowledge of INTERVAL INVERSION is essential knowledge in harmonic and contrapuntal studies. It is useful in spelling and analyzing intervals, especially the larger ones. Only the inversion of Group I intervals will be considered now; the others are treated in frames 6.88–6.91.

        An interval is inverted by rewriting it so that the upper note becomes the lower and vice versa.

        Interval inversion is the process of changing the

notes so that the lower becomes the _____.

upper

6.51   Below is an example of *interval inversion*.

        In (1) the original interval is inverted by writing the upper note (D) an octave lower; in (2) the lower note of the original interval is written an octave higher. The result is the same in either case.

        If an interval is rewritten so that the upper note becomes the lower and vice versa, the interval is said

to be _____.

inverted

6.52   In both (1) and (2) in the preceding frame, the displaced note was moved the interval of an octave. This is called *inversion at the octave*. Inversion can take place at other intervals,* but here the discussion will deal only with octave inversion, since it is by far the most common and useful type.

        The most common interval of inversion is the

_____.

octave

---

* Inversion at the 10th and the 12th is encountered frequently in contrapuntal music of the sixteenth, seventeenth, and eighteenth centuries.

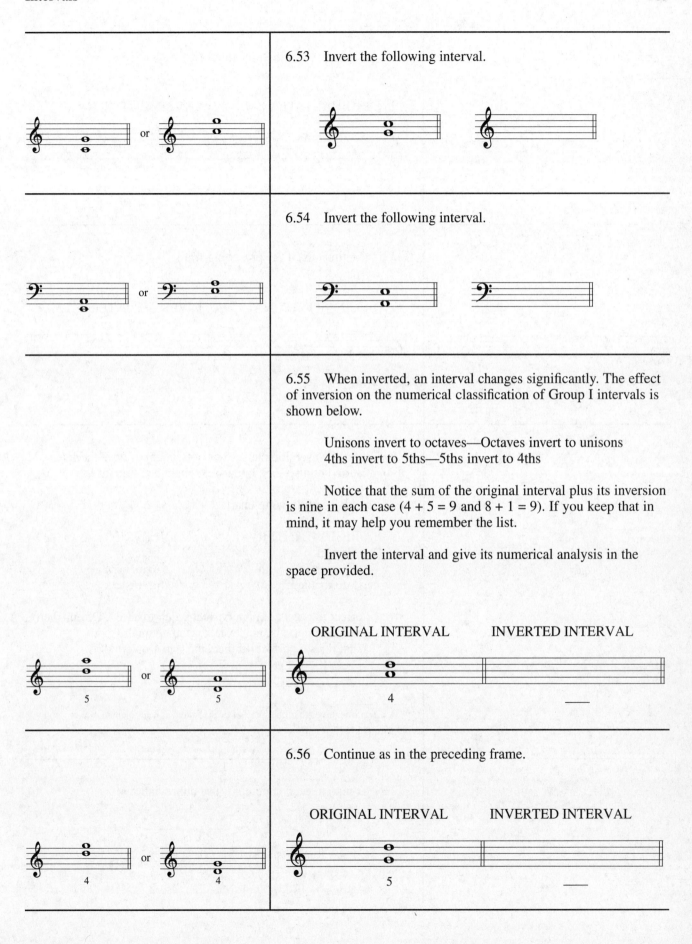

6.53   Invert the following interval.

6.54   Invert the following interval.

6.55   When inverted, an interval changes significantly. The effect of inversion on the numerical classification of Group I intervals is shown below.

Unisons invert to octaves—Octaves invert to unisons
4ths invert to 5ths—5ths invert to 4ths

Notice that the sum of the original interval plus its inversion is nine in each case ($4 + 5 = 9$ and $8 + 1 = 9$). If you keep that in mind, it may help you remember the list.

Invert the interval and give its numerical analysis in the space provided.

ORIGINAL INTERVAL   INVERTED INTERVAL

4

6.56   Continue as in the preceding frame.

ORIGINAL INTERVAL   INVERTED INTERVAL

5

6.57 Continue as in the preceding frame.

ORIGINAL INTERVAL   INVERTED INTERVAL

8   ____

6.58 Continue as in the preceding frame.

ORIGINAL INTERVAL   INVERTED INTERVAL

1   ____

6.59 Interval inversion causes not only changes of numerical classification but also, in some cases, changes of quality.

Study the following chart:

ORIGINAL INTERVAL	INVERTS TO
Perfect	Perfect
Diminished	Augmented
Augmented*	Diminished

Perfect intervals remain perfect when inverted. Diminished and augmented intervals, however, exchange quality.

What does a perfect 4th become when inverted?

_____

_____

* Because it is larger than the interval of inversion, the augmented octave cannot be inverted at the octave.

Perfect 5th

6.60 Complete each statement (use abbreviations).

(1) A d5 inverts to a(n) _____.

(2) A P8 inverts to a(n) _____.

(3) An A1 inverts to a(n) _____.

(1) A4

(2) P1

(3) d8

6.61 Continue as in the preceding frame.

(1) d5

(1) an A4 inverts to a(n) _____ .

(2) P4

(2) A P5 inverts to a(n) _____ .

(3) A1

(3) A d8 inverts to a(n) _____ .

6.62 Invert each interval, and give its correct analysis.

ORIGINAL INTERVAL   INVERTED INTERVAL

(1)

d8   or   d8

(1)

A1   _____

(2)

P4   or   P4

(2)

P5   _____

(3)

d5   or   d5

(3)

A4   _____

6.63 We shall now learn to use the terms applied to the intervals of Group II (2nds, 3rds, 6ths, and 7ths). These intervals can be MAJOR, MINOR, DIMINISHED, and AUGMENTED. The abbreviations for these terms are shown below.

Augmented	A
Major	M
Minor	m
Diminished	d

The intervals of both Group I and Group II use the terms *diminished* and *augmented*. Which term used by intervals of Group I is not used by those of

Perfect

Group II? _____

major (and) minor
(any order)

6.64   Instead of the term *perfect,* the intervals of Group II

use the terms _____ and _____.

6.65   Observe the relation between the terms that apply to 2nds, 3rds, 6ths, and 7ths.

larger ——————————————→

$\boxed{d}$ half step $\boxed{m}$ half step $\boxed{M}$ half step $\boxed{A}$

←————————————————— smaller

The intervals of Group II have four classifications. The smallest is diminished, and the largest is augmented. A

two

minor interval is _____ half step(s) smaller than an augmented interval.

6.66   A major interval is made minor by decreasing

one

its size by _____ half step.

6.67   The interval below is a diminished 3rd. Change this interval in (1), (2), and (3) as directed. *Apply accidentals to the upper notes only.*

(1) m3   (2) M3   (3) A3

d3   (1) m3   (2) M3   (3) A3

6.68   The interval below is a diminished 6th. Change this interval in (1), (2), and (3) as directed. *Apply accidentals to the lower notes only.*

(1) m6   (2) M6   (3) A6

d6   (1) m6   (2) M6   (3) A6

6.69   The example below shows the basic (unaltered) 2nds.

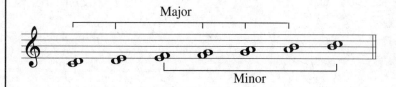

       There should be little difficulty remembering the quality of basic 2nds because it has already been learned that on the staff, half steps occur between the notes E and F and the notes B and C. *(It is useful to remember that a minor 2nd consists of a half step, and a major 2nd consists of a whole step.)*

       Except for E–F and B–C, all basic 2nds are _____.

major

6.70   A minor 2nd may be made major by *increasing* the difference in pitch between the two tones by one half step. Make the interval below major in two ways by altering first the upper, then the lower note.

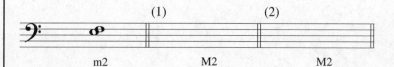

6.71   A major 2nd may be made minor by *reducing* the difference in pitch between the two tones by one half step. Make the major 2nd below minor in two ways by altering first the upper, then the lower note.

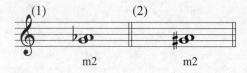

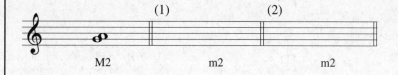

6.72 By referring to the quality of the basic interval and taking into account the effect of accidentals (if any), it is possible to be able to identify the quality of any 2nd. *(Be sure to keep in mind the chart in frame 6.65.)*

Name each interval.

(1)   (2)   (3)

M2   m2   M2

6.73 Name each interval.

(1)   (2)   (3)

M2   A2   m2

6.74 Name each interval.

(1)   (2)   (3)

M2   m2   d2

6.75 If the diminished 2nd in (3) of the preceding frame had been written as either two C-sharps or two D-flats,* the interval would have been analyzed as a

perfect

_____ unison.

* Intervals that sound the same but are notated differently are called *enharmonic*. (See frames 6.102–6.106.)

(1) (2) (3)

m2   M2   M2

6.76   Write the indicated intervals *above* the given notes.

(1)   (2)   (3)

m2   M2   M2

(1) (2) (3)

A2   m2   d2

6.77   Write the indicated intervals *below* the given notes.

(1)   (2)   (3)

A2   m2   d2

6.78   The example below shows the basic 3rds.

Major

Minor

(Do not proceed until the quality of the basic 3rds has been learned.)

A major 3rd may be made *minor* by decreasing

one

the size of the interval by _____ half step(s).

6.79   Which of the intervals are *major* 3rds?

(3) and (5)

_____

(1)   (2)   (3)   (4)   (5)

6.80   Which of the intervals are *minor* 3rds?

(1), (2), and (4)   _____

6.81   The intervals below are minor 3rds. Make each major by altering the *upper* note.

6.82   The intervals below are major 3rds. Make each minor by altering the *lower* note.

6.83   Name each interval.

(1)   (2)   (3)

m3   d3   M3

6.84   Name each interval.

(1)   (2)   (3)

M3   A3   m3

6.85   Name each interval.

(1)   (2)   (3)

m3   M3   M3

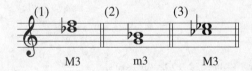

6.86   Write the indicated intervals *above* the given notes.

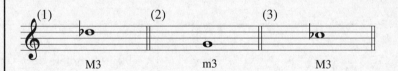

6.87   Write the indicated intervals *below* the given notes.

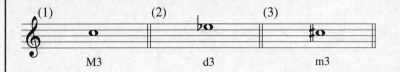

6.88 The use of interval inversion to spell 6ths and 7ths will now be made. When Group II intervals are inverted, their numerical classification changes as below.

2nds invert to 7ths—7ths invert to 2nds
3rds invert to 6ths—6ths invert to 3rds

Invert the intervals and give their numerical classification.

(1) (2)

2 _____ 3 _____

6.89 The effect of inversion on the quality of Group II intervals is shown in the following chart:

ORIGINAL INTERVAL	INVERTS TO
Major	Minor
Minor	Major
Diminished	Augmented
Augmented	Diminished

What does a major 6th become when inverted?

Minor 3rd

_____

6.90 Complete each statement (use abbreviations).

(1) M6

(1) A m3 inverts to a(n) _____.

(2) A6

(2) A d3 inverts to a(n) _____.

(3) m6

(3) A M3 inverts to a(n) _____.

6.91 Complete each statement (use abbreviations).

(1) d3

(1) An A6 inverts to a(n) _____.

(2) M3

(2) A m6 inverts to a(n) _____.

(3) A3

(3) A d6 inverts to a(n) _____.

6.92   This is how inversions are used to spell 6ths and 7ths: (The problem in this frame is to spell a major 6th *above* the note E.)

M6

The solution is reached in two steps: (1) Identify the inversion of the desired interval (a major 6th inverts to a minor 3rd); (2) write a minor 3rd *below* the higher octave of the given note.

M6

If a minor 6th had been desired, it would have been

major

necessary to write a _____ 3rd below the higher octave of the given note.

6.93   To try another example: (The problem this time is to spell a minor 7th *below* the note E.)

m7

M2

Step 1: A m7 inverts to a _____.

6.94   To complete the problem of spelling a minor 7th below E, continue with step 2: Write a major 2nd *above* the lower octave of the given note.

m7

(M2)   ⌐___ Write here

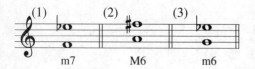

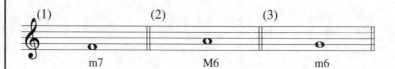

6.95 Write the indicated intervals *above* the given notes.

6.96 Write the indicated intervals *above* the given notes.

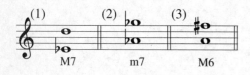

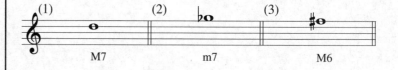

6.97 Write the indicated intervals *below* the given notes.

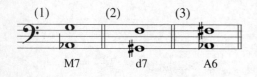

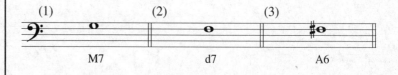

6.98 Write the indicated intervals *below* the given notes.

6.99   The knowledge of inversions to analyze an interval may also be used. The interval E♭ to D can be identified in two steps as shown below:

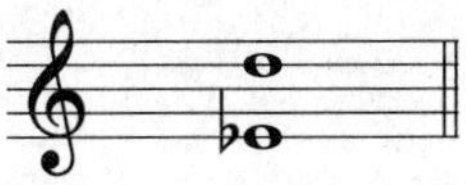

Step 1: Invert the interval

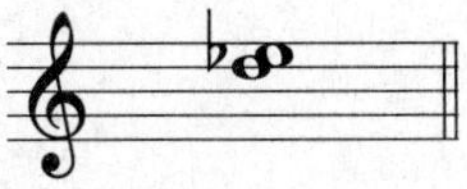

Step 2: Inverted, the interval is a minor 2nd. Thus,

in its original form, it must be a _____ 7th.

Note that intervals can be analyzed by half steps and spelled that way, but it adds unnecessary complications to the process. If the Group I and II concepts are mastered, along with inversions, then the use of half-step calculations is not really necessary.

major

6.100 Name each interval.

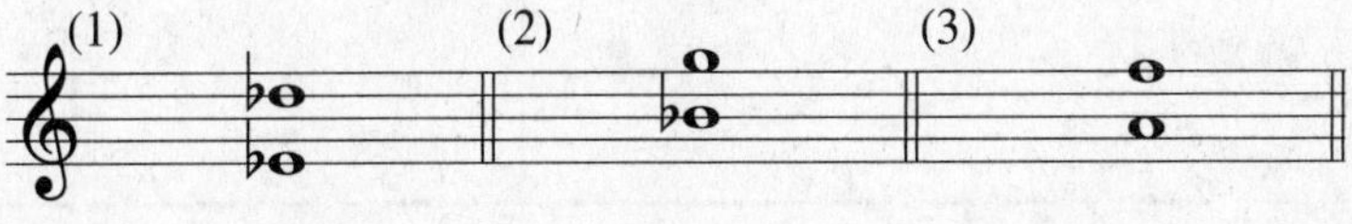

(1)   (2)   (3)

m7   M6   m6

6.101 Name each interval.

(1)   (2)   (3)

d7   m7   A6

6.102 Two intervals that sound the same but are notated differently are said to be ENHARMONIC.

Name each of the intervals below.

(1)   (2)

_____   _____

(1)   (2)

A6   m7

6.103 The preceding frame shows that an augmented

6th is _____ with a minor 7th.

enharmonic

6.104 Apply accidentals to the notes of the second interval to make it *enharmonic* with the first. Also, name each interval.

(1)   (2)

_____   _____

(1)   (2)

A2   m3

6.105 Apply an accidental to one of the notes of the second interval to make it *enharmonic* with the first. Name each interval.

(1)   (2)

_____   _____

(1)   (2)

A4   d5

6.106 The preceding few frames have shown several enharmonic intervals.* Although others are possible, the ones presented are those most frequently encountered in the study of music theory.

Complete this list:

(1) m3

(2) d5

(3) m7

(1) An A2 is enharmonic with a _____.

(2) An A4 is enharmonic with a _____.

(3) An A6 is enharmonic with a _____.

* It is not general musical practice to make enharmonic substitutions when constructing intervals unless the musical context suggests it. *Also, be careful not to confuse these enharmonic applications with the process of inversion.*

6.107 Occasionally, an interval is altered to such an extent that the terms *diminished* and *augmented* do not suffice. In such a case, the interval is referred to as *doubly diminished* or *doubly augmented.*

AA4   dd5

two

The *doubly augmented* 4th is _____ half steps larger than the perfect 4th.

6.108 Write the indicated intervals *above* the given notes.

AA5   dd6   AA4

AA5   dd6   AA4

6.109 Name each interval.

(1)   (2)   (3)

A4   d3   AA5

Summary

The terms used by the intervals of Groups I and II are shown below.

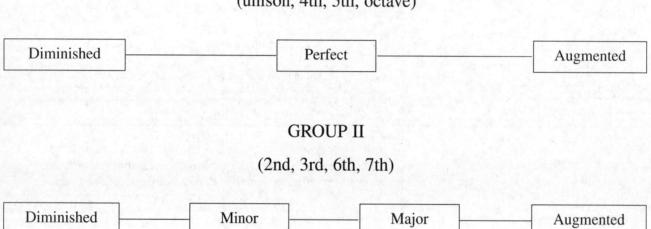

GROUP I

(unison, 4th, 5th, octave)

| Diminished | Perfect | Augmented |

GROUP II

(2nd, 3rd, 6th, 7th)

| Diminished | Minor | Major | Augmented |

Group I intervals have three possible qualities, whereas Group II intervals have four. The term *diminished* represents the smallest interval. Each successive term (left to right) represents an increase in size of one half step.

In addition to its importance for more advanced theory study, knowledge of *interval inversion* may be used to spell larger intervals, such as 6ths and 7ths. When intervals are inverted, their numerical classification and their quality change in the following manner:

ORIGINAL INTERVAL	INVERTED INTERVAL
Perfect	Perfect
Major	Minor
Minor	Major
Augmented	Diminished
Diminished	Augmented
Unison	Octave
2nd	7th
3rd	6th
4th	5th
5th	4th
6th	3rd
7th	2nd
Octave	Unison

Mastery Frames

(b) *(frames 6.1–6.2)*	6–1 Rewrite the interval below as a harmonic interval. (a) (b)
(1) (2) 1 3 6 7 *(6.4–6.16)*	6–2 Write the numerical classification of each interval. (1) (2) (3) (4) ___ ___ ___ ___
perfect, augmented, and diminished *(6.19)*	6–3 Write the terms that are used by intervals of Group I (unison, 4th, 5th, octave). _____ _____
augmented, major, minor, and diminished *(6.63–6.66)*	6–4 Write the terms that are used by intervals of Group II (2nd, 3rd, 6th, 7th). _____ _____
augmented diminished *(6.29–6.31)*	6–5 Write the terms that identify intervals as stated. *Original Interval Perfect* Half step larger: _____ Half step smaller: _____

augmented

minor

diminished

(6.65–6.68)

6–6   Write the terms that identify intervals as stated.

Original Interval	Major
Half step larger:	_____
Half step smaller:	_____
Whole step smaller:	_____

6–7   Provide the missing information.

Original Interval		Inverted Interval
(1) P8	(1) P1	_____
(2) d7	(2) A2	_____
(3) M6	(3) m3	_____
(4) P5	(4) P4	_____
(5) A4	(5) d5	_____
(6) M3	(6) m6	_____
(7) M2	(7) m7	_____
(8) A1	(8) d8	_____

(6.55–6.62; 6.88–6.91)

(1), (3), and (5)   (6.102–6.106)

6–8   Which pairs of intervals are enharmonic?

_____

Supplementary Activities

Note: Supplementary Activities for this chapter are probably best concentrated on ear-training activity after written materials are mastered, but please see other activities listed at the end of the Ear-Training Activities section.

Supplementary Assignments

ASSIGNMENT 6–1   Name: _____

1. Indicate the numerical classification of each interval.

2. List the four intervals that use the term *perfect*.

a. _____ b. _____ c. _____ d. _____

3. List the four intervals that use the terms *major* and *minor,* but not the term *perfect*.

a. _____ b. _____ c. _____ d. _____

4. Invert each interval at the octave, and analyze both the original and the inverted interval.

5. When inverted at the octave:

    Perfect intervals become _____intervals.

    Major intervals become _____intervals.

    Minor intervals become _____intervals.

    Diminished intervals become _____intervals.

    Augmented intervals become _____intervals.

6. When inverted at the octave:

    Unisons become _____ .

    2nds become _____ .

    3rds become _____ .

    4ths become _____ .

    5ths become _____ .

    6ths become _____ .

    7ths become _____ .

    Octaves become _____ .

7. Provide the missing information:

    Original Interval   *Inverted Interval*

    (1) _____   P1

    (2) A2   _____

    (3) m3   _____

    (4) _____   P5

    (5) _____   A4

    (6) m6   _____

    (7) _____   M2

    (8) d8   _____

ASSIGNMENT 6–2   Name: _____

1. Provide the missing information.

    a. All basic 2nds are major except _____ and _____ , which are minor.

    b. All basic 3rds are _____ except C–E, F–A, and G–B, which are _____ .

    c. All basic 4ths are perfect except _____ , which is _____ .

    d. All basic 5ths are _____ except B–F, which is _____ .

    e. All basic 6ths are major except _____ , _____ , and _____ , which are minor.

    f. All basic 7ths are minor, except _____ and _____, which are _____ .

2. Write intervals *above* the given notes.

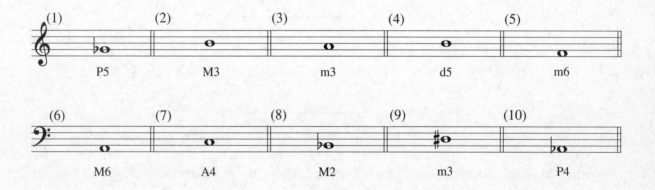

3. Write intervals *below* the given notes.

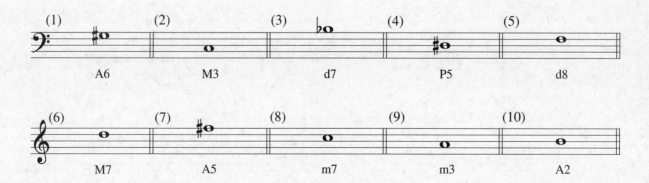

4. Write an *enharmonic* equivalent for each interval.

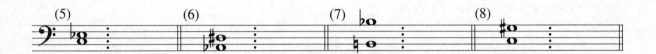

5. Name an *enharmonic* equivalent for each interval.

	Original Interval	*Enharmonic Equivalent*
a.	A1	_____
b.	A2	_____
c.	AA4	_____
d.	d5	_____
e.	A6	_____
f.	d7	_____

6. Now that these various intervals have been learned, try to assemble them in various ways to create some simple melodies based on knowledge thus far.

Ear-Training Activities

The following exercises are quite comprehensive and may take some time to master. Keep working on them even after going ahead to other topics.

1. The numerical classification of intervals stems from the number of basic notes encompassed by the interval. The following exercise will help associate numbers with interval size. Begin on any pitch, but the higher notes must be included in the major scale of the lowest note. (Major scales are presented in Chapter 8.0.)

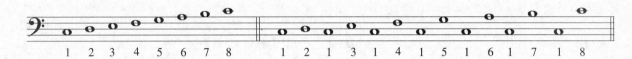

2. In the preceding exercise the intervals are sung upward from the stationary note C. The direction is reversed in the following exercise.

3. *Perfect intervals (unison, 4th, 5th, octave).* The perfect unison and the perfect octave are perhaps the easiest of all intervals to hear. The two notes of the unison have the same pitch, and in the case of the octave, one note is virtually the replica of the other. Nevertheless, when notes lie outside your vocal range, it may be difficult to hear them in your head and duplicate them. It is desirable, therefore, to practice matching pitches both within and outside your range. Play widely spaced notes at the piano so that each will be disassociated from the preceding note.

The following example may serve as a model. Sing after each note.

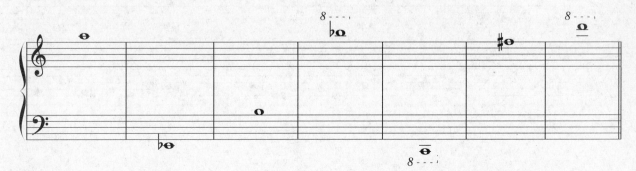

4. *Perfect 4th, perfect 5th.* The numbers associated with the intervals in the next exercise reflect the numerical classification (5th, 4th). Play the first note at the piano; then sing the second two notes. (Check responses if necessary. Note also that only the first example of each interval type is demonstrated on the CD.)

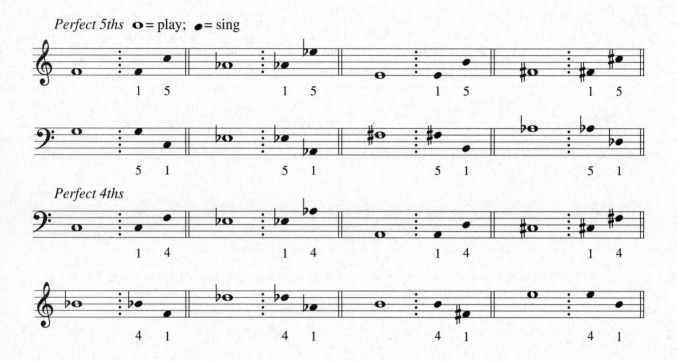

5. *Augmented 4th, diminished 5th (tritones).* The tritone is easy to recognize but sometimes difficult to sing. The peculiar effect of this interval stems from the facts that the interval encompasses three whole tones and that it divides the octave into two equal parts. The augmented 4th and the diminished 5th are enharmonic. It is useful, however, to approach them as related to perfect 4ths and 5ths. Sing the following exercises.

5ths

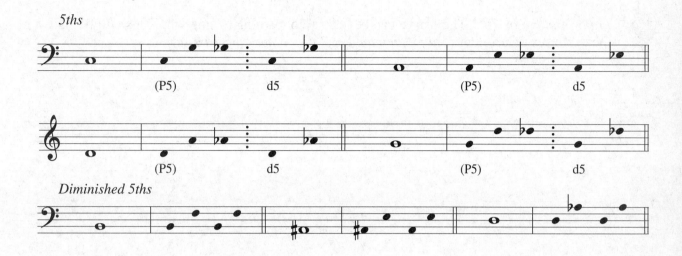

Diminished 5ths

6. *Major and minor 2nds.*

7. *Major and minor 7ths.* The octave can be helpful in learning to sing 7ths. This will be shown in the exercises that follow. *(Sing with numbers if they help; otherwise, use* la.*)*

8. *Major and minor 3rds.*

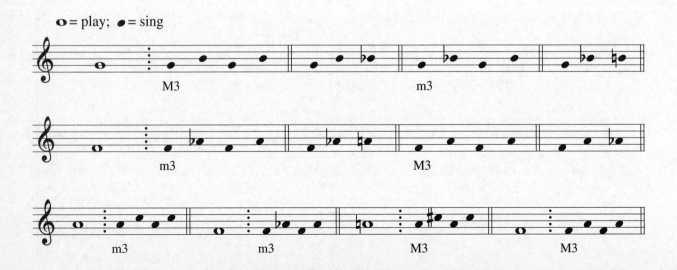

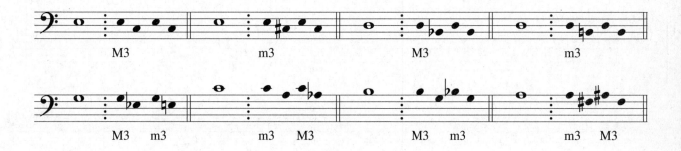

9. *Major and minor 6ths.* The first few exercises show the relationships of major and minor 3rds to their inversions (minor and major 6ths, respectively).

Major 6ths

Minor 6ths

An additional hint: Sometimes remembering the opening phrase of a favorite or well-known song can help to aurally identify intervals. To see how this might work, here are some folk songs with the intervals identified: (*Any song will work; just remember it!*)

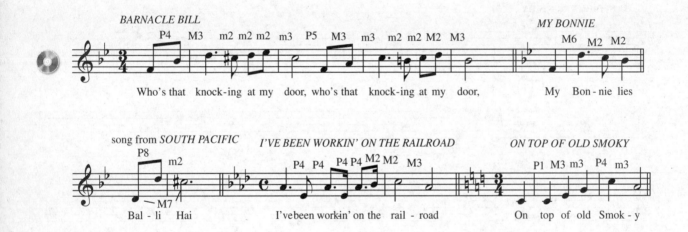

Additional Supplementary Activities

1. Once these ear-training activities have been thoroughly practiced, play short improvised phrases at a keyboard or on an instrument and immediately try singing them back spontaneously. If you are a vocalist (and don't play an instrument readily), get together with a vocal partner and practice singing phrases back and forth in a "dueling banjo" style. Try to do ever longer phrases to see how much can be remembered and temporarily memorized.

2. If some interesting phrases are created in the preceding practice, go to a further step and try to notate what has been improvised. Check it for accuracy by playing it back on a keyboard or on an instrument or by singing.

3. Form an improvisatory ensemble to practice all the preceding ideas or to explore and practice the topics presented thus far in the text. Consider organizing a concert to present some improvisations (by in turn improvising on the spot for the concert itself).

Chapter 7.0
The Basic Scales

The word *scale* is derived from the Latin *scala,* which means "ladder." It refers to an orderly ascending or descending arrangement of successive pitches within the limit of an octave. There are many kinds of scales, depending on the intervallic relation of the notes. This chapter is concerned with the scales formed by only the seven basic (unaltered) notes. Because no accidentals are used, these are called *basic scales.* Other music theorists (writers) may also refer to these *basic scales* as "modes."

7.1   A STEPWISE arrangement of the tones contained in one octave is called a SCALE. *Stepwise* means an alphabetical arrangement of the letters that represent tones.

    Write the letters that produce a *stepwise* series of tones starting and ending on A.

A B C D E F G A

__ __ __ __ __ __ __ __

7.2   Write the letters representing a *stepwise* series of tones starting and ending on E.

E F G A B C D E

__ __ __ __ __ __ __ __

7.3   In a *scale,* the tones contained in one octave are organized stepwise. In a stepwise series of tones, the letters representing the sounds appear in

alphabetical

_____ order.

7.4   A stepwise arrangement of tones is also said to be DIATONIC. To form a *diatonic* scale, all of the seven basic notes must be present plus the octave duplication of the first note. Thus, eight notes are required to form a *diatonic scale.* Also, the notes must be stated in alphabetical order; none may be repeated (except for the octave duplication of the first note), *and none may be omitted.*

How many notes are needed to form a *diatonic*

Eight

scale? _____
_____

Note: The discussion here and in the following chapters is aimed at building elementary knowledge of basic scales (modes), diatonic and chromatic scales, and major and minor scales. Other scales, such as blues, Gypsy, pentatonic, octatonic, and whole-tone, as well as transpositions of these, could be included at an instructor's discretion, but they are outside the study intended here. *See* "Scales," *The New Harvard Dictionary of Music,* ed. Don Randel (Cambridge, Mass.: The Belknap Press of Harvard University Press, 1986), pp. 728–729 for further information on scales.

7.5   The CHROMATIC SCALE arranges *all* the sounds contained in one octave (in the system of equal temperament) and consists of thirteen tones (including the octave duplication of the first tone).
        Other scales are limited to eight tones, including the octave duplication of the first tone. These are called *diatonic scales.*

All the tones normally contained in one octave are

chromatic

included in the _____ scale.

Play the chromatic scale at a keyboard from C up to C. Note that all the intervals are half steps. Sing the same scale.

7.6   Scales that include only basic (unaltered) notes are called BASIC SCALES.

Write the letters representing the *basic scale* starting on C.

C D E F G A B C

—   —   —   —   —   —   —   —

7.7   Write on the staff the *basic* scale starting on F.

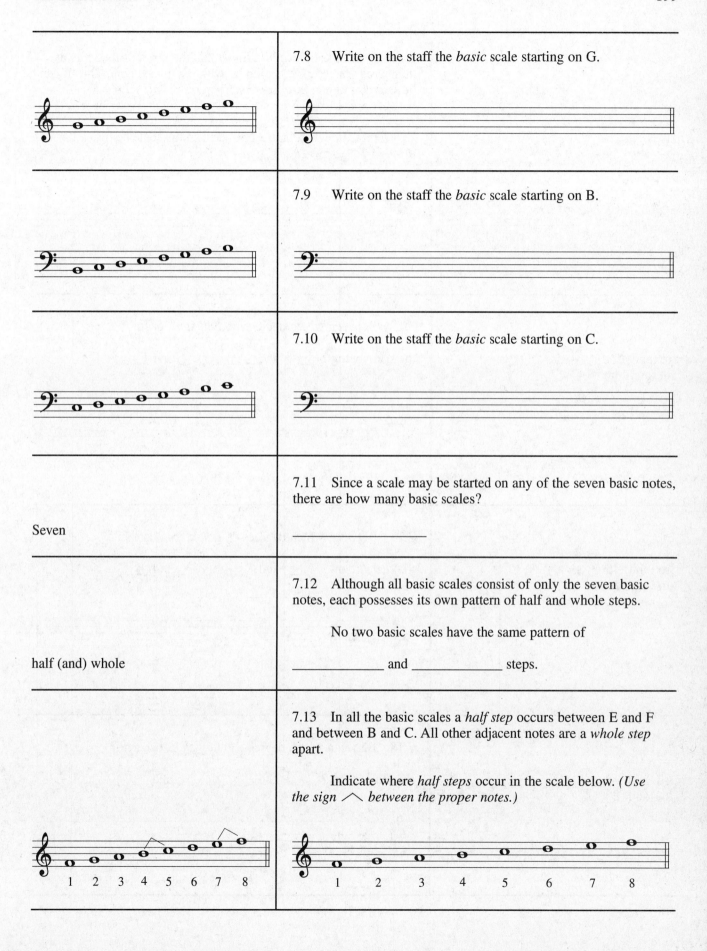

7.8   Write on the staff the *basic* scale starting on G.

7.9   Write on the staff the *basic* scale starting on B.

7.10   Write on the staff the *basic* scale starting on C.

7.11   Since a scale may be started on any of the seven basic notes, there are how many basic scales?

Seven

_____

7.12   Although all basic scales consist of only the seven basic notes, each possesses its own pattern of half and whole steps.

No two basic scales have the same pattern of

half (and) whole

_____ and _____ steps.

7.13   In all the basic scales a *half step* occurs between E and F and between B and C. All other adjacent notes are a *whole step* apart.

Indicate where *half steps* occur in the scale below. *(Use the sign ⌒ between the proper notes.)*

7.14   Note in the preceding frame that the notes of the scale are numbered from 1 to 8, beginning with the lowest note. Thus it can be said that in the *basic scale* starting on F, *half steps* occur between the 4th and 5th and between the 7th and 8th degrees.

Indicate where *half steps* occur in the scale below. *(Use the sign ⌒ between the proper notes.)*

1st (and) 2nd
5th (and) 6th

7.15   Between which degrees do *half steps* occur in

the scale below? _____ and _____ ; _____ and _____

3rd (and) 4th
6th (and) 7th

7.16   Between which degrees do *half steps* occur in

the scale below? _____ and _____ ; _____ and _____

3rd (and) 4th
7th (and) 8th

7.17   Between which degrees do *half steps* occur in

the scale below? _____ and _____ ; _____ and _____

7.18   The pattern of half and whole steps gives each basic scale its own unique intervallic structure. For this reason, no two basic scales sound alike.

When tonal material is limited to the basic notes,

Seven

how many diatonic scales are possible? _____

Sing, or play at a keyboard, the seven basic scales. Note the effect that each scale has because of its particular pattern of half and whole steps.

Modal Melody Ex.: Dorian Mode

Anon. 13th Cen.

p

7.19   Each of the *basic scales* can also be identified by a modal name.*

BASIC SCALE	MODAL NAME
A B C D E F G A	**AEOLIAN**
B C D E F G A B	**LOCRIAN**
C D E F G A B C	**IONIAN**
D E F G A B C D	**DORIAN**
E F G A B C D E	**PHRYGIAN**
F G A B C D E F	**LYDIAN**
G A B C D E F G	**MIXOLYDIAN**

The *Dorian mode* is the same as the basic

D

scale starting on the note _____.

Study the list of modal names above before continuing with the next frame.

---

* These names are derived from tonal structures known as the Church modes. Dorian, Phrygian, Lydian, and Mixolydian date from about the eighth century. Ionian and Aeolian were added to the system by the theorist Glareanus in his treatise *Dodekachordon* (1547). The Locrian mode existed at that time merely as a theoretical possibility. The Church modes served as the tonal basis of Western music until about 1600, after which time they were gradually modified to form the major-minor tonal system, which is the basis of most music heard today. There are also many composers, over this same time period, who have continued to use these modes, or modifications of them, as well as the major-minor scale systems. See "Modes," *The New Harvard Dictionary of Music,* ed. Don Randel (Cambridge: The Belknap Press of Harvard University Press, 1986), pp. 499–502, for further information on modes.

7.20   Do not think that *modal scales* can be written only with basic (unaltered) notes. By use of accidentals, any mode can be constructed on any pitch. But learning to associate the various *modes* with their equivalent *basic scale* can serve as a useful point of reference when transposition to other pitches is desired.* The concern here is that the variety of scale structures available with merely the seven basic notes is appreciated.

Ionian

What is the *modal* name of the *basic scale* starting

on C? _____

_____

* It is also possible to deal with transposition by relating modes to a particular scale degree of the Ionian mode (or the major scale). Thus the second scale degree is Dorian mode, the third is Phrygian, and so forth, and any Ionian (major) scale degree can be used accordingly from any pitch. Please see Chapters 8.0 and 10.0 for related information.

7.21   The *Aeolian mode* is the same as the *basic scale*

A

starting on the note _____.

7.22   The *Phrygian mode* is the same as the *basic scale*

E

starting on the note _____.

7.23   The *Ionian mode* is the same as the *basic scale*

C

starting on the note _____.

7.24   What is the *modal* name of the *basic scale*

Lydian

starting on F? _____

Dorian	7.25 What is the *modal* name of the *basic scale* starting on D? _____
Mixolydian	7.26 What is the *modal* name of the *basic scale* starting on G? _____
Locrian	7.27 What is the *modal* name of the *basic scale* starting on B? _____
	7.28 Write the Dorian mode. *(Use basic notes only.)*
	7.29 Write the Mixolydian mode. *(Use basic notes only.)*
	7.30 Write the Phrygian mode. *(Use basic notes only.)*

7.31   Write the Locrian mode. *(Use basic notes only.)*

7.32   Write the Lydian mode. *(Use basic notes only.)*

7.33   Write the Ionian mode. *(Use basic notes only.)*

7.34   Write the Aeolian mode. *(Use basic notes only.)*

4th (and) 5th

7th (and) 8th

7.35   In the Lydian mode a *half step* occurs between

the _____ and _____ degrees and between the

_____ and _____ degrees. *(Reference may be made to the scale written in frame 7.32.)*

3rd (and) 4th

7th (and) 8th

7.36   In the Ionian mode a *half step* occurs between

the _____ and _____ degrees and between the

_____ and _____ degrees. *(Reference may be made to the scale written in frame 7.33.)*

	7.37 In the Phrygian mode a *half step* occurs between
1st (and) 2nd	the _____ and _____ degrees and between the
5th (and) 6th	_____ and _____ degrees. *(Reference may be made to the scale written in frame 7.30.)*
	7.38 The first and last note of a scale is called the KEYNOTE.* The *keynote* is also called the "tonic note" or the "key center." The *keynote* of the *Dorian mode* (as you have written
D	it in frame 7.28) is _____. _____ * In a completely modal context, the term *final* is preferable to use to identify the keynote. These two terms, along with tonic (note) and key center tend to be used somewhat interchangeably by various writers, theorists, and musicians.
	7.39 What is the *keynote* of the *Mixolydian mode* (as you have written it in frame 7.29)?
G	_____
	7.40 What is the *keynote* of the *basic scale* whose 3rd
G	degree is B? _____
	7.41 What is the *keynote* of the *basic scale* whose 4th
E	degree is A? _____
	7.42 What is the *keynote* of the *basic scale* whose 7th
D	degree is C? _____
	7.43 What is the *keynote* of the *basic scale* whose 6th
A	degree is F? _____

E	7.44 What is the *keynote* of the *basic scale* whose 5th degree is B? _____
keynote	7.45 The note upon which a scale begins and ends is called the _____.

Summary

A *basic scale* may be constructed on each of the seven basic notes. Thus there are seven *basic scales*. No two of these sound alike because the pattern of *half* and *whole steps* is different in each case. *Basic scales* are sometimes identified by their *modal* names.

The following list shows the basic scales and their modal names.

Basic scale starting on A—*Aeolian*

Basic scale starting on B—*Locrian*

Basic scale starting on C—*Ionian*

Basic scale starting on D—*Dorian*

Basic scale starting on E—*Phrygian*

Basic scale starting on F—*Lydian*

Basic scale starting on G—*Mixolydian*

Some additional modal melody examples:

Mastery Frames

True	(frame 7.4)	**7–1**　All of the seven basic notes (A, B, C, D, E, F, G) must be present to form a diatonic scale. (True/False) _____
True	(7.6)	**7–2**　Basic scales are diatonic scales in which no accidentals appear. (True/False) _____
B–C (and) E–F	(7.13–7.18)	**7–3**　All basic scales contain two half steps. The remaining intervals are whole steps. Identify the two half steps. Half steps: _____ – _____ and _____ – _____

7–4　Use the sign ⌒ to indicate where half steps occur in the basic scales below.

All signs should be between B and C and between E and F on all the scale examples.

(7.13–7.18)

| | 7–5   Write the modal names for the basic scales that start on each note below. |

Aeolian   A _____

Locrian   B _____

Ionian   C _____

Dorian   D _____

Phrygian   E _____

Lydian   F _____

Mixolydian   (7.19)   G _____

7–6   What is the keynote of the Aeolian mode?

A   (7.38–7.45)   _____

Supplementary Activities

1. With increased knowledge of the basic scales, continue to create simple melodies as before or even a whole composition. Begin creating a composition and also begin working with the musical terms (found in the *Glossary*) to shape the performance and direction of your pieces.

2. Using *The New Harvard Dictionary of Music,* continue to explore the new terms encountered in this chapter: for example, modes, scales, Aeolian, Phrygian.

3. In creative work, how might the new information be utilized on modes and scales? Must only a particular keynote be used for a particular mode or scale? Can a mode or scale start on other notes?

4. Explore in an essay the effects different modes may have on a person, or does it make any difference? Is one mode as good as another? Hint: The ancient Greeks didn't think so. What do you think?

5. At this point, one may wish to explore the specific role pitch and pitch levels play in music. How important is it anyway? Seek out some references and write an essay on the topic. In the late twentieth century a whole field of music has been developed called psychoacoustics that also might be explored. It ties in directly with an earlier, ongoing musical field called music therapy (the healing effects music may have), which might provide another topic to explore.

Supplementary Assignments

ASSIGNMENT 7–1

Name: _____

1. Show with the sign ⌃ where half steps occur in the scales below.

2. Write a basic scale beginning with each note, and indicate where half steps occur with the sign ⌃ .

3. The first and last note of a scale is called the _____.

4. No accidentals may occur in a basic scale. (True/False) _____

5. All basic scales are diatonic scales. (True/False) _____

6. Indicate between which scale degrees half steps occur in each of the seven basic scales. *(Use the sign ⌃ .)*

KEYNOTE   SCALE DEGREES

A   1   2   3   4   5   6   7   8

B   1   2   3   4   5   6   7   8

C   1   2   3   4   5   6   7   8

D   1   2   3   4   5   6   7   8

E   1   2   3   4   5   6   7   8

F   1   2   3   4   5   6   7   8

G   1   2   3   4   5   6   7   8

7. Explain why no two basic scales sound alike, even though the same notes occur in each.

_____

_____

_____

8. Complete the following information:

MODE   BASIC SCALE ON THE NOTE

Lydian   =   _____

Ionian   =   _____

Dorian   =   _____

Mixolydian   =   _____

Locrian   =   _____

Aeolian   =   _____

Phrygian   =   _____

Ear-Training Activities

By associating the numbers 1–8 with the various scale degrees, a feeling for tonal relations and for the keynote will be developed. Also, letter names or a syllable, such as *la* may be used.

Sing the various basic scales. Be alert to the half and whole steps. (Half steps are indicated by the sign ⌃ .)

 All examples below are recorded on the CD.

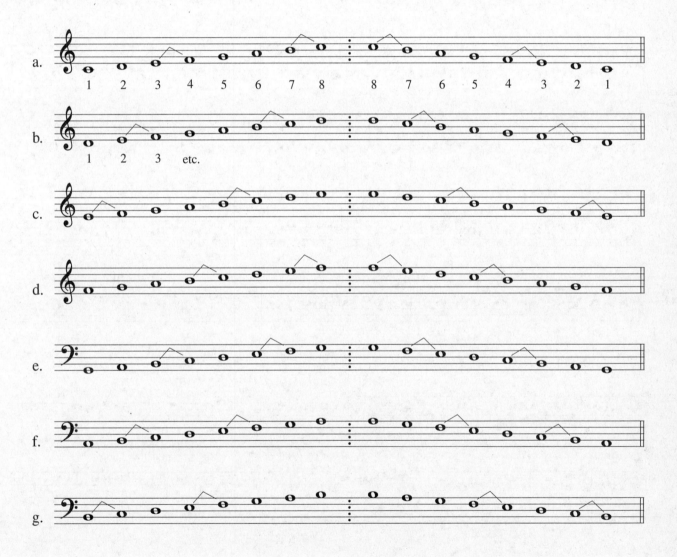

Search for materials that will give visual and aural practice (hearing in your head or singing) in identifying basic scales and modes. Look for compositions, select from those you may be performing, or ask for suggestions. If you have been improvising, try incorporating these basic scales (or modes) into your improvisatory activities.

The following patterns can be sung and practiced on each of the mode keynotes in turn as the basis for the given pattern. These are patterns for the keynote C (or Ionian mode). Listen carefully as practiced to clearly distinguish the differing patterns of whole and half steps for each mode and the unique quality or "sound" for each mode.

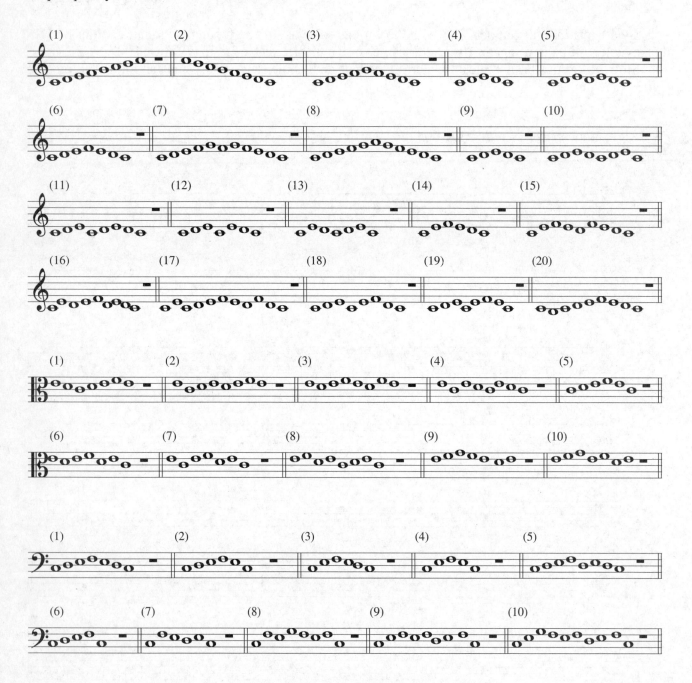

Chapter 8.0
The Major Scale

The character of each type of scale is determined by the pattern of intervals that occur between the successive scale degrees. The *basic scale* on the note C is called the *C major scale*. It may also be referred to as the *key* of C major. (*Keys* and *key signatures* are discussed in Chapter 10.0.) The same pattern of intervallic relationships can be produced beginning on any note by applying the appropriate accidentals. This chapter will illustrate how this is done.

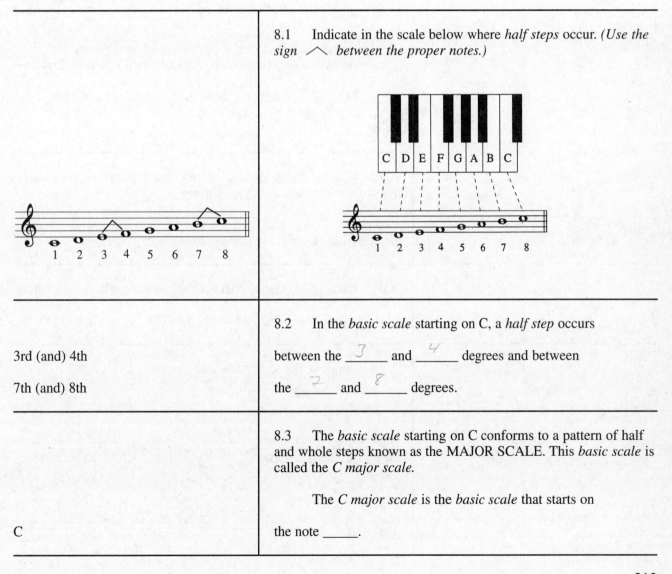

8.1   Indicate in the scale below where *half steps* occur. (*Use the sign ⌃ between the proper notes.*)

3rd (and) 4th

7th (and) 8th

8.2   In the *basic scale* starting on C, a *half step* occurs

between the ___3___ and ___4___ degrees and between

the ___7___ and ___8___ degrees.

C

8.3   The *basic scale* starting on C conforms to a pattern of half and whole steps known as the MAJOR SCALE. This *basic scale* is called the *C major scale*.

The *C major scale* is the *basic scale* that starts on

the note _____.

8.4   The *major scale* may be represented as a series of steps, as below.

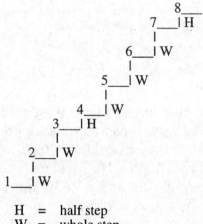

```
                                    8___
                                7___| H
                                  |
                             6___| W
                               |
                          5___| W
                            |
                       4___| W
                     3___| H
                       |
                  2___| W
                    |
               1___| W
```

                    H = half step
                    W = whole step

Try to sing this scale saying the numbers of the degrees. Be careful to sing a half step between 3 and 4 and between 7 and 8.

    The *major scale* is the same as the (Dorian/Aeolian/Ionian)

Ionian   mode. _____

8.5   A major scale may start on any note. However, whole steps must occur between all adjacent notes

3rd (and) 4th   except the _____ and _____ and the _____ and _____
7th (and) 8th   degrees. *This scale is the **same**, ascending and descending.*

8.6   What interval occurs between the 3rd and 4th and the 7th

half   and 8th degrees of the major scale? The _____ step

8.7   Which of the scales below is a major scale?

(2)   _____

```
      (1)
 1   2   3   4   5   6   7   8

      (2)
 1   2   3   4   5   6   7   8
```

(1)

8.8   Which of the scales below is a major scale?

_____

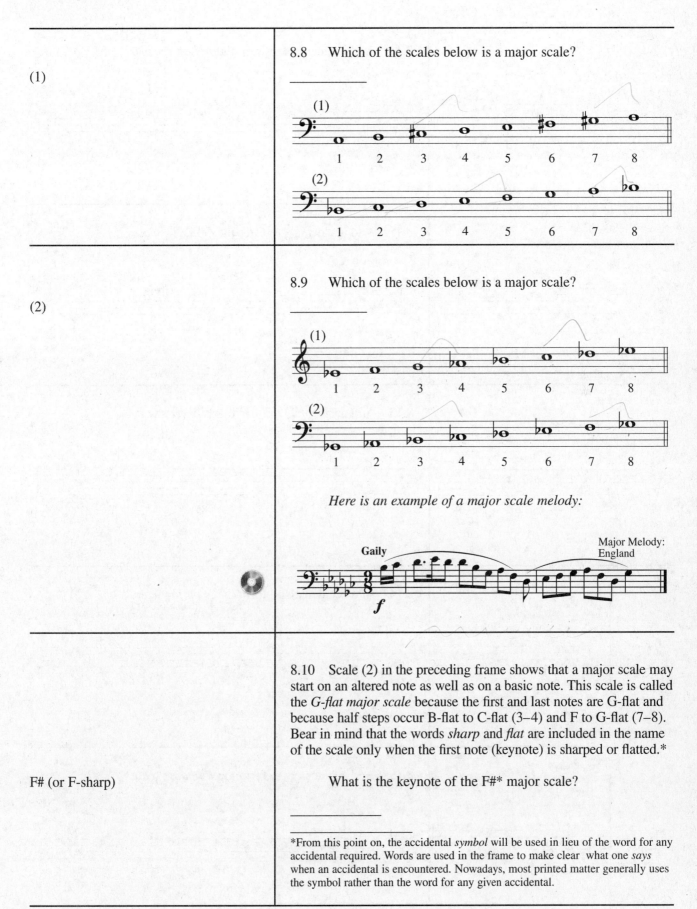

(1)

(2)

Here is an example of a major scale melody:

Gaily

Major Melody:
England

f

8.10   Scale (2) in the preceding frame shows that a major scale may start on an altered note as well as on a basic note. This scale is called the *G-flat major scale* because the first and last notes are G-flat and because half steps occur B-flat to C-flat (3–4) and F to G-flat (7–8). Bear in mind that the words *sharp* and *flat* are included in the name of the scale only when the first note (keynote) is sharped or flatted.*

F# (or F-sharp)   What is the keynote of the F#* major scale?

_____

*From this point on, the accidental *symbol* will be used in lieu of the word for any accidental required. Words are used in the frame to make clear what one *says* when an accidental is encountered. Nowadays, most printed matter generally uses the symbol rather than the word for any given accidental.

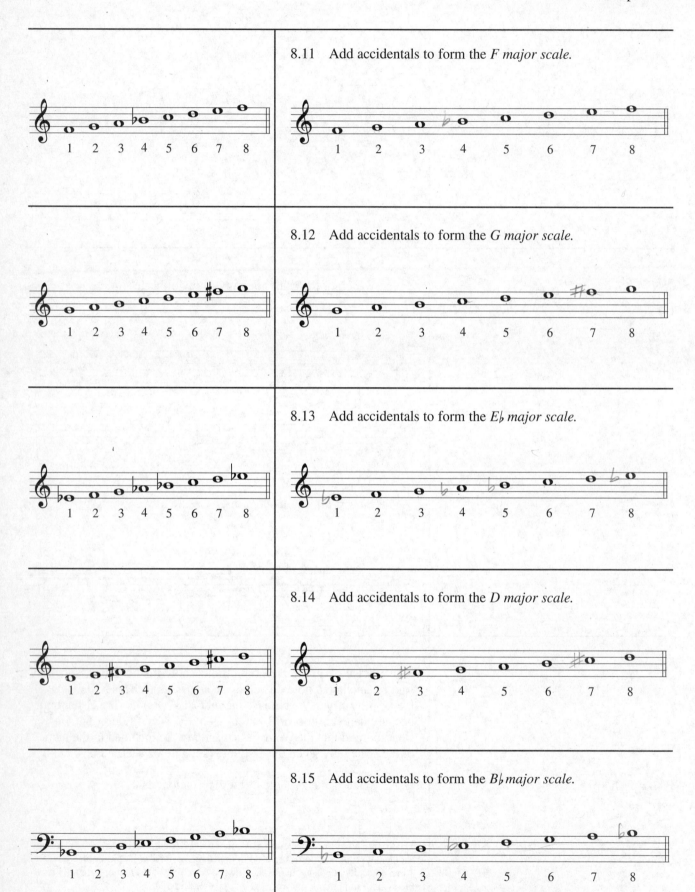

8.11   Add accidentals to form the *F major scale.*

8.12   Add accidentals to form the *G major scale.*

8.13   Add accidentals to form the *E♭ major scale.*

8.14   Add accidentals to form the *D major scale.*

8.15   Add accidentals to form the *B♭ major scale.*

8.16   Add accidentals to form the *A major scale.*

8.17   Add accidentals to form the *A♭ major scale.*

8.18   Write the *E major scale.*

8.19   Write the *D♭ major scale.*

8.20   Write the *F♯ major scale.*

8.21   Write the *G♭ major scale.*

8.22   Write the *B major scale.*

8.23   Write the *C♯ major scale.*

8.24   Write the *C♭ major scale.*

8.25   The basic scale that conforms to the pattern of half and whole steps of the major scale begins and ends on the note

_____.

C

True	8.26 All adjacent scale degrees in the major scale are separated by either a whole step or a half step. (True/False) _____
False *(Half steps occur between 3 and 4, and between 7 and 8 in the major scale.)* True	8.27 In the major scale a half step occurs between the 3rd and 4th and between the 6th and 7th degrees. (True/False) _____ Major scales are the same, ascending and descending. (True/False) _____
B♭	8.28 What accidental must be added to the Lydian mode (F up to F) to form a major scale? _____
F♯	8.29 What accidental must be added to the Mixolydian mode (G up to G) to form a major scale? _____
E Major	8.30 F♯ is the *second* degree of what *major scale*? _____
G♭ Major	8.31 B♭ is the *third* degree of what *major scale*? _____
A♭ Major	8.32 D♭ is the *fourth* degree of what *major scale*? _____

E Major

8.33   B is the *fifth* degree of what *major scale*?

_____

F Major

8.34   D is the *sixth* degree of what *major scale*?

_____

D Major

8.35   C# is the *seventh* degree of what *major scale*?

_____

8.36   It may be helpful to regard the major scale as consisting of two groups of four notes each called TETRACHORDS.

D MAJOR SCALE — lower tetrachord / upper tetrachord

Examine the succession of intervals contained in each *tetrachord*. The *lower tetrachord* consists of two whole steps followed by a half step; the *upper tetrachord* consists of

two whole steps followed
by a half step
(or equivalent)

_____

_____ .

8.37 The example in the preceding frame shows that the *upper* and *lower tetrachords* of the major scale contain the same successions of intervals (two whole steps followed by a half step). The interval separating the two *tetrachords* is a (half/whole)

whole

_____ step.

8.38 Write the *lower tetrachord* of the A♭ *major scale.*

8.39 Write the *upper tetrachord* of the A♭ *major scale.*
Remember: The first note of the upper tetrachord is a whole step above the last note of the lower.

8.40 Any tetrachord consisting of two whole steps followed by a half step may be either the upper or the lower tetrachord of a major scale. The tetrachord

Lower: C

Upper: F

C D E F is the lower tetrachord of the _____ major

scale, and also the upper tetrachord of the _____ major scale.

8.41 The tetrachord below is the lower tetrachord of

Lower: B

Upper: E

the _____ major scale, and also the upper tetrachord

of the _____ major scale.

C	8.42 The lower tetrachord of the G major scale is the same as the upper tetrachord of the ___ major scale.
A	8.43 The upper tetrachord of the D major scale is the same as the lower tetrachord of the ___ major scale.

Summary

A *tetrachord* is a four-note scale pattern. Two *tetrachords* combine to make a *scale.* In *major scales,* the *upper* and the *lower tetrachords* contain the same *intervals:* two *whole steps* followed by a *half step.* Any *tetrachord* that has this pattern may be either the *upper* or the *lower tetrachord* of a *major scale.* In *major scales,* a *whole step* separates the *upper* from the *lower tetrachord.* Considered as a whole, the *major scale* consists of *whole steps,* except for *half steps* between the 3rd and 4th and the 7th and 8th degrees. By use of *accidentals* to produce this pattern, a *major scale* can be constructed on any note.

The intervallic pattern of the *major scale* is shown schematically below.

Additional major scale melodies:

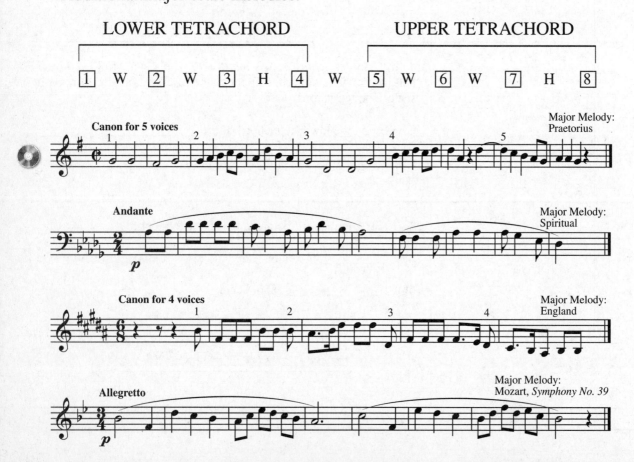

Mastery Frames

	8–1 Which basic scale contains the same intervallic pattern as a major scale?
C (frames 8.1–8.4)	The scale beginning on the note _____
	8–2 Use the sign ⌒ to show where half steps occur in the major scale.
1 2 3̂ 4 5 6 7̂ 8 (8.1–8.6)	1 2 3 4 5 6 7 8
	8–3 Write the lower tetrachord of the C major scale.
(8.36)	
	8–4 Write the upper tetrachord of the C major scale.
(8.36–8.37)	

8–5   Write accidentals to produce major scales.

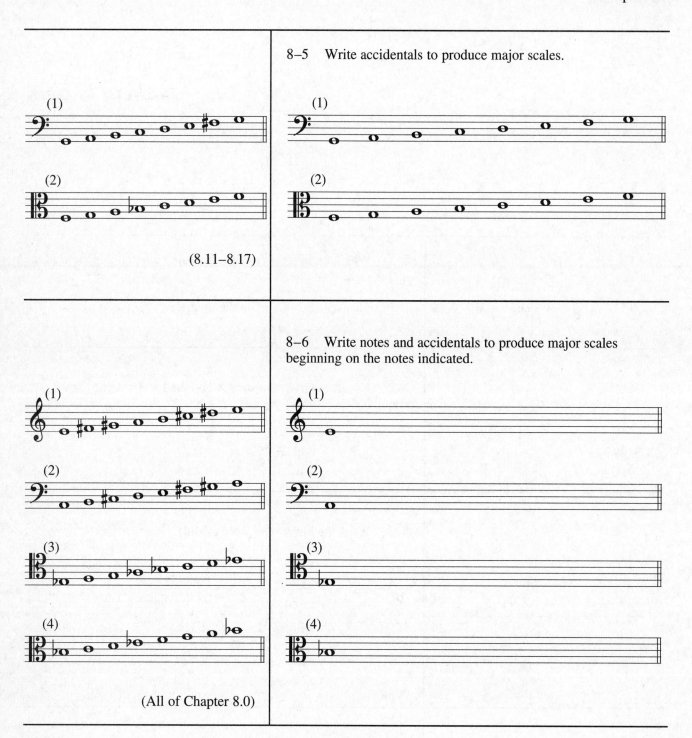

(1)

(2)

(8.11–8.17)

(1)

(2)

8–6   Write notes and accidentals to produce major scales beginning on the notes indicated.

(1)

(2)

(3)

(4)

(1)

(2)

(3)

(4)

(All of Chapter 8.0)

Supplementary Activities

Continue activities similar to those outlined previously in exploring topics from the chapter and writing about them, and also continue creative activities in composition.

Supplementary Assignments

ASSIGNMENT 8–1   Name: _____

1. Between which scale degrees do half steps occur in the major scale?

    _____

2. Indicate the intervals that occur within the two tetrachords of the major scale. (Use abbreviations:

    W = whole step; H = half step.)

    Lower tetrachord: 1 _____   2 _____   3 _____

    Upper tetrachord: 1 _____   2 _____   3 _____

3. What interval separates or connects the lower and upper tetrachords of a major scale?

    _____

4. Add two accidentals to produce the F♯ major scale.

5. Which is a major scale?_____

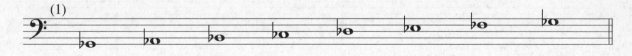

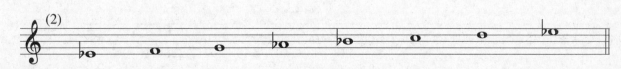

6.   Notate an ascending and descending major scale on each note.

7.   Compose some major-scale melodies. *(Basic hints: Establish a keynote from which to work and also a time signature to guide the duration of the notes chosen for the melody. Generally begin and end the melody on the keynote and make the last note of the melody longer than the other notes. For purposes here, use only the notes found in the key chosen for the melody. Sing or play on an instrument or keyboard as the melody is created to know how the melody is going to sound.)*

ASSIGNMENT 8–2   Name: _____

1. A basic scale beginning on the note _____ contains the same intervallic pattern as a

    _____ scale. It also may be called the _____ mode.

2. D E F♯ G is the lower tetrachord of the _____ major scale, and also the upper tetrachord of

    the _____ major scale.

3. a. Notate the lower tetrachord of the B♭ major scale.

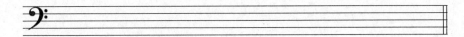

    b. Notate the upper tetrachord of the B♭ major scale.

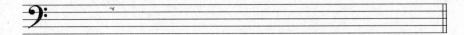

4. Notate accidentals to produce major scales.

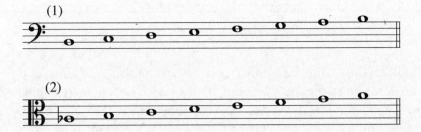

5. Which is a major scale? _____

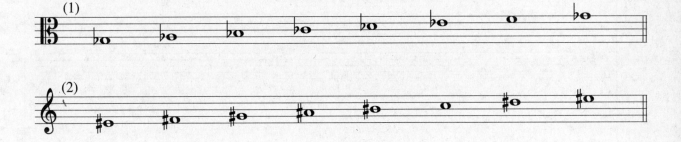

6. Notate an ascending and descending major scale on each note.

7. Compose some major-scale melodies. *(Basic hints: Establish a keynote from which to work and also a time signature to guide the duration of the notes chosen for the melody. Generally begin and end the melody on the keynote and make the last note of the melody longer than the other notes. For purposes here, use only the notes found in the key chosen for the melody. Sing or play on an instrument or keyboard as the melody is created to know how the melody is going to sound.)*

Ear-Training Activities

1. Sing the following scales. Be alert to the half steps that occur between 3 and 4 and between 7 and 8.

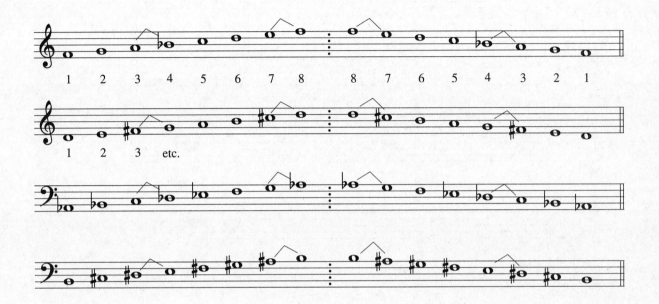

2. Use the note A as the 1st, 2nd, 3rd, and 4th degrees of a major scale as indicated in the following exercise. Try to do this exercise by ear. Use your knowledge of the half- and whole-step pattern of the major scale. Resort to a keyboard for aid, if necessary.

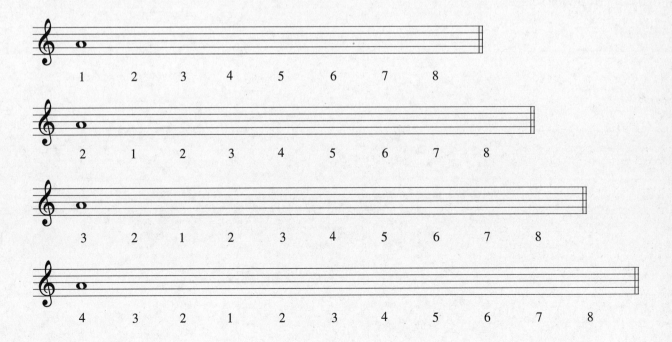

3. Use the note C as the 5th, 6th, 7th, and 8th degrees of a major scale as indicated in the following exercise. Proceed as in the last exercise.

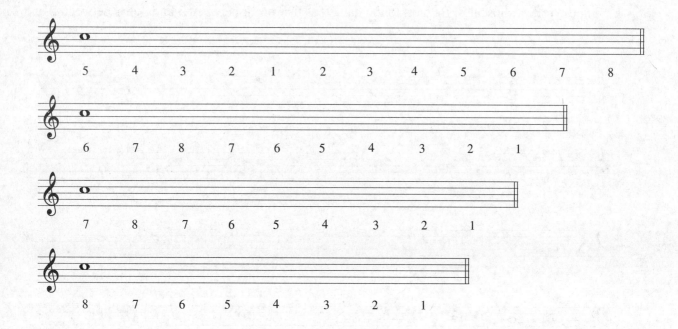

4. Search for materials that will give visual and aural practice (hearing in your head or singing) in identifying major scales and modes. Look for compositions, select from those you may be performing, or ask for suggestions. If you have been improvising, try incorporating the major scales into your improvisatory activities.

5. The singing patterns given in Chapter 7.0, p. 212, also can be used as a basis for aural practicing of major scales.

The handwritten annotations at the top of the page read:

natural = aeilon, pure minor
natural minor

harmonic minor - great impact

Harmonic ♭3 → ♭6 7♯8

♮3 7♯8 melodic

1 tetord
2 t chr

Harmonic
minor

Chapter 9.0
The Minor Scales

The character of a scale results from the intervals that occur between the various scale degrees. Unlike the major scale, which has a single pattern of half and whole steps, the *minor scale* has three forms, each with a distinctive arrangement of intervals, as will be presented in this chapter. The three types of minor scales are called *natural*, *harmonic*, and *melodic*. These scales ultimately derive from actual musical practice (contained in Western musical traditions) and as a result of the varying melodic and harmonic contexts within which they are used.

	9.1 Indicate in the scale below where *half steps* occur. *(Use the sign � between the proper notes.)*
2nd (and) 3rd	9.2 In the *basic scale* starting on the note A, *half* steps occur between the _____ and _____ degrees
5th (and) 6th	and between the _____ and _____ degrees.

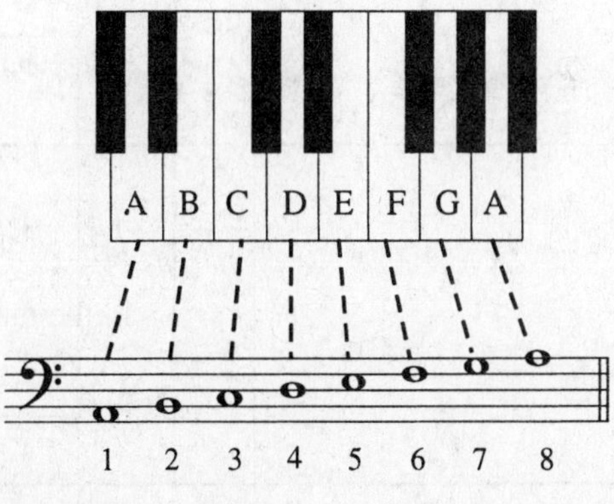

231

9.3   The *basic scale* starting on the note A conforms to the pattern of half and whole steps of the NATURAL MINOR SCALE.*

The *natural minor scale* may be represented as a series of steps, as below.

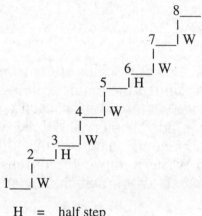

H = half step
W = whole step

Try to sing this natural minor scale. Be careful to observe the correct pattern of half and whole steps.

The *natural minor scale* is the same as the basic

scale starting on the note _____.

_____

* The natural minor scale is also called the *pure, normal,* or *Aeolian* minor.

A

9.4   Between which scale degrees do half steps occur

in the natural minor scale? _____ and _____; _____

and _____

2nd (and) 3rd

5th (and) 6th

9.5   The natural minor scale is the same as the

_____ mode.

Aeolian

9.6   There are three types of minor scales:
(1) *harmonic minor*, (2) *melodic minor*,

and (3) _____ *minor.*

natural

(2)

(1)

9.7 Which of the scales below is a natural minor scale? _____

(1)

1   2   3   4   5   6   7   8

(2)

1   2   3   4   5   6   7   8

9.8 Which of the scales below is a natural minor scale? _____

(1)

1   2   3   4   5   6   7   8

(2)

1   2   3   4   5   6   7   8

Here is an example of a natural minor scale melody:

Expressively

Natural Minor Melody: "Snake Charmer"

9.9 The *lower* tetrachord of the *c natural minor scale* is notated below. Analyze the intervals contained in this tetrachord as indicated.

W = whole step   H = half step

W   H   W

___   ___   ___

9.10 Analyze the intervals contained in the *upper* tetrachord of the *c natural minor scale.*

W = whole step   H = half step

___   ___ ___

H   W   W

9.11 In the *natural minor scale,* the *lower* tetrachord consists of a whole step followed by a half step followed by a whole step; the *upper* tetrachord consists of a half step followed by two whole steps. As in the major scale, the two tetrachords are separated by the interval of a _____ step.

whole

9.12 Add accidentals to form the *d natural minor scale.*

1   2   3   4   5   6   7   8

9.13 Add accidentals to form the *e natural minor scale.*

1   2   3   4   5   6   7   8

9.14 Add accidentals to form the *g natural minor scale.*

1   2   3   4   5   6   7   8

9.15 Add accidentals to form the *b natural minor scale.*

9.16 Write the *f♯ natural minor scale.*

9.17 Write the *c natural minor scale.*

9.18 Write the *c♯ natural minor scale.*

9.19 Write the *f natural minor scale.*

9.20   The HARMONIC MINOR SCALE has half steps between the 2nd and 3rd, 5th and 6th, and 7th and 8th degrees.

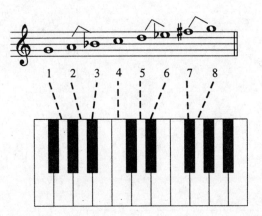

How many half steps are contained in the *harmonic minor scale*? _____

Three

9.21   What is the interval separating the 6th and 7th degrees of the *harmonic minor scale*?

_____

(Refer to the scale in the preceding frame.)

Augmented 2nd

9.22   A unique feature of the harmonic minor scale is the *augmented 2nd* that occurs between the 6th and 7th degrees. The *augmented 2nd* is the same as a

whole step plus a _____ step or _____ half steps.

half, three

9.23   Show the degrees between which half steps occur in the harmonic minor scale.

_____ and _____; _____ and _____; _____ and _____.

2nd (and) 3rd
5th (and) 6th
7th (and) 8th

9.24 The *harmonic minor scale* may be represented as a series of steps, as below.

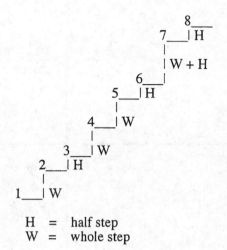

H = half step
W = whole step

Try to sing this harmonic minor scale. Be careful to observe the correct pattern of half and whole steps.

In the *harmonic minor scale,* half steps occur between the 2nd and 3rd, 5th and 6th, and 7th and 8th degrees. The interval between the 6th and 7th degrees is a *step-and-a-half.* The remaining intervals are all

whole

_____ steps.

9.25 Is the scale below a harmonic minor scale?

Yes

_____

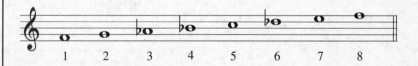

9.26 Is the scale below a harmonic minor scale?

Yes

_____

9.27   Is the scale below a harmonic minor scale?

No

_____

9.28   What type of scale is shown in the preceding

Natural minor

frame? _____

9.29   Rewrite the proper accidentals for the scale in frame 9.27 so that it is a *c harmonic minor scale.*

9.30   As originally written, the scale in frame 9.27 was a natural minor scale. What alteration was necessary to transform it into a harmonic minor scale?*

The 7th scale degree

_____

was raised a half step.

_____

_____
* Please note that a *natural* sign is *not* needed here to indicate the raised 7th degree. It would be needed if there was a key signature present. (*See* Key Signatures, Chapter 10.0.)

9.31   The harmonic minor scale differs from the natural minor scale only in that the 7th degree is raised a

half

_____ step.

9.32   To write a harmonic minor scale: (1) write a natural minor scale; (2) raise the 7th degree a half step.

Transform the natural minor scale below into a harmonic minor scale in the manner described above.

9.33   Transform the natural minor scale below into a harmonic minor scale.

9.34   Add accidentals to form the *d harmonic minor scale. (Check all intervals.)*

9.35   Add accidentals to form the *e harmonic minor scale. (Check all intervals.)*

9.36   Add accidentals to form the *c harmonic minor scale.*
(Check all intervals.)

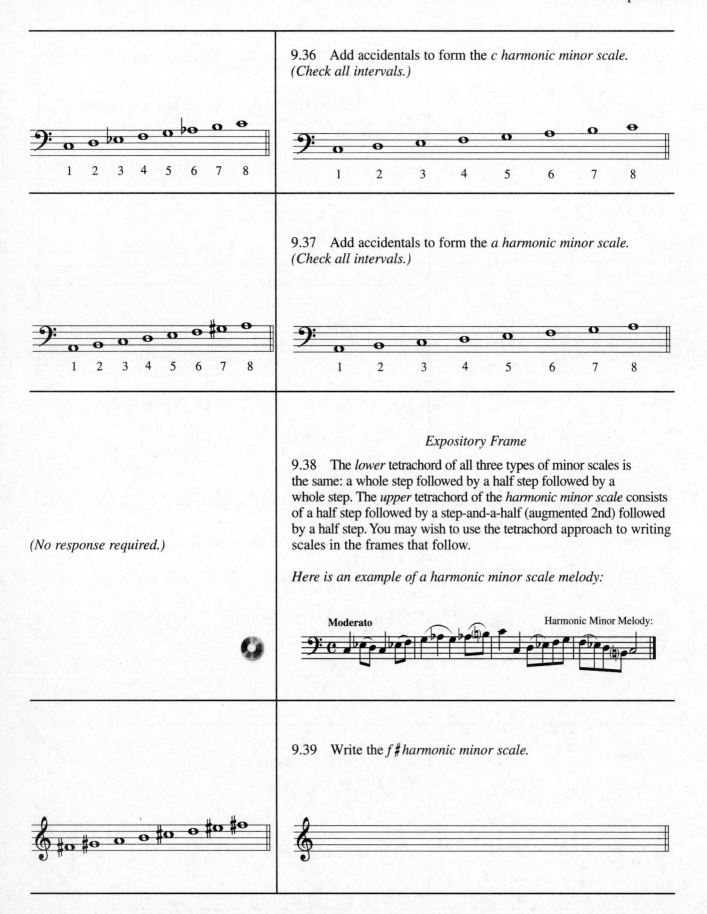

9.37   Add accidentals to form the *a harmonic minor scale.*
(Check all intervals.)

(No response required.)

Expository Frame

9.38   The *lower* tetrachord of all three types of minor scales is the same: a whole step followed by a half step followed by a whole step. The *upper* tetrachord of the *harmonic minor scale* consists of a half step followed by a step-and-a-half (augmented 2nd) followed by a half step. You may wish to use the tetrachord approach to writing scales in the frames that follow.

Here is an example of a harmonic minor scale melody:

Moderato   Harmonic Minor Melody:

9.39   Write the *f♯ harmonic minor scale.*

9.40   Write the *f harmonic minor scale.*

9.41   Write the *c♯ harmonic minor scale.*

9.42   Write the *b♭ harmonic minor scale.*

9.43   Write the *g♯ harmonic minor scale.*

9.44   Write the *e♭ harmonic minor scale.*

9.45   Write the *d♯ harmonic minor scale.*

9.46   Write the *a♭ harmonic minor scale.*

9.47   Write the *a♯ harmonic minor scale.*

9.48   The minor scale that has half steps between the
2nd and 3rd and the 5th and 6th degrees is called

natural

the _____ minor scale.

9.49   The minor scale that has half steps between
the 2nd and 3rd, 5th and 6th, and 7th and 8th degrees

harmonic

is called the _____ minor scale.

9.50   In all the scales studied to this point, the *ascending*
and *descending* forms have contained the same notes. The
MELODIC MINOR SCALE, however, has one pattern of
half and whole steps for its *ascending* form and another for
its *descending* form.

     The only scale that has different patterns of half
and whole steps for its *ascending* and *descending*

melodic

forms is called the _____ minor scale.

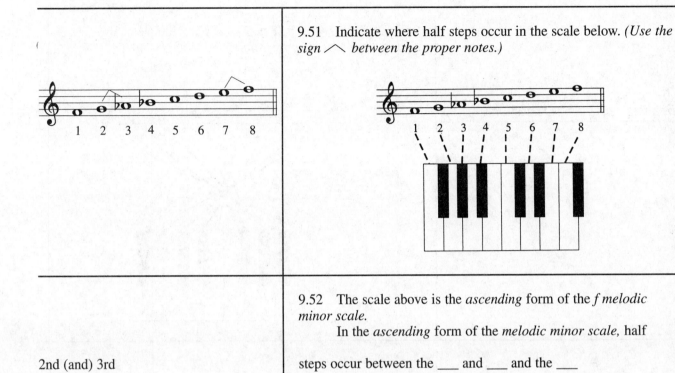

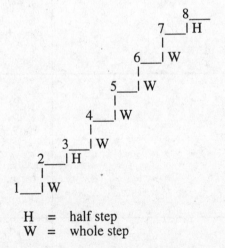

9.51 Indicate where half steps occur in the scale below. *(Use the sign ⌒ between the proper notes.)*

9.52 The scale above is the *ascending* form of the *f melodic minor scale.*

In the *ascending* form of the *melodic minor scale,* half

steps occur between the ___ and ___ and the ___

and ___ degrees. *(Refer to the scale in the preceding frame.)*

2nd (and) 3rd

7th (and) 8th

9.53 The *ascending* form of the *melodic minor scale* may be represented as a series of steps, as below.

```
                                      8___
                                  7___|H
                                   |
                              6___|W
                               |
                          5___|W
                           |
                      4___|W
                       |
                  3___|W
                   |
              2___|H
               |
          1___|W
```

        H = half step
        W = whole step

Try to sing an* ascending *form of the melodic minor scale. Be careful to observe the correct pattern of half and whole steps.

Any scale that has a half step between the 2nd and 3rd degrees and between the 7th and 8th degrees corresponds to the pattern of half and whole steps known as the

ascending form of the _____ minor scale.

melodic

9.54   Indicate where half steps occur in the scale below. *(Use the sign ⌢ between the proper notes.)*

9.55   In the scale above, a half step occurs between the 2nd and 3rd and between the 5th and 6th degrees. This is the *descending* form of the *melodic minor scale.*

A comparison of the *ascending* and *descending* forms of the *melodic minor scale (refer to frames 9.51 and 9.54)* shows that the two degrees that differ in the two forms

6th (and) 7th

are the _____ and _____ degrees.

9.56   The 6th and 7th degrees of the *ascending* form of the *melodic minor scale* are a half step (higher/lower)

higher

_____ than the same degrees of the *descending* form.

9.57   In the *descending* form of the *melodic minor scale,* half steps occur between the 2nd and 3rd and between the 5th and 6th degrees.

This pattern of half and whole steps is identical with that of another minor scale previously studied.

natural

This scale is called the _____ minor scale.

9.58   The *descending* form of the *melodic minor scale* may be represented as a series of steps, as below.

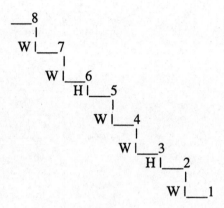

H   =   half step
W   =   whole step

Try to sing a descending form of the melodic minor scale. Be careful to observe the correct pattern of half and whole steps.

The pattern of half and whole steps in the *natural*

descending

minor scale is the same as that of the _____ form of the *melodic minor scale.*

9.59   Which of the scales below is the *descending*

(1)

form of the d melodic minor scale? _____

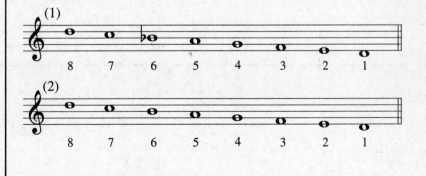

(2)

9.60   Which of the scales below is the *ascending*

form of the c♯ melodic minor scale? _____

(2)

9.61   Which of the scales below is the *ascending*

form of the g melodic minor scale? _____

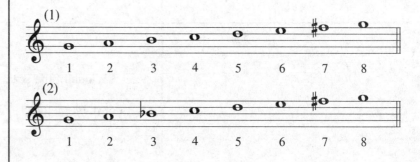

9.62   Scale (1) in the preceding frame is what type of

Major   scale? _____

The 3rd

9.63   Compare scale (1) with scale (2) in frame 9.61.

What scale degree is different? _____

---

half

9.64   The ascending form of the melodic minor scale
is the same as a major scale, except that the

3rd degree is a _____ step lower.

True

9.65   The lower tetrachord of all three types of minor scales
consists of a whole step followed by a half step followed by a
whole step. In the melodic minor scale, the *ascending* upper
tetrachord is the same as in the major scale (whole step, whole
step, half step); the *descending* upper tetrachord is the same as in
the natural minor scale (whole step, whole step, half step).

The tetrachord below is the upper tetrachord of the
b melodic minor scale, *ascending* form. (True/False)

_____

9.66   Write the upper tetrachord of the *d melodic minor scale,
descending* form.

9.67   Write the upper tetrachord of the *e melodic minor scale, ascending* form.

Here is an example of a melodic minor scale melody:

Moderato

Melodic Minor Melody:
from Greensleeves

9.68   Use accidentals to form the *c melodic minor scale.*

ASCENDING FORM

1   2   3   4   5   6   7   8

DESCENDING FORM

8   7   6   5   4   3   2   1

9.69   Use accidentals to form the *f melodic minor scale.*

ASCENDING FORM

1   2   3   4   5   6   7   8

DESCENDING FORM

8   7   6   5   4   3   2   1

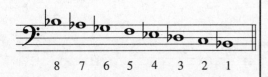

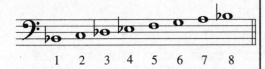

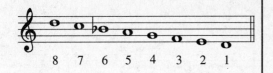

9.70 Use accidentals to form the *g melodic minor scale.*

ASCENDING FORM

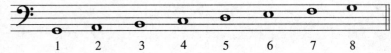

DESCENDING FORM

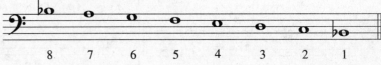

9.71 Use accidentals to form the *b♭ melodic minor scale.*

ASCENDING FORM

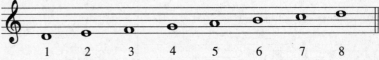

DESCENDING FORM

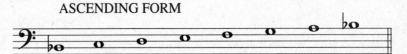

9.72 Use accidentals to form the *d melodic minor scale.*

ASCENDING FORM

DESCENDING FORM

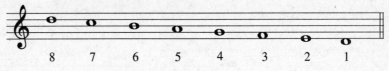

9.73   Use accidentals to form the *e♭ melodic minor scale.*

ASCENDING FORM

DESCENDING FORM

9.74   Use accidentals to form the *a melodic minor scale.*

ASCENDING FORM

DESCENDING FORM

9.75   Write the *a♭ melodic minor scale.*

ASCENDING FORM

DESCENDING FORM

9.76   Write the *e melodic minor scale.*

ASCENDING FORM

DESCENDING FORM

9.77   Write the *c♯ melodic minor scale.*

ASCENDING FORM

DESCENDING FORM

9.78   Write the *b melodic minor scale.*

ASCENDING FORM

DESCENDING FORM

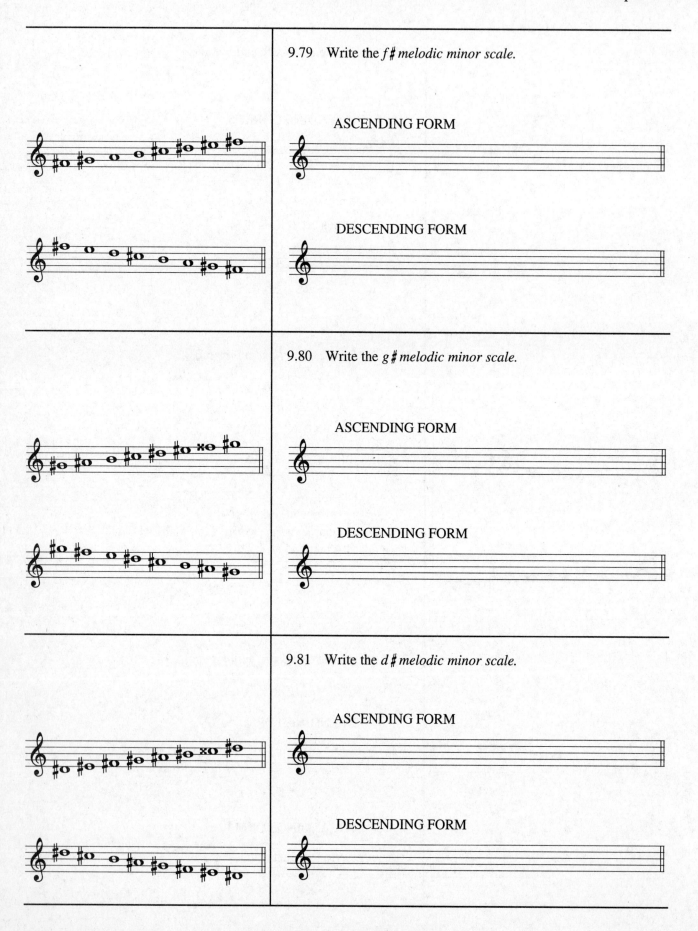

9.79 Write the *f♯ melodic minor scale.*

ASCENDING FORM

DESCENDING FORM

9.80 Write the *g♯ melodic minor scale.*

ASCENDING FORM

DESCENDING FORM

9.81 Write the *d♯ melodic minor scale.*

ASCENDING FORM

DESCENDING FORM

9.82   Write the *a♯ melodic minor scale.*

ASCENDING FORM

DESCENDING FORM

(2)

9.83   Which of the scales below is a *pure* minor scale?

_____

(1)

(2)

(2)

9.84   Which of the scales below is a *harmonic* minor scale?

_____

(1)

(2)

(1)

9.85   Which of the scales below is the *ascending* form of a *melodic* minor scale?

_____

(1)

9.86   Which of the scales below is the *descending* form of a *melodic* minor scale?

_____

No

9.87   All *major* and *minor* scales are *diatonic* scales. A diatonic scale consists of eight notes (including the octave duplication of the keynote) arranged stepwise. Does the chromatic half step occur in any of the

diatonic scales? _____

Summary

In all three forms of the *minor scale,* the *lower tetrachord* is the same. The *intervals* are a *whole step* followed by a *half step* followed by a *whole step.* The *upper tetrachord,* however, is different in each case. This is shown in the schematic below. Notice that in each pattern, the two *tetrachords* are separated by a *whole step.*

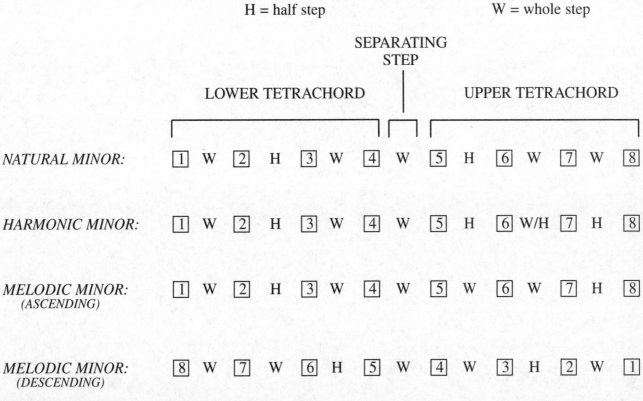

H = half step   W = whole step

SEPARATING STEP

LOWER TETRACHORD | UPPER TETRACHORD

NATURAL MINOR: 1 W 2 H 3 W 4 W 5 H 6 W 7 W 8

HARMONIC MINOR: 1 W 2 H 3 W 4 W 5 H 6 W/H 7 H 8

MELODIC MINOR:
(ASCENDING) 1 W 2 H 3 W 4 W 5 W 6 W 7 H 8

MELODIC MINOR:
(DESCENDING) 8 W 7 W 6 H 5 W 4 W 3 H 2 W 1

Additional minor scale melodies:

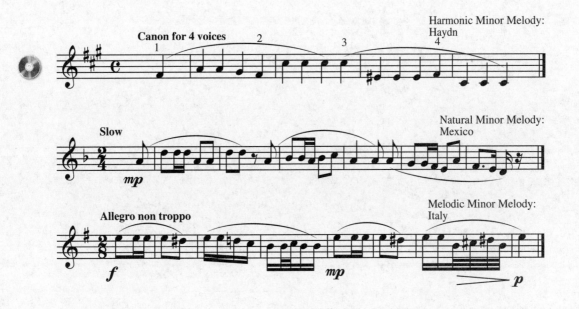

Canon for 4 voices

Harmonic Minor Melody:
Haydn

Slow

Natural Minor Melody:
Mexico

Allegro non troppo

Melodic Minor Melody:
Italy

Mastery Frames

Natural   (frame 9.3)

9–1   Name the type of minor scale that has the same pattern of half and whole steps as the Aeolian mode.

_____

9–2   Add accidentals to produce natural minor scales.

(9.12–9.15)

9–3   Which type of minor scale contains three half steps?

Harmonic   (9.20)   _____

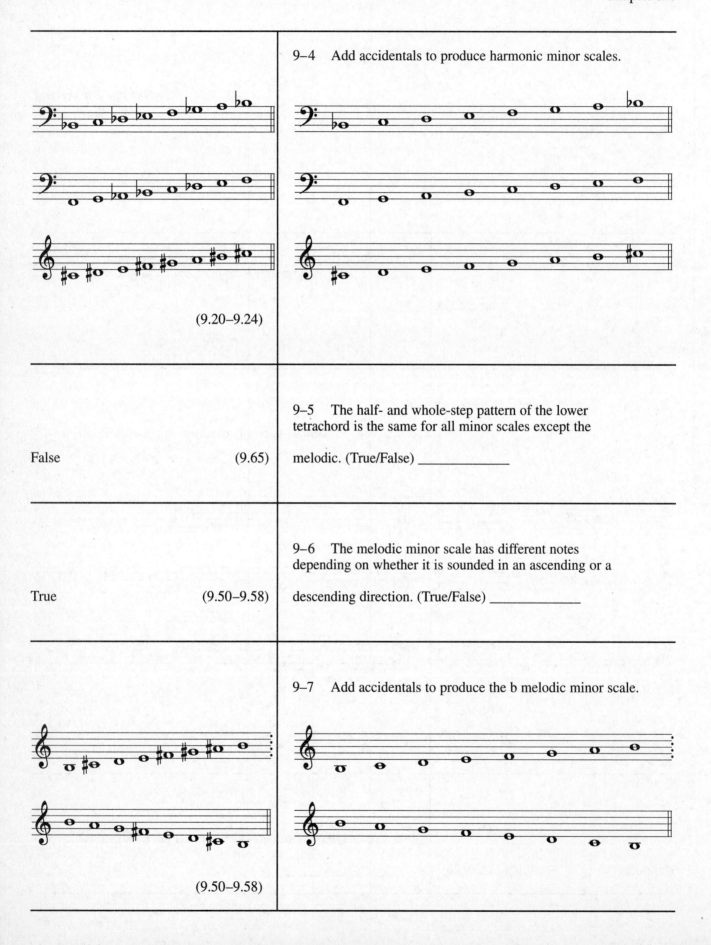

9–4   Add accidentals to produce harmonic minor scales.

(9.20–9.24)

False   (9.65)

9–5   The half- and whole-step pattern of the lower tetrachord is the same for all minor scales except the

melodic. (True/False) _____

True   (9.50–9.58)

9–6   The melodic minor scale has different notes depending on whether it is sounded in an ascending or a

descending direction. (True/False) _____

9–7   Add accidentals to produce the b melodic minor scale.

(9.50–9.58)

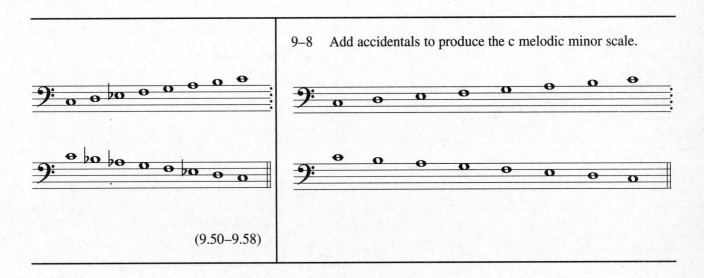

9–8   Add accidentals to produce the c melodic minor scale.

(9.50–9.58)

Supplementary Activities

Continue activities similar to those outlined previously in exploring topics from the chapter and writing about them, and also continue creative activities in composition.

Supplementary Assignments

ASSIGNMENT 9–1   Name: _____

1. What type of minor scale contains the interval of an augmented second? _____

2. Between which scale degrees do half steps occur in the natural minor scale? _____

3. Add one accidental to change the natural minor scale below to a harmonic minor scale.

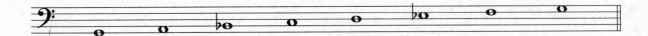

4. Which of the scales is a natural minor scale? _____

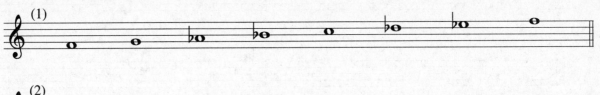

5. Which of the scales is a harmonic minor scale? _____

6. Add accidentals to produce natural minor scales.

7. Add accidentals to produce harmonic minor scales.

8. What interval occurs between the 6th and 7th degrees of the harmonic minor scale?_____

9. Which scale degrees have alternate forms in the melodic minor scale, depending on whether the

   scale is ascending or descending? _____

10. Add accidentals to produce melodic minor scales.

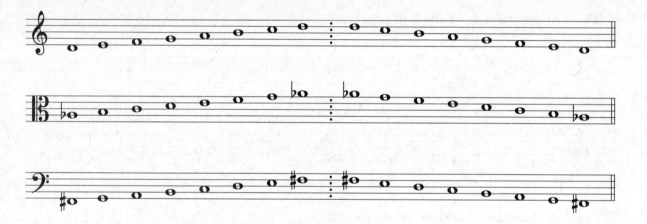

11. Between which scale degrees do half steps occur in the ascending form of the melodic minor scale?

   _____

12. Between which scale degrees do half steps occur in the descending form of the melodic minor

   scale? _____

13. Compose some minor-scale melodies. (*Utilize the hints from Chapter 8.0, Major Scales.*)

ASSIGNMENT 9–2   Name: _____

1. Select the statement that applies to each tetrachord.

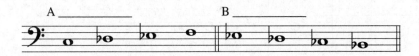

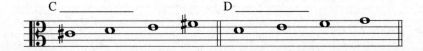

(1) Lower tetrachord c minor   (2) Upper tetrachord e♭ minor (melodic, descending)

(3) Upper tetrachord f♯ minor (natural)   (4) Lower tetrachord d minor (harmonic)

(5) None of these

2. The _____ minor scale contains three half steps.

3. The _____ minor scale has the same half- and whole-step patterns as the _____ mode.

4. The _____ minor scale has three different notes depending on whether it is sounded in an

ascending or a descending direction.

5. Where do half steps occur in the harmonic minor scale? _____

Where do they occur in the melodic minor scale (up and down)?

6. Select the statement that applies to each tetrachord.

(1) Upper tetrachord e minor (natural)   (2) Upper tetrachord a minor (harmonic)

(3) Upper tetrachord f minor (melodic, ascending)   (4) Lower tetrachord a♭ minor

(5) None of these

7. Notate minor scales on each note as indicated.

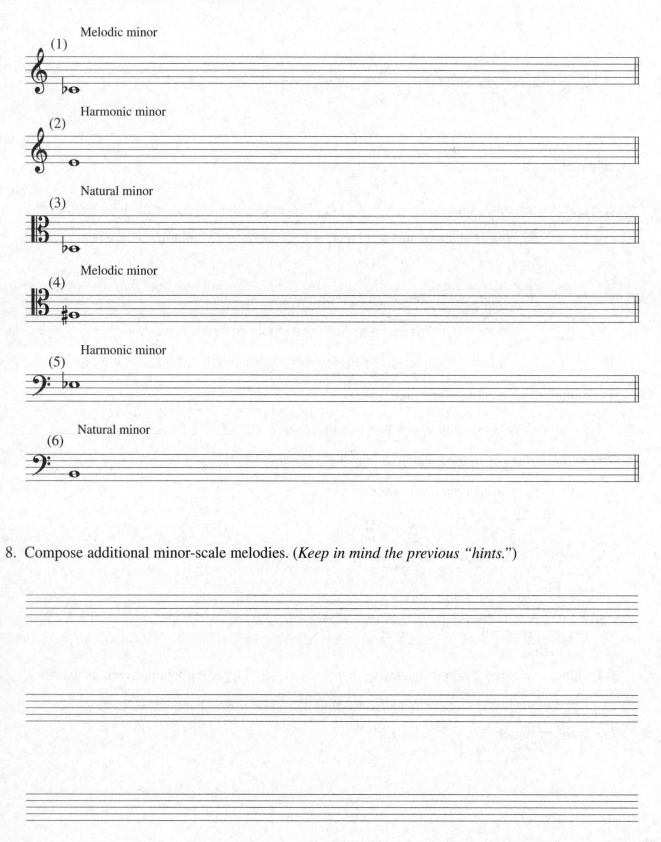

8. Compose additional minor-scale melodies. (*Keep in mind the previous "hints."*)

Ear-Training Activities

1. The *lower* tetrachord (scale degrees 1–4) of all three forms of the minor scale is the same. The interval pattern is whole step/half step/whole step. Sing the following tetrachords:

2. Focus attention on the *upper* tetrachord as the following three minor scales are sung:

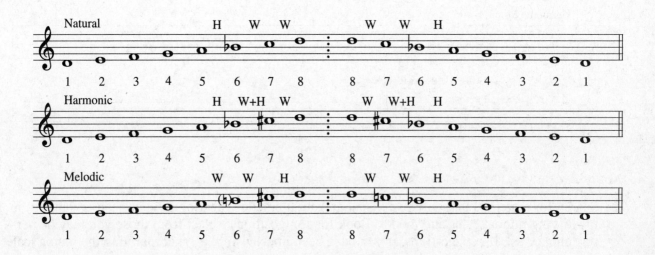

3. Practice singing the three forms of the minor scale beginning on various notes to achieve accuracy and fluency. Always be conscious of the half- and whole-step pattern. Check at a keyboard, if necessary.

4. Using the notes given, sing the various minor scales as directed. Rely on the ear and the knowledge of the intervallic pattern of each scale. Resort to a keyboard for aid, if necessary. End by writing out the notes of the scale.

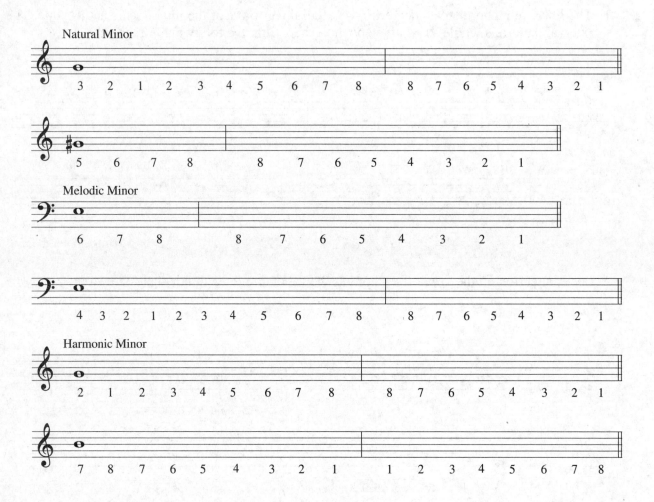

5. Search for materials that will give visual and aural practice (hearing in your head or singing) in identifying minor scales and modes. Look for compositions; select from those you may be performing, or ask for suggestions. If you have been improvising, try incorporating the minor scales into your improvisatory activities.

6. Again, the singing patterns given in Chapter 7.0, p. 212, can be used as a basis for aural practicing of minor scales.

Chapter 10.0
Key Signatures

The writing of *major* and *minor* scales by applying *accidentals* to produce the *half-* and *whole-step* patterns has been demonstrated. The *sharps* and *flats* used in a particular *scale* may be grouped together and placed on the *staff* immediately after the *clef sign*. This is called a *key signature*. With a key signature in place, it is unnecessary to apply accidentals to each note; a sharp or a flat in the key signature affects all such notes in any octave, unless superseded by an accidental. The music notation is thus less cluttered and easier to read. In this "gathering" of the recurring accidentals at the beginning of each staff, a system of key signatures, which will be explained in this chapter, has developed over the centuries. The concept of key signatures dates approximately from the late 1600s and is rooted in European art music practices of the time.

	10.1 A scale (a stepwise series of notes) organizes the tonal material of a particular KEY. The first and last note of a scale is called the KEYNOTE (or TONIC).
A	The *keynote* of the A major scale is _____.
	10.2 The *key* of a composition is the same as the *keynote* of its principal scale. If a composition is based primarily on the E♭ major scale, it is said to be in the key of
E♭	_____ Major.
	10.3 *Key* is practically synonymous with TONALITY. Regardless of the term used, the *keynote* is the center to which the other tones of the scale relate.
	Tonality is the result of a *keynote* (or *tonic*) predominating over the remaining tones of the
scale	_____.

10.4   Reiteration of the keynote is one way of causing it to predominate over the remaining tones of the scale, for any note that occurs more frequently than others automatically has special status. Another way is to use the keynote in strategic positions, such as on metrical stresses, or at structural points, such as beginnings and endings of phrases. Thus, *tonality*, or *tonal* music, is created whenever the *keynote* or *tonic note* predominates or is more important than other notes in a musical texture. *Harmonic relationships* also help establish *tonality*, which is demonstrated in the study of harmony. (*The study of melody and harmony is outside the scope of this book*.)

Tonality

What is another word for key? _____

10.5   Much of the music heard today is based on major and minor scales. Either of these can be written beginning on any note, provided the appropriate basic notes are adjusted by the use of accidentals.

Accidentals are used to produce the desired pattern

half (and) whole

of _____ and _____ steps.

10.6   The *sharps* or *flats* necessary to produce the desired *half-* and *whole-step* pattern in a given *scale* are grouped together to form the KEY SIGNATURE. The *key signature* is placed on the *staff* immediately after the *clef* sign, as shown below.

The *key signature* consists of a group of either

sharps (or) flats

_____ or _____.

10.7   The sharps or flats of a key signature apply to *all* notes of that name in the composition, unless superseded by additional accidentals.

A B♭ in the key signature means that each B appearing

B♭ (or B-flat)

in the composition will be played as a _____.

10.8 The group of sharps or flats that appears just to the right of the clef sign is called the

key signature

_____.

10.9 Does a sharp or a flat in the key signature affect all notes of that name regardless of where they may appear?

Yes

_____

10.10 The sharps or flats that constitute a key signature always occur in a specific order. The order of the sharps is F–C–G–D–A–E–B, or an intervallic pattern of ascending perfect fifths.

    Key signatures consist of either sharps or flats.* The sharps are placed on the staff in the following order:

F–C–G–D–A–E–B

____ – ____ – ____ – ____ – ____ – ____ – ____

Learn the order of the sharps before proceeding with the next frame.

_____

* Two keys (C major and a minor) have a key signature of no sharps or flats. Mnemonics to remember the order of sharps and flats are **F**at **C**ats **G**o **D**own **A**lleys **E**ating **B**agels; **F**at **C**ows **G**raze **D**aily **A**t **E**lmer's **B**arn; **F**oreign **C**ars **G**et **D**ents **A**fter **E**ach **B**ump. The reverse of these gives the order of flats.

10.11 The sharps are placed on the staff in a particular order, creating this pattern:

    On which line of the treble staff does the fourth

The fourth

sharp appear? _____

The third

10.12 In which space does the sixth sharp appear on the

bass staff? _____

10.13 Write the seven sharps on the *grand* staff. **Observe correct order and placement.**

No
(The third sharp on the bass staff should be an octave higher.)

10.14 Are the sharps placed correctly in the example below?

_____

10.15 When the C-clefs are used, the sharps are placed on the staff this way:

Alto Clef

Tenor Clef

Do the sharps occur in the same order in each case

Yes *(See the next frame.)*   above? _____

10.16 Even though they appear in a different pattern, the sharps occur in the *same order* on both the *alto* and the *tenor* clefs. Write the order of the seven sharps as they occur in a key signature.

F–C–G–D–A–E–B

_____–_____–_____–_____–_____–_____–_____

10.17 Write the seven sharps on the alto clef.

10.18 Write the seven sharps on the tenor clef.

10.19 The flats are placed on the staff in the following order: B–E–A–D–G–C–F. Observe that the order of the flats is the reverse of the order of the sharps* or an intervallic pattern of ascending perfect fourths. Write the order of the flats.

B–E–A–D–G–C–F

_____–_____–_____–_____–_____–_____–_____

Learn the order of the flats before proceeding with the next frame.

The reverse of "sharp" mnemonics gives the order of flats, or **B**ig **E**lephants **A**t **D**inner **G**obble **C**urly **F**ries, **B**uy **E**ight **A**pple **D**onuts **G**et **C**offee **F**ree, and **B**efore **E**very **A**utumn **D**ay, **G**odzilla **C**hases **F**rankenstein.

10.20 The flats are placed on the staff in a particular order, creating this pattern:

On which line of the treble staff does the fifth

The second

flat appear? _____

10.21 Where on the bass staff is the seventh flat placed?

In the first space
below the staff.

_____

_____

10.22 Write the seven flats on the *grand* staff. ***Observe correct order and placement.***

10.23 Are the flats placed correctly in the example below?

No
*(The last flat on
both the treble
and the bass staff
should be an
octave lower.)*

_____

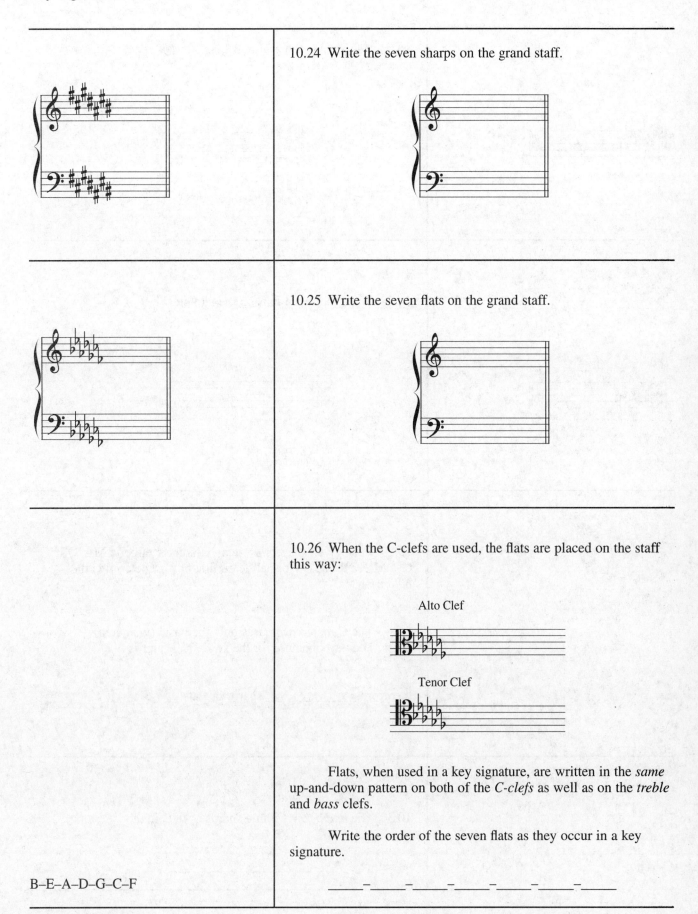

10.24 Write the seven sharps on the grand staff.

10.25 Write the seven flats on the grand staff.

10.26 When the C-clefs are used, the flats are placed on the staff this way:

Alto Clef

Tenor Clef

Flats, when used in a key signature, are written in the *same* up-and-down pattern on both of the *C-clefs* as well as on the *treble* and *bass* clefs.

Write the order of the seven flats as they occur in a key signature.

B–E–A–D–G–C–F   ____ – ____ – ____ – ____ – ____ – ____ – ____

10.27 Write the seven flats on the tenor clef.

10.28 Write the seven flats on the alto clef.

10.29 Each given *key signature* may indicate either a MAJOR or a MINOR KEY. We shall learn first how to determine the *major key.*

 The C major scale uses only the basic (unaltered) notes. The key signature for the key of C Major is

no

therefore _____ sharps or flats.

10.30 The *major key* with no sharps or flats in the

C Major

signature is _____.

	10.31 If the *key signature* consists of *sharps,* the *major key* can be determined by referring to the *last* sharp in the signature. This sharp indicates the *7th* scale degree, also known as the *leading tone.* The *keynote,* therefore, is a half step higher. (The interval of a half step separates the 7th and 8th degrees of the major scale.) If the last sharp in the key signature is D♯, E the key is _____ Major.
the 7th	10.32 Which degree of the major scale is indicated by the last sharp of the key signature? _____
A	10.33 If the last sharp in the key signature is G♯, the key is _____ Major.
D	10.34 If the last sharp in the key signature is C♯, the key is _____ Major
B	10.35 What *major key* is indicated by the signature below? _____ Major
G	10.36 What *major key* is indicated by the signature below? _____ Major.

F#

10.37 What *major key* is indicated by the signature below?

_____ Major

E

10.38 What *major key* is indicated by the signature below?

_____ Major

D

10.39 What *major key* is indicated by the signature below?

_____ Major

A

10.40 What *major key* is indicated by the signature below?

_____ Major

C#

10.41 What *major key* is indicated by the signature below?

_____ Major

10.42 To write a key signature consisting of sharps for a given key, the process described in frame 10.31 is reversed. For example, the signature for the key of E Major can be determined as follows:

(1) The 7th degree of the E major scale is D♯.
(2) D♯ will be the last sharp in the key signature.
(3) The order of sharps up to and including D♯ is F–C–G–D.
(4) Therefore, the signature for the key of E Major is four sharps.

The *last* sharp of the key signature is on which degree

of the major scale? _____

The 7th

10.43 Write the *key signature* for A Major on the *grand* staff.

10.44 Write the *key signature* for D Major on the *grand* staff.

10.45 Write the *key signature* for E Major on the *grand* staff.

10.46 Write the *key signature* for G Major on the *grand* staff.

10.47 Write the *key signature* for B Major on the *grand* staff.

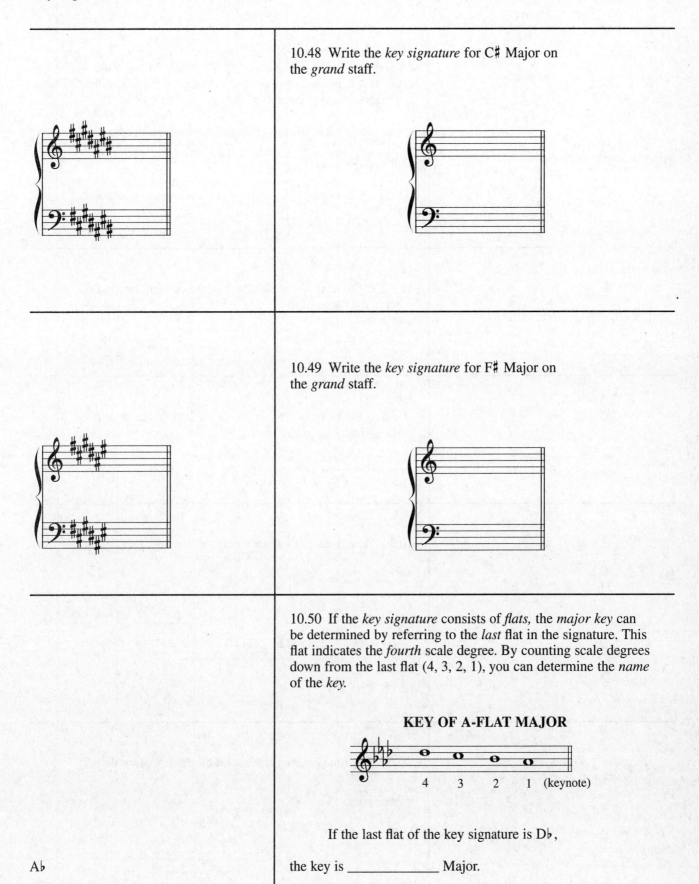

10.48 Write the *key signature* for C♯ Major on the *grand* staff.

10.49 Write the *key signature* for F♯ Major on the *grand* staff.

10.50 If the *key signature* consists of *flats,* the *major key* can be determined by referring to the *last* flat in the signature. This flat indicates the *fourth* scale degree. By counting scale degrees down from the last flat (4, 3, 2, 1), you can determine the *name* of the *key.*

KEY OF A-FLAT MAJOR

4   3   2   1   (keynote)

If the last flat of the key signature is D♭,

the key is _____ Major.

A♭

The 1st

10.51 Notice in the preceding frame that the *name* of the *key* (A♭) is the *same* as the *next-to-the-last* flat. *This will always be the case.* You may wish to make use of this method when identifying *key signatures* that contain *flats.**

The next-to-the-last flat indicates which degree

of the major scale? _____
_____

* The key with one flat (F Major) is the only key that cannot be identified in this way.

D♭

10.52 If the next-to-the-last flat in the key signature is D♭, what is the name of the key?

_____ Major

E♭

10.53 If the next-to-the-last flat in the key signature is E♭, what is the name of the key?

_____ Major

D♭

10.54 What *major key* is indicated by the signature below?

_____ Major

F

10.55 What *major key* is indicated by the signature below?

_____ Major

Gb

10.56 What *major key* is indicated by the signature

below? _____ Major

Ab

10.57 What *major key* is indicated by the signature

below? _____ Major

Bb

10.58 What *major key* is indicated by the signature

below? _____ Major

Eb

10.59 What *major key* is indicated by the signature

below? _____ Major

Cb

10.60 What *major key* is indicated by the signature

below? _____ Major

10.61 The signature of a key containing flats can be determined as follows:

> (1) Go through the order of the flats until you reach the flat that is identical with the name of the key.
>
> (2) Add the next flat in the series of flats.

The *next-to-the-last* flat is on which degree of

The 1st   the major scale? _____

10.62 The *last* flat is on which degree of the major scale?

The 4th   _____

10.63 Write the *key signature* for E♭ Major on the *grand* staff.

10.64 Write the *key signature* for B♭ Major on the *grand* staff.

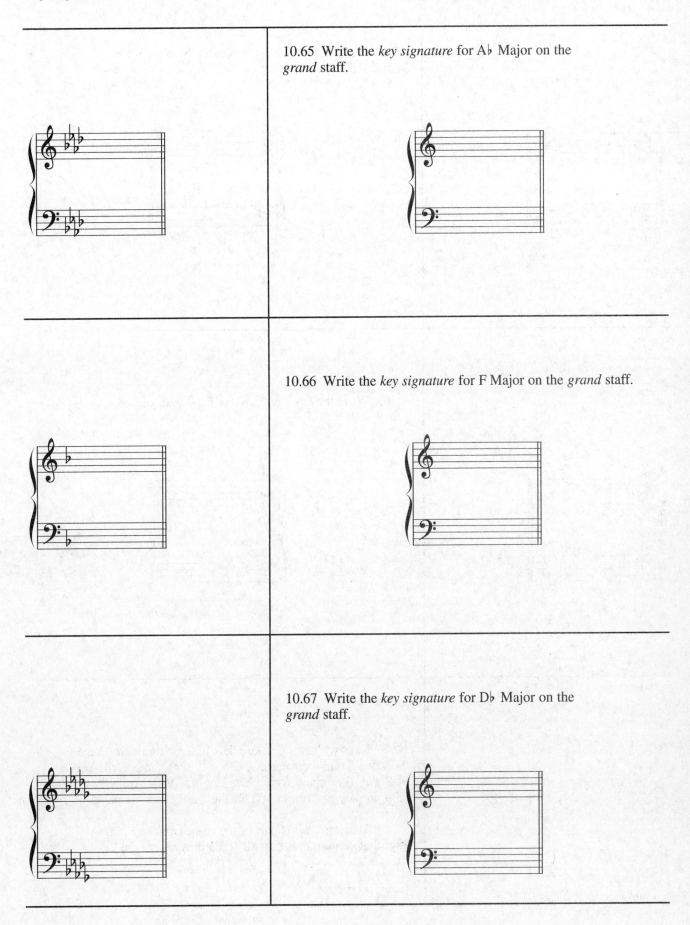

10.65 Write the *key signature* for A♭ Major on the *grand* staff.

10.66 Write the *key signature* for F Major on the *grand* staff.

10.67 Write the *key signature* for D♭ Major on the *grand* staff.

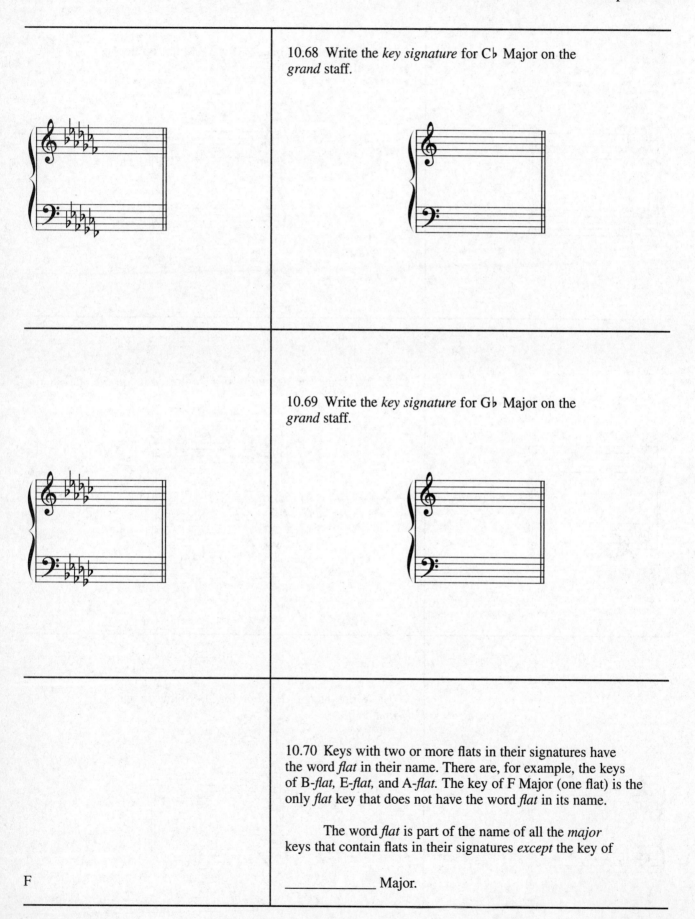

10.68 Write the *key signature* for C♭ Major on the *grand* staff.

10.69 Write the *key signature* for G♭ Major on the *grand* staff.

10.70 Keys with two or more flats in their signatures have the word *flat* in their name. There are, for example, the keys of B-*flat*, E-*flat*, and A-*flat*. The key of F Major (one flat) is the only *flat* key that does not have the word *flat* in its name.

The word *flat* is part of the name of all the *major* keys that contain flats in their signatures *except* the key of

_____ Major.

F

Sharps

10.71 Would the signature for the key of E Major consist of sharps or flats?

_____

Flats

10.72 Would the signature for the key of A♭ Major consist of sharps or flats?

_____

Flats

10.73 Would the signature for the key of G♭ Major consist of sharps or flats?

_____

Sharps

10.74 Would the signature for the key of B Major consist of sharps or flats?

_____

10.75 Write the *key signature* for D Major on the *grand* staff.

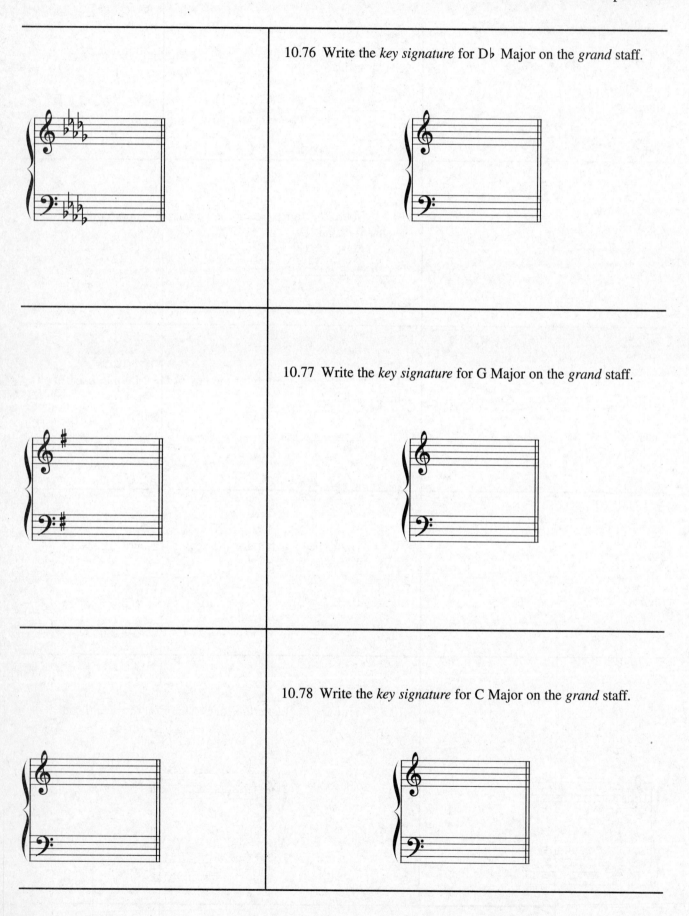

10.76 Write the *key signature* for D♭ Major on the *grand* staff.

10.77 Write the *key signature* for G Major on the *grand* staff.

10.78 Write the *key signature* for C Major on the *grand* staff.

10.79 Write the *key signature* for F Major on the *grand* staff.

10.80 Write the *key signature* for B Major on the *grand* staff.

10.81 Write the *key signature* for B♭ Major on the *grand* staff.

10.82 The *system* of *major keys* may be arranged in a *pattern* called the CIRCLE OF FIFTHS.

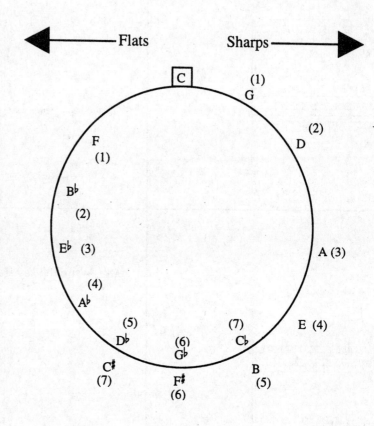

You may find the *circle of fifths* to be an aid in remembering the various *major key signatures.* Examine the order in which the sharp keys occur (reading clockwise from C Major).

Each sharp added to the signature produces a key the interval

perfect 5th

of a _____ higher than the preceding key.

10.83 Refer again to the *circle of fifths* in the preceding frame. Examine the order in which the flat keys occur (reading counterclockwise from C Major).

Each flat added to the signature produces a key

lower

the interval of a perfect 5th _____ than the preceding key.

C♭ Major

10.84 The *circle of fifths* makes it clear that some of the flat keys sound the same as some of the sharp keys. The key of five flats (D♭), for example, sounds the same as the key of seven sharps (C♯). Keys that contain the same pitches but are notated differently are ENHARMONIC KEYS.

Which key is *enharmonic* with B Major?

_____

Six sharps
(F♯ Major)

10.85 What is the signature of the key that is

enharmonic with G♭ Major? _____

---

major

10.86 Each *key signature* may indicate either a *major* key or a *minor* key. The *major* and *minor* keys that share the *same signature* are called RELATIVE KEYS.

Each *major* key has a *relative* minor key, and

each *minor* key has a *relative* _____ key.

3rd

10.87 The relation between a *major* key and its *relative minor* is shown in the example below.

White note = major keynote.
Black note = minor keynote.

The *keynote* of the *relative minor* key is located on the *6th* degree of the *major* scale. The *keynote* of

the *relative major* key is located on the _____ degree of the *minor* scale.

below

10.88 The *keynotes* of *relative major* and *minor* keys are a *minor 3rd* apart. The *keynote* of a *minor* key

is a *minor 3rd* (above/below) _____ the *keynote* of its *relative major.*

relative

10.89 The two keys (one major and one minor) that

use the same key signature are called _____ keys.

The 6th

10.90 *There is a relative minor key for each major key.* Upon which degree of the major scale is the keynote of its relative minor located?

_____

The 3rd

10.91 *There is a relative major key for each minor key.* Upon which degree of the minor scale is the keynote of its relative major located?

_____

The minor 3rd

10.92 You must not think that because the keynote of the relative minor is located below the keynote of the major or because major key signatures have been presented first, minor keys are inferior to major keys. On the contrary, composers have long treated minor keys as in every way equal to major keys. A minor key does not *borrow* its signature from the relative major; a *single* signature is *shared* by the two keys.

What is the interval that separates the keynotes of relative major and minor keys?

_____

(1)

(2)

(3)

10.93 Indicate (with a black note) the keynote of the *relative minor* for each *major* key below.

(1) (2) (3)

White note = major keynote.
Black note = minor keynote.

(1)

(2)

(3)

10.94 Indicate (with a black note) the keynote of the *relative minor* for each *major* key below.

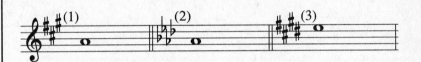

(1) (2) (3)

White note = major keynote.
Black note = minor keynote.

(1)

(2)

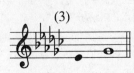

(3)

10.95 Indicate (with a white note) the keynote of the *relative major* for each *minor* key below.

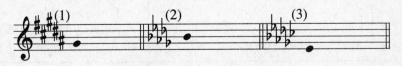

(1) (2) (3)

White note = major keynote.
Black note = minor keynote.

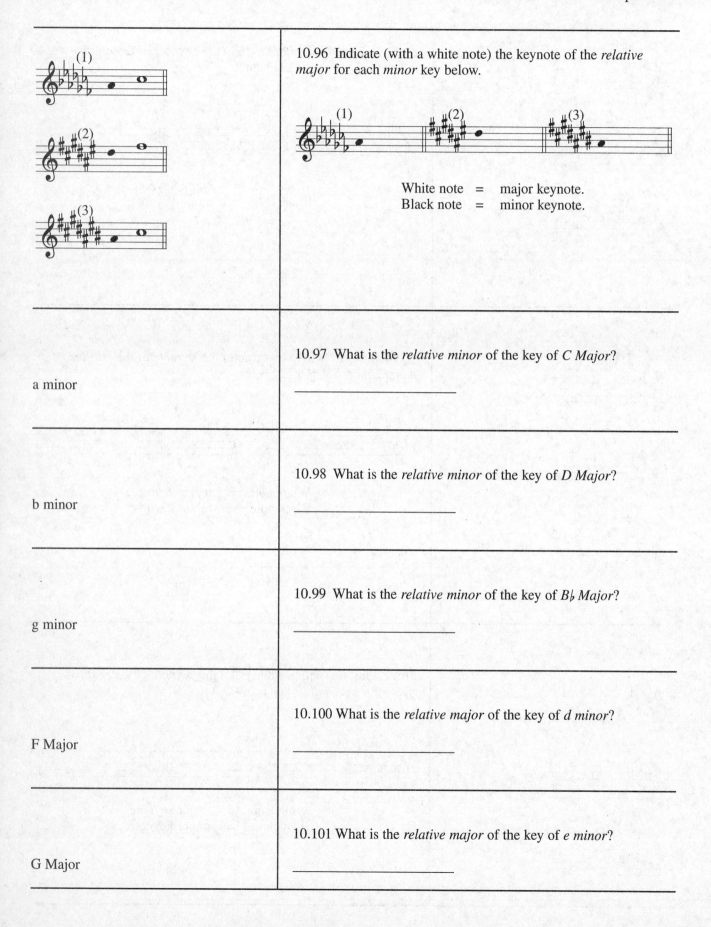

10.96 Indicate (with a white note) the keynote of the *relative major* for each *minor* key below.

White note = major keynote.
Black note = minor keynote.

a minor

10.97 What is the *relative minor* of the key of *C Major*?

_____

b minor

10.98 What is the *relative minor* of the key of *D Major*?

_____

g minor

10.99 What is the *relative minor* of the key of *B♭ Major*?

_____

F Major

10.100 What is the *relative major* of the key of *d minor*?

_____

G Major

10.101 What is the *relative major* of the key of *e minor*?

_____

	10.102 What is the *relative major* of the key of *f♯ minor*?
A Major	_____
	10.103 What is the *relative minor* of the key of *E♭ Major*?
c minor	_____
	10.104 A *circle of fifths* can be written for *minor* keys as well as for *major* keys.

You may use the *circle of fifths* above as an aid in remembering *minor key signatures*. As in the case of major keys, each additional sharp in the signature produces a key a perfect 5th higher than the preceding key.

The keys of e♭ minor and d♯ minor are

enharmonic	_____ keys.

10.105 Write the *key signature* for c♯ minor on the *grand* staff.

10.106 Write the *key signature* for f minor on the *grand* staff.

10.107 Write the *key signature* for b♭ minor on the *grand* staff.

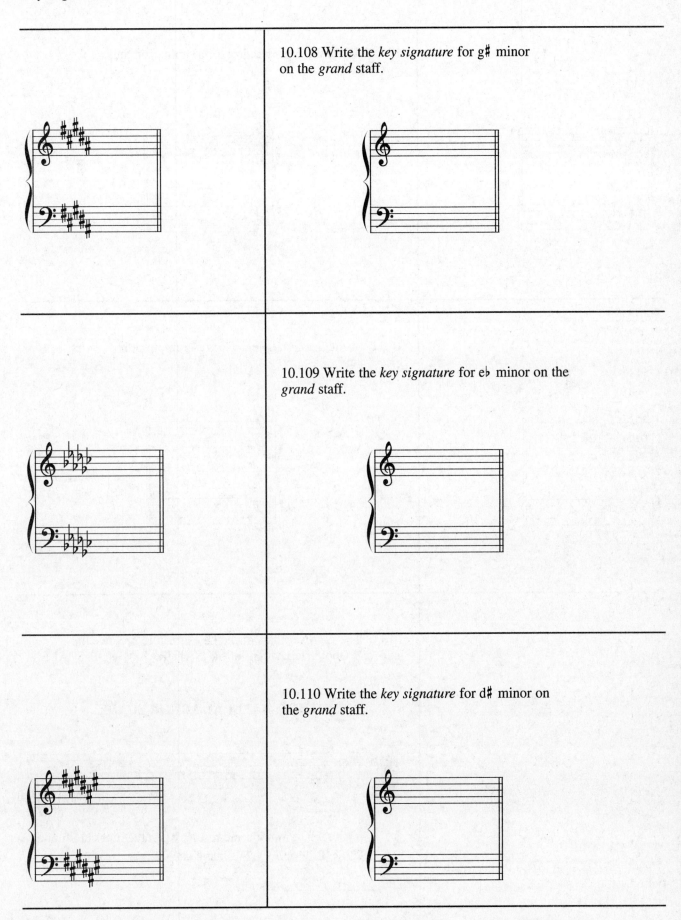

10.108 Write the *key signature* for g♯ minor on the *grand* staff.

10.109 Write the *key signature* for e♭ minor on the *grand* staff.

10.110 Write the *key signature* for d♯ minor on the *grand* staff.

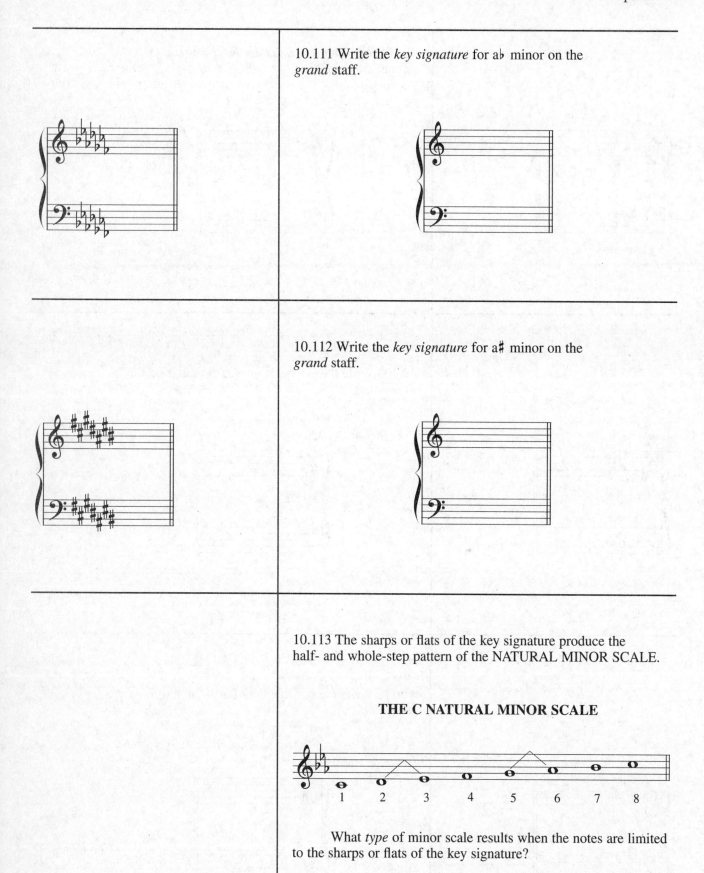

10.111 Write the *key signature* for a♭ minor on the *grand* staff.

10.112 Write the *key signature* for a♯ minor on the *grand* staff.

10.113 The sharps or flats of the key signature produce the half- and whole-step pattern of the NATURAL MINOR SCALE.

THE C NATURAL MINOR SCALE

1   2   3   4   5   6   7   8

What *type* of minor scale results when the notes are limited to the sharps or flats of the key signature?

natural

The _____ minor

10.114 *Accidentals in addition* to the sharps or flats of the key signature are necessary to transform the *natural* minor scale into the *harmonic* and *melodic* types. These accidentals are applied to the individual notes as needed.

THE C HARMONIC MINOR SCALE

1   2   3   4   5   6   7   8

If the 7th degree of a natural minor scale is raised

harmonic

a half step, the result is the _____ minor scale.

10.115 Transform the *natural* minor scale below into a *harmonic* minor scale.

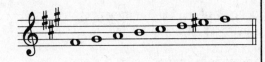

10.116 Transform the *natural* minor scale below into a *harmonic* minor scale.

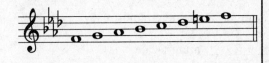

10.117 Transform the *natural* minor scale below into a *harmonic* minor scale.

10.118 Transform the *natural* minor scale below into a *harmonic* minor scale.

10.119 The *melodic* minor scale (*ascending* form) is formed by *raising* the 6th and 7th degrees of the *natural* minor scale each by a *half step*.

THE C MELODIC MINOR SCALE, ASCENDING FORM

If the 6th and 7th degrees of the natural minor scale are raised each by a half step, the result is the

ascending   _____ form of the melodic minor scale.

10.120 Since the *descending* form of the *melodic* minor scale is identical with the *natural* minor scale, the 6th and 7th degrees *must be returned to their previous state* by the use of accidentals.

THE C MELODIC MINOR SCALE

The descending form of the melodic minor scale

natural   is the same as the _____ minor scale.

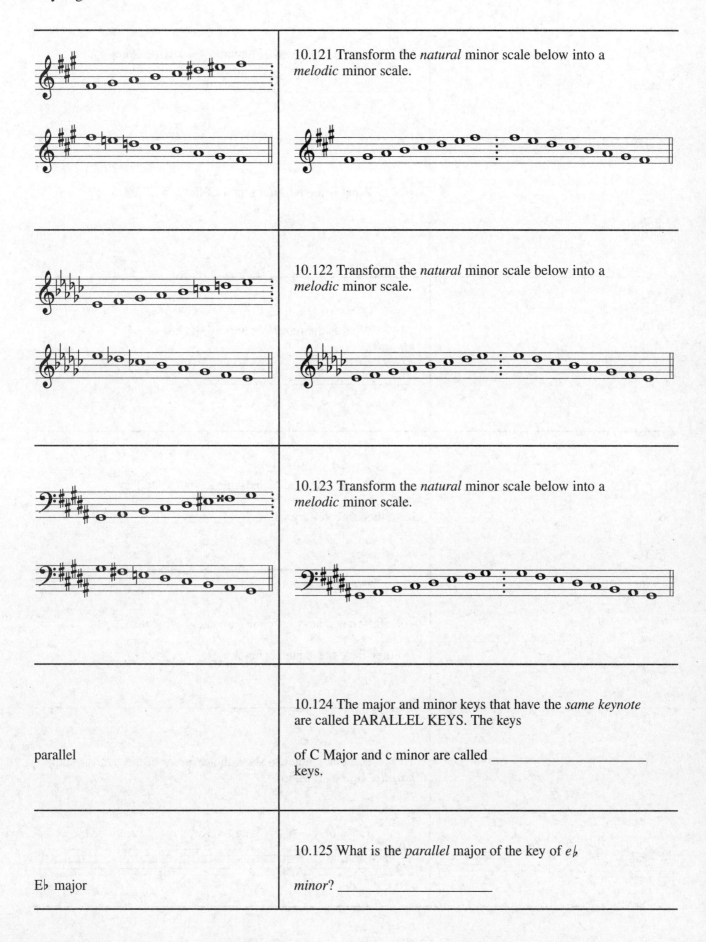

10.121 Transform the *natural* minor scale below into a *melodic* minor scale.

10.122 Transform the *natural* minor scale below into a *melodic* minor scale.

10.123 Transform the *natural* minor scale below into a *melodic* minor scale.

10.124 The major and minor keys that have the *same keynote* are called PARALLEL KEYS. The keys

parallel

of C Major and c minor are called _____ keys.

10.125 What is the *parallel* major of the key of e♭

E♭ major

minor? _____

B Major	10.126 What is the *parallel* major of the key of *b minor*? _____
e minor	10.127 What is the *parallel* minor of the key of *E Major*? _____
f♯ minor	10.128 What is the *parallel* minor of the key of *F♯ Major*? _____
No	10.129 Parallel keys have the same keynote. Do they have the same key signature? _____
No	10.130 Relative keys have the same key signature. Do they have the same keynote? _____
	10.131 Use black notes to show the *keynotes* of the *relative* and *parallel keys* of E Major.

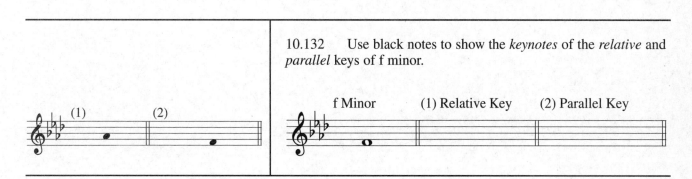

10.132   Use black notes to show the *keynotes* of the *relative* and *parallel* keys of f minor.

Summary

The signature of no sharps or flats denotes the keys of C Major and a minor. All other keys have signatures of one or more sharps or flats. If there are *sharps* in the signature, the *last* sharp falls on the *seventh* degree of the major scale; if there are *flats,* the *last* flat falls on the *fourth* degree of the major scale, or the key may be derived from the *next-to-the-last flat,* except for the key of F Major.

Any *key signature* serves for both a *major* and a *minor key.* The two *keys* that use the *same signature* are called *relative keys.* The *keynote* of the *relative minor* is located a *minor* 3rd **below** the *keynote* of the *major* (on the sixth scale degree); the *keynote* of the *relative major* is located a *minor* 3rd **above** the *keynote* of the *minor* (on the third scale degree). *Parallel keys* must not be confused with *relative keys. Parallel keys* have the *same keynotes* but **not** the *same signatures.*

Mastery Frames

10–1 Write the seven sharps on the treble and tenor clefs as they would appear in a key signature.

Treble

Treble

Tenor

Tenor

(frames 10.11, 10.15)

10–2 Write the seven flats on the bass and alto clefs as they would appear in a key signature.

Bass

Bass

Alto

Alto

(10.20, 10.26)

10–3 If sharps appear in the key signature, the major keynote is located a half step above the next-to-the-last

False   (10.31)   sharp. (True/False) _____

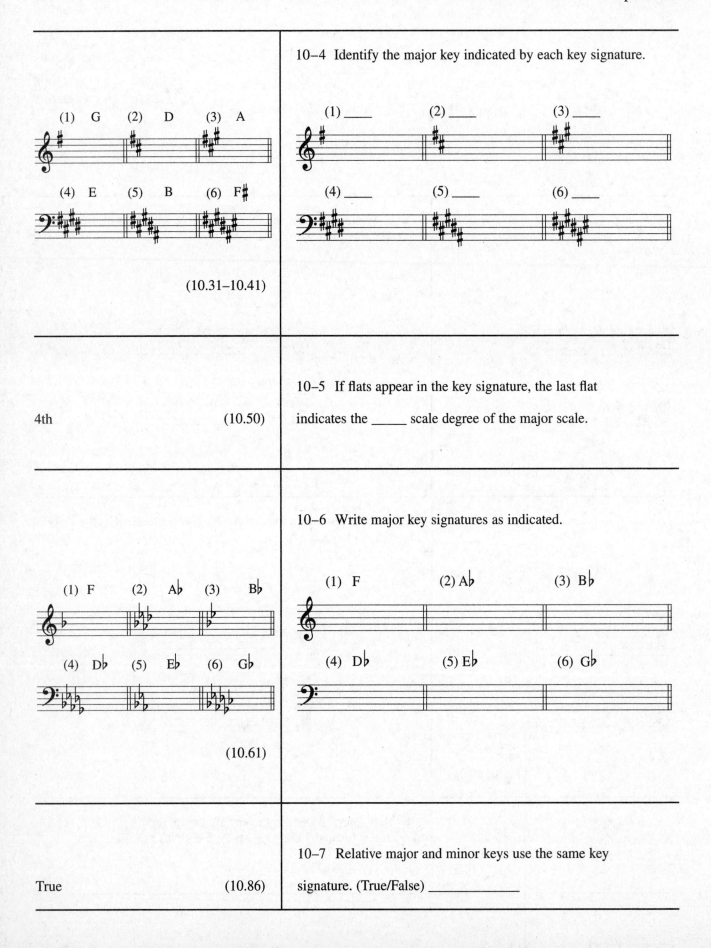

10–4 Identify the major key indicated by each key signature.

(1) ____   (2) ____   (3) ____

(4) ____   (5) ____   (6) ____

(10.31–10.41)

4th   (10.50)

10–5 If flats appear in the key signature, the last flat indicates the _____ scale degree of the major scale.

10–6 Write major key signatures as indicated.

(1) F   (2) A♭   (3) B♭

(4) D♭   (5) E♭   (6) G♭

(10.61)

True   (10.86)

10–7 Relative major and minor keys use the same key signature. (True/False) _____

10–8 Use a black note to indicate the keynote of the relative minor in each case.

Write here

(1)   (2)   (3)

Major Keynotes

(10.87–10.91)

10–9 Write minor key signatures as indicated. *Notice the use of lowercase letters to denote minor keys.*

(1) b   (2) f♯   (3) f

(4) c♯   (5) c   (6) g

(10.86–10.104)

10–10 Parallel major and minor keys share the same keynote but have different signatures.

True   (10.124–10.129)   (True/False) _____

Supplementary Activities

Continue activities similar to those outlined in the previous two chapters in exploring and writing about topics from this chapter (in this case, key signatures and their history and usage), and also continue activities in composition. At this point melodies and short compositions can and should be done with appropriate key signatures.

Supplementary Assignments

ASSIGNMENT 10–1   Name: _____

1. Write the seven sharps and seven flats on the staffs below as they would appear in a key signature. *(Use correct order and placement.)*

SHARPS   FLATS

2. What is the key signature for the key of C Major? _____

3. Explain how the major key is determined if the signature contains flats.

   _____

   _____

4. Explain how the major key is determined if the signature contains sharps.

   _____

   _____

5. Each major key has a relative minor key, which uses the same signature. The minor key is located a

   minor 3rd (above/below) _____ the major key.

6. Which key signature indicates the relative major of f♯ minor? _____

7. Name the major and minor keys indicated by each of the key signatures below.

   (1)   (2)

   Major: _____   Major: _____

   Minor: _____   Minor: _____

   (3)   (4)

   Major: _____   Major: _____

   Minor: _____   Minor: _____

   (5)   (6)

   Major: _____   Major: _____

   Minor: _____   Minor: _____

8. Compose melodies using a major key signature.

ASSIGNMENT 10–2   Name: _____

1. Which key signature indicates the parallel major of b♭ minor? _____

2. Which key signature indicates the relative minor of D Major? _____

3. Write key signatures on the grand staff as directed. *(Capital letters indicate major keys; lowercase letters indicate minor keys.)*

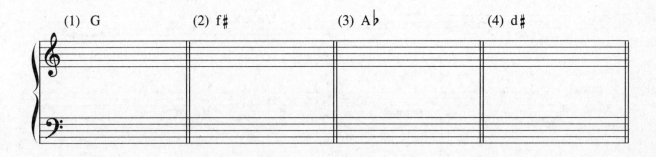

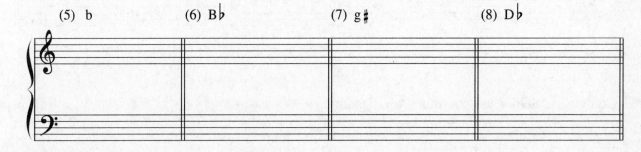

4. What form of the minor scale uses only the notes provided by the key signature? _____

5. What form of the minor scale requires that the seventh scale degree be raised a half step? _____

6. Transform the scales below into harmonic minor scales by applying the necessary accidentals.

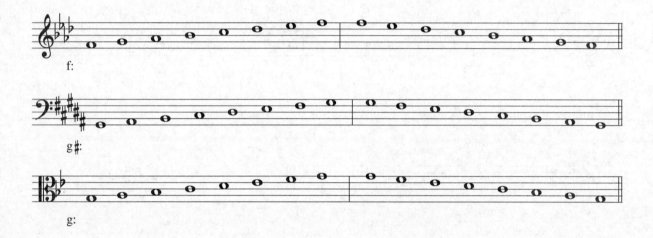

7. Transform the scales below into melodic minor scales by applying the necessary accidentals.

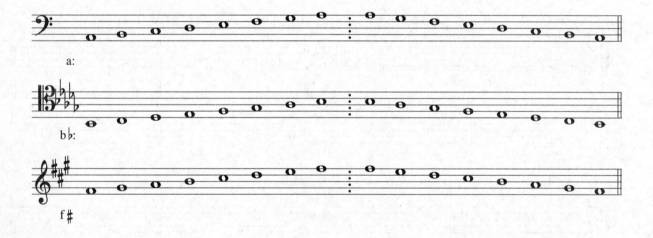

8. Compose melodies using a minor key signature.

Ear-Training Activities

1. The circle of fifths (frames 10.82 and 10.104 in the text) is helpful in remembering the various key signatures. It is also helpful for understanding harmonic relations such as chord progressions and modulations, topics of more advanced theory study (covered in Steinke, *Harmonic Materials in Tonal Music,* Parts I and II). Beginning on the lowest C of the piano or a full-size keyboard, the entire series of fifths in ascending motion may be played.

2. As a more advanced exercise for those wishing the challenge, the series can be sung within vocal range by bringing all the notes within a limited range. Sing the circle of fifths as notated below (or transpose to a more convenient level).

3. Continue with any other musical activities that involve performing from music or improvisationally along with which the knowledge of key signatures can be applied simultaneously or after the fact.

4. For those wishing to get started with melodic dictation, here is a short discussion about how to get started and some helpful tips to perfect one's abilities in this technique.

Melodic Dictation

Melodic dictation is an essential part of the study of music reading as it is actually music reading in reverse. That is to say that when the printed music is seen, the symbols must be translated into sound in a manner so as to include all elements peculiar to the rendition of that particular musical phrase. In melodic dictation, on the other hand, the sound is heard and the appropriate symbols for its representation must be ascertained. Thus, for a complete understanding of the problems involved, it is necessary to study the process from both directions.

One of the most important items in the taking down of melodic dictation is one's ability to memorize quickly and accurately at least a small portion of the melody. In the case of a long or complicated phrase it is often futile to attempt to retain the entire melody. In such cases the attention should be focused upon only a small portion at a time, perhaps only a few notes. Improvement in this technique may be made only at the expense of considerable effort in actual practice. One way to practice memorization is to play or sing a short phrase of an unfamiliar melody, being careful to notice all elements that may facilitate its memorization (i.e., implied harmonic background, phrase structure, melodic patterns, sequential usages, characteristic rhythmic patterns, etc.). Then repeat the phrase at once without music; and, finally, check to see which elements were retained and which were forgotten. This drill will point out weaknesses as well as improve the general memorization technique.

The following procedure is recommended for the development of melodic dictation technique.

A. Selection of the Time Signature

    1. Recognize the beat.

    2. Listen for the succession of strong and weak beats. (This will give the first part of the time classification; duple, triple, quadruple, etc.).

    3. Listen for the division of the beat. (This will give the second part of the time classification; simple or compound).

    4. Select an appropriate time signature.

B. Indication of Pitch Relationships

    1. Memorize a portion of the melody.

    2. Write these pitches on the staff devoid of rhythm in the form of dots by relating each tone to the key center.

    3. Repeat steps 1 and 2 above until the entire melody is completed.

C. Indication of Rhythmic Patterns

    1. Listen again for the beat, observing where each beat occurs in relation to the pitches that have been transcribed.

    2. Write appropriate numbers representing beats over the correct notes.

    3. Draw bar lines before each primary beat (i.e., before each note associated with the number 1).

    4. Listen to each beat and deduce the correct notation for the rhythmic pattern involved.

Chapter 11.0
Triads

The three basic elements of most Western music are *melody, rhythm,* and *harmony.* The harmonic element is based on three-note chords called *triads.* The major-minor scale system generates four types of triads: *major, minor, diminished,* and *augmented.* These names reflect the *intervals* contained in the triads. Triads may be built on any note of a scale. They vary not only in quality but also in the way they function within a tonality. Because of the important role harmony plays in much of Western art music, there must be a thorough knowledge of triads. It is also essential that sensitivity to their sounds is cultivated.

three	11.1 Three or more tones sounding together form a CHORD. 　　　An *interval* consists of *two* tones, but a *chord* consists of _____ or more tones.
chord	11.2 Three or more tones sounding together form a _____, or more specifically, a *trichord.*
trichord, triad	11.3 The term TRIAD refers specifically to a three-note chord composed of thirds. A *chord* of three tones is called a _____ but a _____ is composed of thirds.
triad	11.4 *Triads* are based on the TERTIAN system of harmony. In this system the tones of the *triad* are related to one another by the interval of the 3rd, and the only thirds found in triads are major or minor thirds. 　　　A *chord* consisting of two superimposed 3rds is called a _____.

11.5   A triad may be constructed on any note of the basic scale.

These triads are called BASIC TRIADS. What

is the total number of *basic triads*? _____

Seven

11.6   Spell the *basic triad* based on C. _____

C E G

11.7   Spell the *basic triad* based on D. _____

D F A

11.8   Spell the *basic triad* based on E. _____

E G B

11.9   Spell the *basic triad* based on F. _____

F A C

11.10 Spell the *basic triad* based on G. _____

G B D

11.11 Spell the *basic triad* based on A. _____

A C E

11.12 Spell the *basic triad* based on B. _____

B D F

Expository Frame

11.13 Play the seven basic triads at a keyboard or from the CD and compare the sounds. It is apparent that the triads do not all sound alike. This is because the intervallic structure is not the same for all basic triads, and that is due to the *half steps* that occur between E and F and between B and C in the *basic scale.*

(No response required.)

11.14 There are four types of triads that originate in the major-minor scale system: MAJOR, MINOR, DIMINISHED, and AUGMENTED. We shall examine each type separately.

    Name the four types of triads.

(1) major

(2) minor

(3) diminished

(4) augmented
(any order)

(1) _____

(2) _____

(3) _____

(4) _____

11.15 While the three tones of the MAJOR TRIAD easily correspond to the 1st, 3rd, and 5th degrees of the *major scale,* they may also be rooted on other scale degrees in both major and minor scales.

    When sounding together, the 1st, 3rd, and 5th degrees

major

of the major scale can produce a _____ triad.

11.16 The *lowest* tone of a triad, when the tones are arranged in 3rds, is called the ROOT. It may be thought of as a tone generating the triad. It also exerts a strong influence over the other two members (the 3rd and the 5th).

    The lowest tone of a triad (when arranged in 3rds)

root

is called the _____.

5th	11.17 The *uppermost* tone of a triad (when the tones are arranged in 3rds) is called the _____.
3rd	11.18 The tone between the *root* and the 5th of a triad is called the _____.
1st, 3rd, (and) 5th	11.19 The major triad may consist of the _____, _____, and _____ degrees of the major scale.
Perfect 5th	11.20 Observe in the example below the *intervals* that constitute the *major triad*. In the major triad the interval from the root up to the 3rd is a major 3rd, the interval from the 3rd up to the 5th is a minor 3rd, and the interval from the root up to the 5th is a _____.
minor 3rd	11.21 What is the *interval* between the 3rd and the 5th of a *major triad*? _____
Major 3rd	11.22 What is the *interval* between the root and the 3rd of a *major triad*? _____

11.23 What is the *interval* between the root and the 5th of a *major triad*?

Perfect 5th

_____

11.24 Three of the *basic triads* are *major triads*. These are C E G, F A C, and G B D.

Observe that the tones of each triad fall into the *major scale* of the *root*.

When sounding together, the 1st, 3rd, and 5th degrees

major

of the major scale produce a _____ triad.

11.25 A *major triad* may be written on any note either *by relating the three tones of the triad to the major scale of the root* or *by observing the correct intervallic relationship between the triad tones*. Try both methods; check one against the other. Depending on the musical context, both methods are effective.

Write *major triads* (the given note is the *root*).

(1)   (2)   (3)

(1)   (2)   (3)

11.26 Write *major triads* (the given note is the *root*).

(1)   (2)   (3)

(1)   (2)   (3)

11.27 Write *major triads* (the given note is the *root*).

11.28 Write *major triads* (the given note is the *root*).

11.29 Write *major triads* (the given note is the *root*).

11.30 Write *major triads* (the given note is the *3rd*).

11.31 Write *major triads* (the given note is the *3rd*).

11.32 Write *major triads* (the given note is the *3rd*).

11.33 Write *major triads* (the given note is the *3rd*).

11.34 Write *major triads* (the given note is the *5th*).

11.35 Write *major triads* (the given note is the *5th*).

11.36 Write *major triads* (the given note is the *5th*).

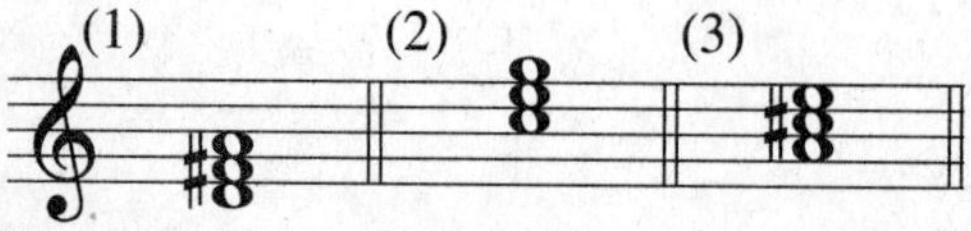

(1)   (2)   (3)

11.37 Write *major triads* (the given note is the *5th*).

(1)   (2)   (3)

C E G; F A C; G B D

11.38 List the three *basic triads* that are *major*.

_____ _____ _____

11.39 A MINOR TRIAD may consist of the 1st, 3rd, and 5th degrees of the *minor scale*.

1 2 3 4 5 6 7 8   5
                                         3
                                         1

minor

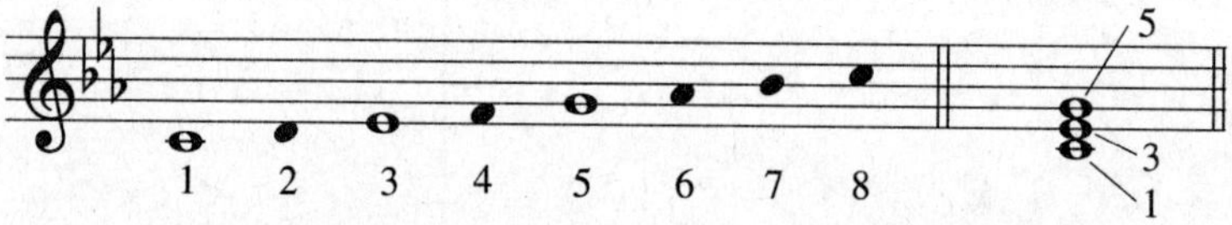

When sounding together, the 1st, 3rd, and 5th degrees

of the minor scale produce a _____ triad.

minor

11.40 A minor triad consists of the 1st, 3rd, and 5th

degrees of a _____ scale.

11.41 The *intervals* that constitute the *minor triad* are shown below.

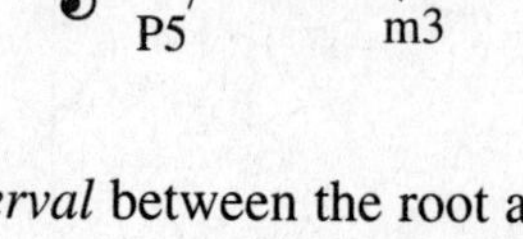

M3

P5   m3

What is the *interval* between the root and the 3rd of a *minor triad*?

minor 3rd

_____

	11.42 What is the *interval* between the 3rd and the 5th of a *minor triad*?
Major 3rd	_____
	11.43 What is the *interval* between the root and the 5th of a *minor triad*?
Perfect 5th	_____

11.44 As compared with the major triad, the *order* of major and minor 3rds is *reversed* in the minor triad.

	MAJOR TRIAD	MINOR TRIAD
root up to 3	major 3rd	minor 3rd
3 up to 5	minor 3rd	major 3rd
root up to 5	perfect 5th	perfect 5th

The interval between the root and the 5th is a perfect 5th in both the major and the minor triad. The interval between the 3rd and the 5th in the major triad is a minor 3rd; but in the minor triad

major   the interval between the 3rd and 5th is a _____ 3rd.

11.45 Three of the *basic triads* are *minor triads*. These are D F A, E G B, and A C E.

1st, 3rd,   The minor triad may consist of the _____, _____,

(and) 5th   and _____ degrees of the minor scale.

11.46 Write *minor triads* (the given note is the *root*).

11.47 Write *minor triads* (the given note is the *root*).

11.48 Write *minor triads* (the given note is the *root*).

11.49 Write *minor triads* (the given note is the *root*).

11.50 Write *minor triads* (the given note is the *root*).

11.51 Write *minor triads* (the given note is the *3rd*).

11.52 Write *minor triads* (the given note is the *3rd*).

11.53 Write *minor triads* (the given note is the *3rd*).

11.54 Write *minor triads* (the given note is the *3rd*).

11.55 Write *minor triads* (the given note is the *5th*).

11.56 Write *minor triads* (the given note is the *5th*).

11.57 Write *minor triads* (the given note is the *5th*).

11.58 Write *minor triads* (the given note is the *5th*).

(2)

11.59 Which of the *triads* below is *minor*? _____

(3)

11.60 Which of the *triads* below is *major*? _____

11.61 List the three *basic triads* that are *minor.*

D F A ; E G B ; A C E

_____ _____ _____

11.62 The DIMINISHED TRIAD can be produced by *lowering* the *5th* of a *minor* triad one *chromatic half step.*

MINOR   DIMINISHED

If the 5th of a minor triad is lowered a half step,

diminished

the result is a _____ triad.

11.63 Transform the *minor* triads below into *diminished* triads by *lowering* the *5th* a *chromatic half step.*

Apply the proper accidentals to the second triad in each case.

(1)   (2)   (3)

(1)   (2)   (3)
MINOR DIM.   MINOR DIM.   MINOR DIM.

11.64 The *diminished* triad can be produced by *raising* the *root* and the *3rd* of a *minor* triad one *chromatic half step.*

MINOR   DIMINISHED

If a root and the 3rd of a minor triad are raised a chromatic

diminished

half step, the result is a _____ triad.

11.65 Transform the *minor* triads below into *diminished* triads by *raising* the *root* and the *3rd* a *chromatic half step.*

Apply the proper accidentals to the second triad in each case.

11.66 The diminished triad is the same as a minor triad whose 5th has been lowered a chromatic half step or whose root

raised

and 3rd have been _____ a chromatic half step.

11.67 Observe the *intervals* that constitute the *diminished triad.*

The diminished triad is named for the diminished 5th between the root and the 5th of the triad. What is

minor 3rd

the *interval* between the 3rd and the 5th? _____

11.68 What is the *interval* between the root and the 3rd of a

minor 3rd

diminished triad? _____

minor	**11.69** The diminished triad consists of two superimposed _____ 3rds.
B D F	**11.70** One of the *basic triads* is a *diminished triad.* Spell this triad. _____

11.71 Write *diminished triads* (the given note is the *root*).

11.72 Write *diminished triads* (the given note is the *root*).

11.73 Write *diminished triads* (the given note is the *root*).

11.74 Write *diminished triads* (the given note is the *root*).

11.75 Write *diminished triads* (the given note is the *3rd*).

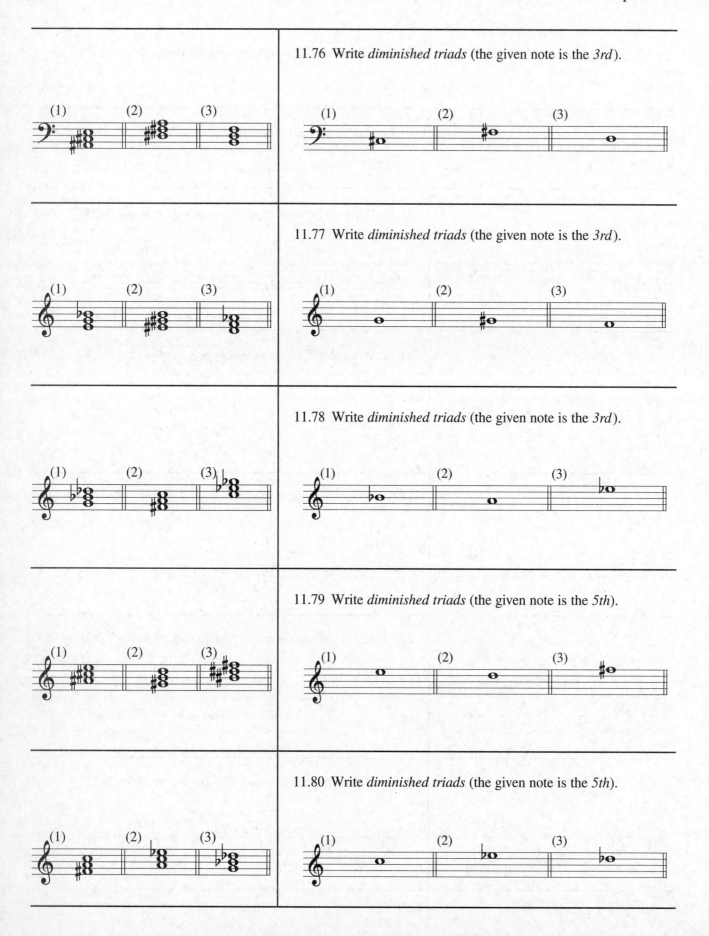

11.76 Write *diminished triads* (the given note is the *3rd*).

11.77 Write *diminished triads* (the given note is the *3rd*).

11.78 Write *diminished triads* (the given note is the *3rd*).

11.79 Write *diminished triads* (the given note is the *5th*).

11.80 Write *diminished triads* (the given note is the *5th*).

(1) (2) (3)

11.81 Write *diminished triads* (the given note is the *5th*).

(1) (2) (3)

11.82 Write *diminished triads* (the given note is the *5th*).

(1) (2) (3)

(4)

11.83 Which of the *triads* below is *diminished*?

_____

(1) (2) (3) (4)

(3)

11.84 Which of the *triads* below is *minor*?

_____

(1) (2) (3) (4)

(3)

11.85 Which of the *triads* below is *major*?

_____

(1) (2) (3) (4)

11.86 The AUGMENTED TRIAD can be produced by *raising* the *5th* of a *major* triad by one *chromatic half step.*

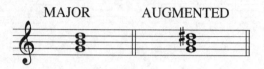

If the 5th of a major triad is raised a chromatic half step,

augmented   the result is a(n) _____ triad.

11.87 Transform the *major* triads below into *augmented* triads by *raising* the *5th* a *chromatic half step.*

Apply the proper accidentals to the second triad in each case.

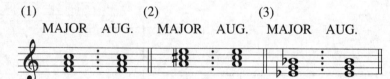

11.88 The *augmented* triad can be produced by *lowering* the *root* and the *3rd* of a *major* triad one *chromatic half step.*

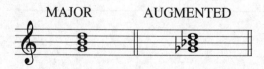

If the root and the 3rd of a major triad are lowered a

augmented   chromatic half step, the result is a(n) _____ triad.

11.89 Transform the *major* triads below into *augmented* triads by *lowering* the *root* and the *3rd* a *chromatic half step.*

Apply the proper accidentals to the second triad in each case.

(1)   (2)   (3)
MAJOR   AUG.   MAJOR   AUG.   MAJOR   AUG.

(1)   (2)   (3)

lowered

11.90 The augmented triad is the same as a major triad whose 5th has been raised a chromatic half step or whose root

and 3rd have been _____ a chromatic half step.

11.91 Observe the *intervals* that constitute the *augmented triad.*

In the augmented triad the *intervals* between the root and the 3rd and between the 3rd and the 5th are both major 3rds.

What is the *interval* between the root and the 5th?

An augmented 5th

_____

major

11.92 The augmented triad consists of two

superimposed _____ 3rds.

11.93 The *augmented triad* **does not exist** as a *basic triad*. List the three types of triads that do occur as *basic triads*.

major; minor;

diminished

_____

_____

11.94 Write *augmented triads* (the given note is the *root*).

(1)   (2)   (3)

11.95 Write *augmented triads* (the given note is the *root*).

(1)   (2)   (3)

11.96 Write *augmented triads* (the given note is the *root*).

(1)   (2)   (3)

11.97 Write *augmented triads* (the given note is the *root*).

(1)   (2)   (3)

11.98 Write *augmented triads* (the given note is the *3rd*).

11.99 Write *augmented triads* (the given note is the *3rd*).

11.100 Write *augmented triads* (the given note is the *3rd*).

11.101 Write *augmented triads* (the given note is the *3rd*).

11.102 Write *augmented triads* (the given note is the *5th*).

11.103 Write *augmented triads* (the given note is the *5th*).

(1)   (2)   (3)

11.104 Write *augmented triads* (the given note is the *5th*).

(1)   (2)   (3)

11.105 Write *augmented triads* (the given note is the *5th*).

(1)   (2)   (3)

(2)

11.106 Which of the *triads* below is *augmented*?

_____

(1)   (2)   (3)   (4)

(3)

11.107 Which of the *triads* below is *major*?

_____

(1)   (2)   (3)   (4)

(4)

11.108 Which of the *triads* below is *diminished*?

_____

(1)   (2)   (3)   (4)

---

(3)

11.109 Which of the *triads* below is *minor*?

_____

(1)   (2)   (3)   (4)

---

major

11.110 The *major triad* consists of a major 3rd (root up to the 3rd) and a minor 3rd (3rd up to the 5th). The *minor triad* consists of a

minor 3rd (root up to the 3rd) and a _____ 3rd (3rd up to 5th).

---

minor

11.111 The two 3rds that constitute the major and minor triads are "unequal." One is major and one

is _____.

---

major

11.112 The *diminished triad* consists of two minor 3rds (root up to the 3rd and the 3rd up to the 5th). The *augmented triad*

consists of two _____ 3rds (root up to the 3rd and the 3rd up to the 5th).

---

minor

11.113 The diminished and augmented triads are composed of "equal" intervals. Both of the 3rds in

the diminished triad are _____ 3rds.

augmented

11.114 The triad that consists of two superimposed major 3rds is the _____ triad.

(as follows or with accidental signs)

(1) D F♯ A

(2) D F A

(3) D F A♭

(4) D F♯ A♯

11.115 Spell triads as directed.

    (1) D is the root of the *major* triad   _____

    (2) D is the root of the *minor* triad   _____

    (3) D is the root of the *diminished* triad _____

    (4) D is the root of the *augmented* triad _____

---

(1) E♭ G B♭

(2) E G B

(3) E G B♭

(4) E♭ G B

11.116 Spell triads as directed.

    (1) G is the 3rd of the *major* triad   _____

    (2) G is the 3rd of the *minor* triad   _____

    (3) G is the 3rd of the *diminished* triad _____

    (4) G is the 3rd of the *augmented* triad _____

---

(1) F A C

(2) F A♭ C

(3) F♯ A C

(4) F♭ A♭ C

11.117 Spell triads as directed.

    (1) C is the 5th of the *major* triad   _____

    (2) C is the 5th of the *minor* triad   _____

    (3) C is the 5th of the *diminished* triad _____

    (4) C is the 5th of the *augmented* triad _____

---

(1) B♭ D♭ F

(2) A♭ C E♭

(3) F A♭ C♭

(4) C E G♯

11.118 Spell triads as directed.

    (1) B♭ is the root of the *minor* triad _____

    (2) E♭ is the 5th of the *major* triad _____

    (3) A♭ is the 3rd of the *diminished* triad_____

    (4) G♯ is the 5th of the *augmented* triad_____

(1) C♯ E G

(2) B♭ D F♯

(3) D♭ F♭ A♭

(4) C♯ E♯ G♯

11.119 Spell triads as directed.

    (1) G is the 5th of the *diminished* triad _____

    (2) D is the 3rd of the *augmented* triad _____

    (3) A♭ is the 5th of the *minor* triad _____

    (4) C♯ is the root of the *major* triad _____

11.120 The example below shows triads built on each degree of the D major scale. Indicate the quality of each triad.

Use the following abbreviations: M = major; m = minor; d = diminished; A = augmented.

11.121 The previous frame shows that the major scale produces three major triads, three minor triads, and one diminished triad.

    List the scale degrees on which the various triad types occur.

Triad Types	Scale Degrees
Major:	1, 4, 5
Minor:	2, 3, 6
Diminished:	7

Triad Types	Scale Degrees
Major	_____
Minor	_____
Diminished	_____

Expository Frame

11.122 ROMAN NUMERALS may be used to *identify* the *scale degrees* on which triads are built. This is shown in the following example based on the major scale:

Notice that major triads are represented by *capital roman numerals,* minor triads are represented by *lowercase roman numerals,* and the diminished triad is represented by a *small circle added to a lowercase roman numeral.*

(No response required.)

11.123 Write *roman numerals* to identify the triads built on the tones of the E♭ major scale.

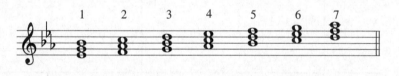

___ ___ ___ ___ ___ ___ ___

11.124 The example below shows triads built on each degree of the e harmonic minor scale. Indicate the *quality* of each triad.

Use the abbreviations M, m, d, and A, as needed.

___ ___ ___ ___ ___ ___ ___

11.125 The harmonic minor scale produces *a different array of triad* types than the major scale. There are *two* major triads, *two* minor triads, *two* diminished triads, and *one* augmented triad.

List the scale degrees on which the various triad types occur.

Triad Types	Scale Degrees
Major	_____
Minor	_____
Diminished	_____
Augmented	_____

Triad Types	Scale Degrees
Major:	5, 6
Minor:	1, 4
Diminished:	2, 7
Augmented:	3

Expository Frame

11.126 *Roman numerals* are used to *identify* the *scale degrees* on which triads are built. This is shown below, based on a harmonic minor scale:

KEY OF E MINOR

i   ii°   III⁺   iv   V   VI   vii°

As in the case of the major scale (see frame 11.122), various *roman numerals* are used to represent the *quality* of each triad produced by the minor scale. Notice that the augmented triad* is represented by a *small cross added to a capital roman numeral.*

---

* While an augmented triad can be formed in the context of the harmonic minor scale, its use in musical literature is quite rare but certainly not nonexistent. Nonetheless, the triad on the third scale degree in any minor form tends to appear as a major triad due to its position as the tonic chord in the related major key. This relationship and phenomenon will be made clearer with the further study of tonal principles and harmony.

(No response required.)

11.127 Write roman numerals to identify the triads built on the tones of the c harmonic minor scale.

i   ii°   III⁺   iv   V   VI   vii°

_____ _____ _____ _____ _____ _____ _____

11.128 By using various roman numerals, you are made aware of the *specific quality of each triad.* Your sensitivity to the actual sounds represented by the notes is thereby enhanced.

As an adjunct to roman numerals, the *key* is identified *by an abbreviation of its name followed by a colon (:).*

Compare the following designations:

A-flat Major = A♭:
a-flat minor = a♭:

Notice that a *capital letter* signifies a *major key,* whereas a *lowercase letter* signifies a *minor key.*

Write the proper designation for each key.

(1) f-sharp minor   _____

(2) G Major   _____

(3) E-flat major   _____

(1) f♯:

(2) G:

(3) E♭:

11.129 What key is indicated by each symbol.*

(1) B-flat or (B♭) Major

(2) g-sharp or (g♯) minor

(3) c minor

(1) B♭: _____

(2) g♯: _____

(3) c : _____

_____
*Note: The use of either accidental symbols or written-out symbols (flat, sharp, natural) is okay, and both methods will be found in musical writings and practice.

11.130 Write the proper roman numeral for each triad.

d: V   A: vii°   B♭: ii

d: ____   A: ____   B♭: ____

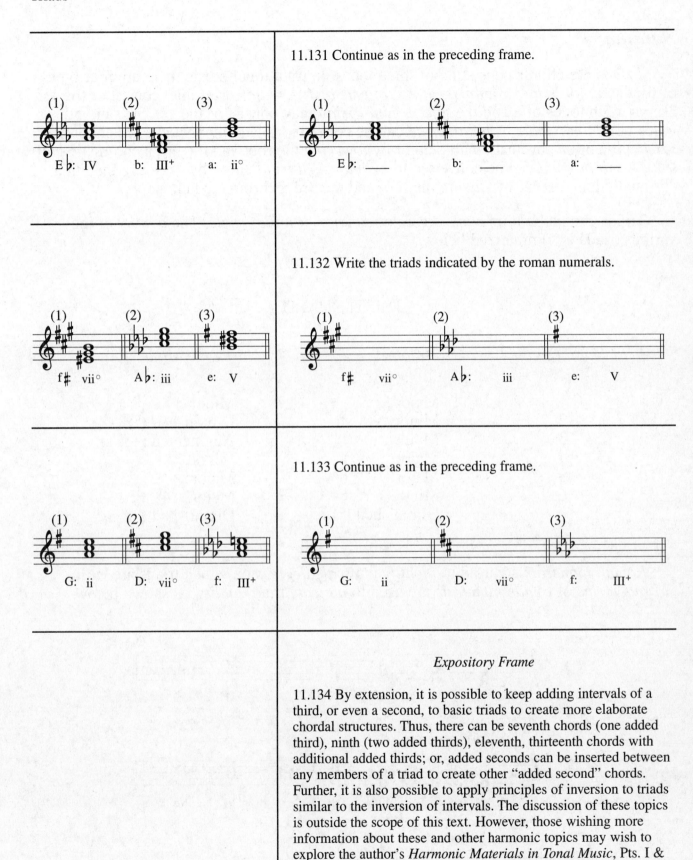

11.131 Continue as in the preceding frame.

(1)   (2)   (3)

E♭: ____   b: ____   a: ____

11.132 Write the triads indicated by the roman numerals.

(1)   (2)   (3)

f♯: vii°   A♭: iii   e: V

11.133 Continue as in the preceding frame.

(1)   (2)   (3)

G: ii   D: vii°   f: III⁺

(No response required.)

Expository Frame

11.134 By extension, it is possible to keep adding intervals of a third, or even a second, to basic triads to create more elaborate chordal structures. Thus, there can be seventh chords (one added third), ninth (two added thirds), eleventh, thirteenth chords with additional added thirds; or, added seconds can be inserted between any members of a triad to create other "added second" chords. Further, it is also possible to apply principles of inversion to triads similar to the inversion of intervals. The discussion of these topics is outside the scope of this text. However, those wishing more information about these and other harmonic topics may wish to explore the author's *Harmonic Materials in Tonal Music*, Pts. I & II or *Bridge to 20th-Century Music* published by Pearson Prentice Hall. *See Bibliography for Further Study* pp. 377ff for more details.

Summary

*T*riads are chords consisting of three tones. In traditional music there are four types of triads: *major, minor, diminished,* and *augmented.* A *major triad* may consist of the 1st, 3rd, and 5th tones of a *major scale;* a *minor triad* may consist of the 1st, 3rd, and 5th tones of a *minor scale.* A *major triad* can be converted to an *augmented triad* either by *raising* the 5th a chromatic half step or by *lowering* the root and the 3rd a chromatic half step. A *minor triad* can be converted to a *diminished triad* either by *lowering* the 5th a chromatic half step or by *raising* the root and the 3rd a chromatic half step.

Triads can be built on *each degree* of a *major* or *minor scale.* The *quality* of the various triads is summarized below.

TRIAD QUALITY

Scale Degree	Major	Harmonic Minor
1	Major	Minor
2	Minor	Diminished (°)
3	Minor	Augmented (+)
4	Major	Minor
5	Major	Major
6	Minor	Major
7	Diminished (°)	Diminished (°)

Roman numerals are used to *identify* the *scale degrees* on which triads are built. *Various forms* of *roman numerals* are used to *indicate* triad *quality,* as shown below.

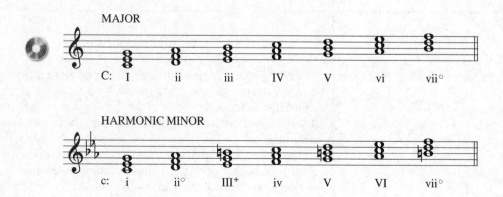

Mastery Frames

11–1 Indicate the quality of each basic triad.

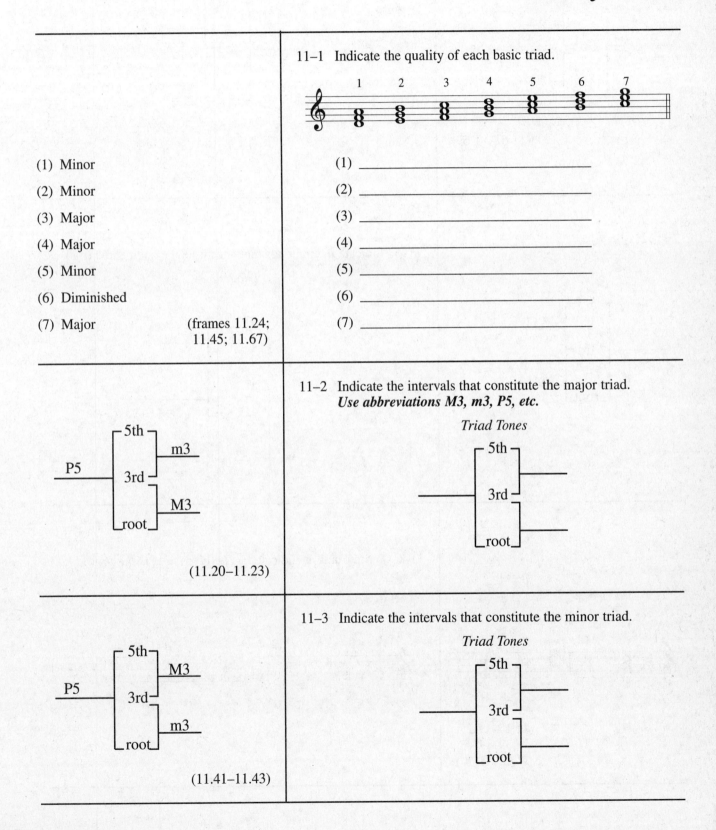

(1) Minor

(2) Minor

(3) Major

(4) Major

(5) Minor

(6) Diminished

(7) Major   (frames 11.24; 11.45; 11.67)

(1) _____

(2) _____

(3) _____

(4) _____

(5) _____

(6) _____

(7) _____

11–2 Indicate the intervals that constitute the major triad.
      Use abbreviations M3, m3, P5, etc.

(11.20–11.23)

11–3 Indicate the intervals that constitute the minor triad.

(11.41–11.43)

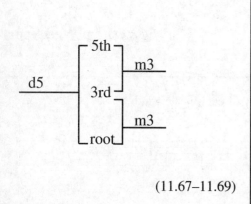

d5

(11.67–11.69)

11–4 Indicate the intervals that constitute the diminished triad.

Triad Tones

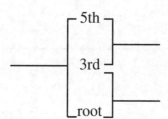

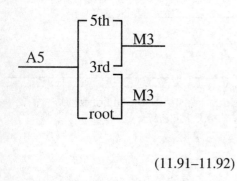

A5

(11.91–11.92)

11–5 Indicate the intervals that constitute the augmented triad.

Triad Tones

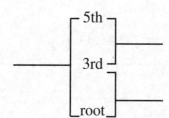

11–6 Write triads as indicated. *(The given note is the root.)*

(11.15–11.25;
11.39–11.43;
11.62–11.70)

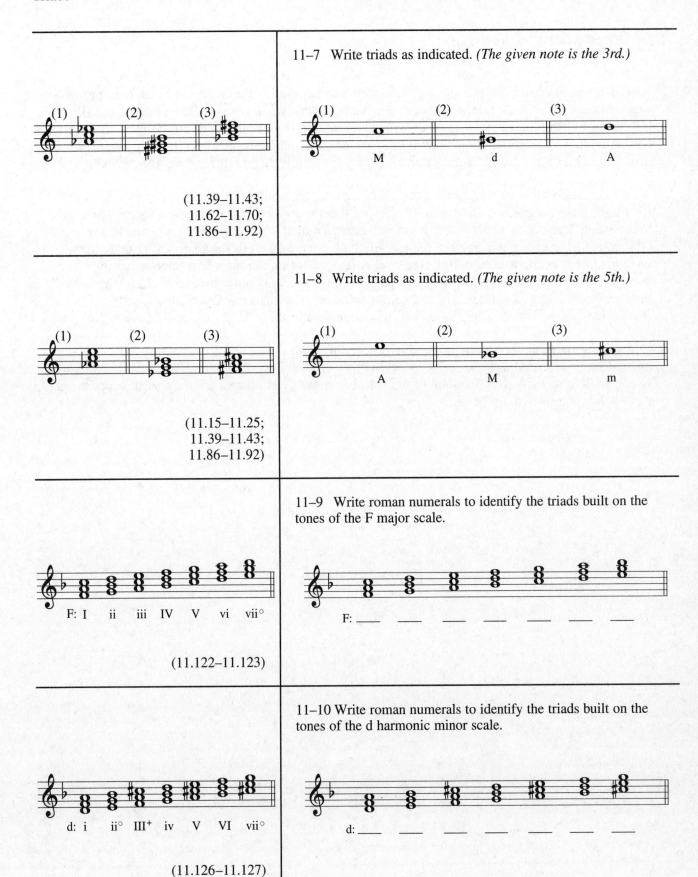

11–7 Write triads as indicated. *(The given note is the 3rd.)*

(11.39–11.43;
11.62–11.70;
11.86–11.92)

11–8 Write triads as indicated. *(The given note is the 5th.)*

(11.15–11.25;
11.39–11.43;
11.86–11.92)

11–9 Write roman numerals to identify the triads built on the tones of the F major scale.

(11.122–11.123)

11–10 Write roman numerals to identify the triads built on the tones of the d harmonic minor scale.

(11.126–11.127)

Supplementary Activities

1. At this point, skills can be practiced in attempting to harmonize the melodies created earlier in these studies. To do this, refer to Steinke, *Harmonic Materials in Tonal Music,* Parts I and II, also published by Pearson Prentice Hall, or work with materials that might be offered by an instructor. Experimentation is certainly encouraged in harmonizing melodies or to put triads together in different combinations and learn to perceive the various effects and differences they evoke.

2. A number of creative writing projects could be developed around the history of the triad and how its usages have become codified into the various theoretical systems in use even today. There are many facets that could be explored, from Rameau's *Treatises* of the eighteenth century to Hindemith's theoretical writings of the twentieth century, as well as the many other theoretical writings in between, or even before Rameau. A review of the literature will uncover many composers and music theorists who have passionately written about music to explain why it has been composed the way it has. Try to explore some of these theoretical writings. Use the *Bibliography for Further Study* as an aid in accomplishing this.

3. Completing these materials should enable proceeding with the study of elementary harmony and music theory or even, in some cases, to begin basic studies in composition. Be encouraged to do so. Along with this, a rigorous program of ear training should continue as a strong aural support for what is learned in written theory.

Supplementary Assignments

ASSIGNMENT 11–1   Name: _____

1. On the staff below, write the seven basic triads. Identify the quality of each triad. *(Use the abbreviations M, m, d, and A, as needed.)*

2. Name the triad that consists of two minor thirds. _____

3. Name the triad that consists of a major third over a minor third. _____

4. Name the triad that consists of a minor third over a major third. _____

5. Name the triad that consists of two major thirds. _____

6. Write major triads as indicated.

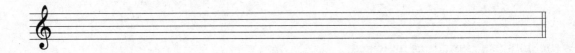

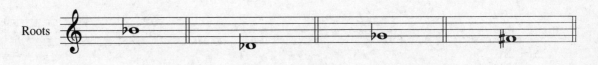

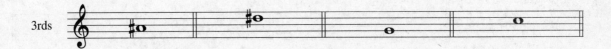

7. Write minor triads as indicated.

8. Write diminished triads as indicated.

9. Write augmented triads as indicated.

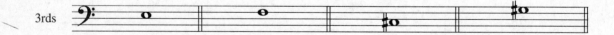

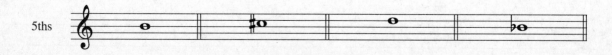

ASSIGNMENT 11–2   Name: _____

1. Spell these triads as indicated.

    (1) C♯ is the root of the *major* triad   _____

    (2) C♯ is the root of the *minor* triad   _____

    (3) C♯ is the root of the *diminished* triad _____

    (4) C♯ is the root of the *augmented* triad _____

2. Spell these triads as indicated.

    (1) D is the 3rd of the *major* triad   _____

    (2) D is the 3rd of the *minor* triad   _____

    (3) D is the 3rd of the *diminished* triad   _____

    (4) D is the 3rd of the *augmented* triad   _____

3. Spell these triads as indicated.

    (1) E is the 5th of the *major* triad   _____

    (2) E is the 5th of the *minor* triad   _____

    (3) E is the 5th of the *diminished* triad   _____

    (4) E is the 5th of the *augmented* triad   _____

4. Spell these triads as indicated.

    (1) A♭ is the 5th of the *minor* triad   _____

    (2) E♭ is the 3rd of the *major* triad   _____

    (3) D is the 5th of the *diminished* triad   _____

    (4) E is the root of the *augmented* triad   _____

5. Write the proper roman numeral for each of the triads in the key of E Major.

E: ___ ___ ___ ___ ___ ___ ___

6. Write the proper roman numeral for each of the triads in the key of g minor.

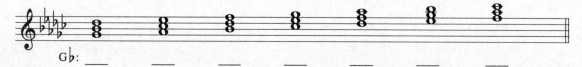

g: ___ ___ ___ ___ ___ ___ ___

7. Write the proper roman numeral for each of the triads in the key of G♭ Major.

G♭: ___ ___ ___ ___ ___ ___ ___

8. Write the proper roman numeral for each of the triads in the key of f♯ minor.

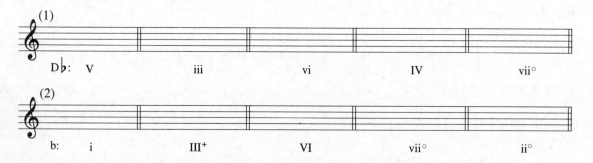

f♯ ___ ___ ___ ___ ___ ___ ___

9. Write the triad indicated by each chord symbol. *(Provide the necessary accidentals.)*

(1)

D♭: V   iii   vi   IV   vii°

(2)

b: i   III⁺   VI   vii°   ii°

10. Provide the correct roman numeral for each chord.

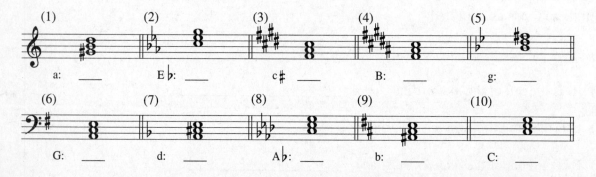

(1)   (2)   (3)   (4)   (5)

a: ___   E♭: ___   c♯ ___   B: ___   g: ___

(6)   (7)   (8)   (9)   (10)

G: ___   d: ___   A♭: ___   b: ___   C: ___

Ear-Training Activities

1. Play the seven *basic* triads at a keyboard, taking note of the effect of each type.

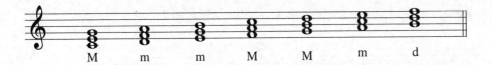

2. Sing the *basic* triads according to the following model:

3. Sing *major* triads as indicated by the following:

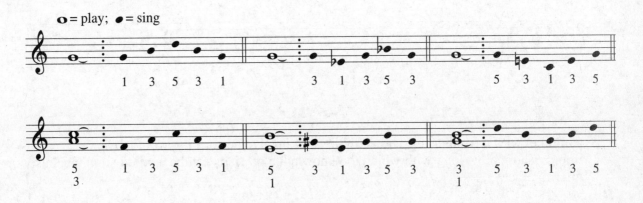

4. Sing *minor* triads as indicated by the following:

5. Sing *diminished* triads as indicated by the following:

6. Sing *augmented* triads as indicated by the following:

7. Continue with any other musical activities that involve performing from music or improvisationally along with which the knowledge of triads can be applied simultaneously or after the fact.

Appendix A
Music Theory Summary

THE BASIC MATERIALS OF TIME AND SOUND

Sound is produced by a vibrating object in the form of a *sound wave*. Four properties of sound concern the musician:

- Pitch—perceived "highness" or "lowness" of sound
- Intensity—"loudness" or "softness" of sound as result of the *amplitude* of the sound wave.
- Timbre—the quality of the sound; its "brightness" or "darkness" and distribution of the *harmonics* present in the sound. Timbre is the tone color of the note.
- Duration—patterns of sound (*rhythms*); the "longness" or "shortness" of tones.

THE NOTATION OF PITCH

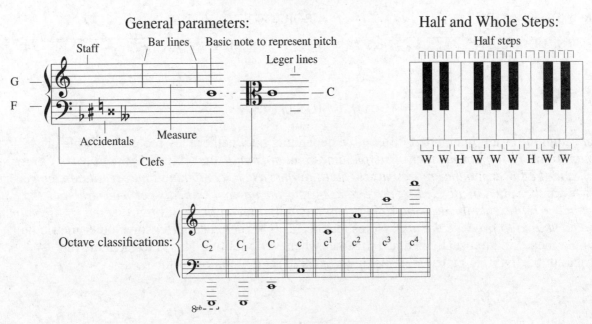

TIME CLASSIFICATION

- *Meter* from patterns of stress that are commonly duple, triple, quadruple, and quintuple
- *Division* of the beat into two parts: simple time; into three parts: compound time
- *Borrowed divisions* that occur from "borrowing" from simple time into compound time and vice versa
- *Subdivisions* are normally into four parts for simple time and six parts for compound time; *irregular groups* of five, seven, eleven, or more may occur in either simple or compound time.

NOTE AND REST VALUES

Notes and rests are the two basic symbols used to notate rhythms of sounds and silences:

𝅝	whole note	𝄻	whole rest
𝅗𝅥	half note	𝄼	whole rest
𝅘𝅥	quarter note	𝄽	quarter rest
𝅘𝅥𝅮	eighth note	𝄾	eighth rest
𝅘𝅥𝅯	sixteenth note	𝄿	sixteenth rest
𝅘𝅥𝅰	thirty-second note	𝅀	thirty-second rest

Head → 𝅘𝅥 ← Stem   𝅘𝅥𝅮 ← Flag

UNIT: 𝅗𝅥 𝅘𝅥 𝅘𝅥𝅮	UNIT: 𝅗𝅥. 𝅘𝅥. 𝅘𝅥𝅮.
DIVISION: 𝅘𝅥 𝅘𝅥 𝅘𝅥𝅮𝅘𝅥𝅮 𝅘𝅥𝅯𝅘𝅥𝅯	DIVISION: 𝅘𝅥 𝅘𝅥 𝅘𝅥 𝅘𝅥𝅮𝅘𝅥𝅮 𝅘𝅥𝅯𝅘𝅥𝅯
BORROWED DIVISION: ⌐3⌐ 𝅘𝅥 𝅘𝅥 𝅘𝅥 3 𝅘𝅥𝅮𝅘𝅥𝅮 3 𝅘𝅥𝅯𝅘𝅥𝅯	BORROWED DIVISION: ⌐2⌐ 𝅘𝅥 𝅘𝅥 2 𝅘𝅥𝅮𝅘𝅥𝅮 2 𝅘𝅥𝅯𝅘𝅥𝅯
SUBDIVISION: 𝅘𝅥𝅮𝅘𝅥𝅮𝅘𝅥𝅮 𝅘𝅥𝅯𝅘𝅥𝅯𝅘𝅥𝅯 𝅘𝅥𝅰𝅘𝅥𝅰𝅘𝅥𝅰	SUBDIVISION: 𝅘𝅥𝅮𝅘𝅥𝅮𝅘𝅥𝅮 𝅘𝅥𝅯𝅘𝅥𝅯𝅘𝅥𝅯 𝅘𝅥𝅰𝅘𝅥𝅰𝅘𝅥𝅰

TIME SIGNATURES

Time signatures are interpreted differently, depending on whether they represent *simple* or *compound* time. *The upper number of simple time signatures indicates the number of beats per measure (meter), and the lower number represents the unit. In the case of compound time signatures, however, the upper number must be divided by three to ascertain the number of beats per measure, and since the lower number represents the division rather than the unit, three of the notes represented by this number must be combined to produce the unit.* Notes that occur in a single beat or in some other metric unit, such as the measure, are usually beamed together whenever possible. This is to facilitate the interpretation of rhythmic patterns by making a graphic representation of the pulse.

INTERVALS

An *interval* consists of the difference in pitch level between two tones.

Group I
(unison, 4th, 5th, octave)

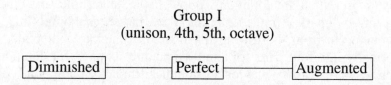

Group II
(2nd, 3rd, 6th, 7th)

| Diminished | — | Minor | — | Major | — | Augmented |

Group I intervals have three possible qualities, whereas Group II intervals have four. The term *diminished* represents the smallest interval. Each successive term (left to right) represents an increase in size of one half step.

In addition to its importance for more advanced theory study, knowledge of *interval inversion* may be used to spell larger intervals, such as 6ths and 7ths. When intervals are inverted, their numerical classification and their quality change in the following manner:

ORIGINAL INTERVAL	INVERTED INTERVAL
Perfect	Perfect
Major	Minor
Minor	Major
Augmented	Diminished
Diminished	Augmented
Unison	Octave
2nd	7th
3rd	6th
4th	5th
5th	4th
6th	3rd
7th	2nd
Octave	Unison

SCALES

Scales are the orderly ascending or descending arrangement of successive pitches within the limit of an octave.

H = half step   W = whole step

Basic Scales:

BASIC SCALE	MODAL NAME
A B C D E F G A	**AEOLIAN**
B C D E F G A B	**LOCRIAN**
C D E F G A B C	**IONIAN**
D E F G A B C D	**DORIAN**
E F G A B C D E	**PHRYGIAN**
F G A B C D E F	**LYDIAN**
G A B C D E F G	**MIXOLYDIAN**

Major Scale:

Lower Tetrachord   Upper Tetrachord

[1] W [2] W [3] H [4] W [5] W [6] W [7] H [8]

Minor Scales:

Lower Tetrachord   Upper Tetrachord

Natural Minor: [1] W [2] H [3] W [4] W [5] H [6] W [7] W [8]

Harmonic Minor: [1] W [2] H [3] W [4] W [5] H [6] W/H [7] H [8]

Melodic Minor (ascending):   [1] W [2] H [3] W [4] W [5] W [6] W [7] H [8]

Melodic Minor (descending): [8] W [7] W [6] H [5] W [4] W [3] H [2] W [1]

KEY SIGNATURES

A key signature is a grouping of sharps or flats used in a particular scale and placed on the staff immediately after the clef used on a staff.

The signature of no sharps or flats denotes the keys of C major and a minor. All other keys have signatures of one or more sharps or flats. If there are *sharps* in the signature, the *last* sharp falls on the *seventh* degree of the major scale; if there are *flats,* the *last* flat falls on the *fourth* degree of the major scale, or the key may be derived from the *next-to-the-last flat,* except for the key of F major.

Any *key signature* serves for both a *major* and a *minor key.* The two *keys* that use the *same signature* are called *relative keys.* The *keynote* of the *relative minor* is located a *minor* 3rd **below** the *keynote* of the *major* (on the sixth scale degree); the *keynote* of the *relative major* is located a *minor* 3rd **above** the *keynote* of the *minor* (on the third scale degree.) *Parallel keys* must not be confused with *relative keys.* *Parallel keys* have the *same keynotes* but **not** the *same signatures.*

TRIADS

Triads are *chords* consisting of three tones. The major-minor scale system generates four types of triads: *major, minor, diminished,* and *augmented.* The names reflect the quality of the intervals contained in the triads. Triads can be built on each degree of a major or minor scale. The qualities are as follows:

TRIAD QUALITY

Scale Degree	Major	Harmonic Minor
1	Major	Minor
2	Minor	Diminished ($^\circ$)
3	Minor	Augmented ($^+$)
4	Major	Minor
5	Major	Major
6	Minor	Major
7	Diminished ($^\circ$)	Diminished ($^\circ$)

Roman numerals are used to *identify* the *scale degrees* on which triads are built. *Various forms* of *roman numerals* (with qualifiers "$^\circ$" or "$^+$" for diminished and augmented) are used to *indicate* triad *quality,* as shown below:

MAJOR

HARMONIC MINOR

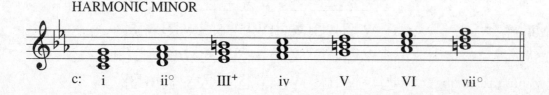

Appendix B
Piano Styles

Creative writing is possibly the best way to demonstrate command of the concepts and materials presented in this text. In original compositions, students may creatively apply the knowledge they have gained. It is desirable that students use a variety of media (piano, voice, small ensembles, etc.), but because of its availability, the piano is the most practical. The brief exposition of piano styles presented here provides a guide for those who have had little experience with keyboard techniques.* Effective writing is possible—even by nonpianists—if typical styles are utilized. The material that follows—used in conjunction with the suggested supplementary activities—facilitates the creative work, that helps develop a heightened sensitivity to the rhetoric of harmonic music.

There are three textures into which all music falls: *monophonic* (a single melodic line), *homophonic* (a melody with accompaniment), and *polyphonic* (several voices approximately equal in melodic interest). Of these, homophonic texture is the most practical for music in which the harmonic element is stressed. Thus, the concentration will be on various homophonic piano styles.

All of the following examples (**1–31**) are reproduced on the compact disc.

I. FIGURATED BLOCK CHORDS. In the example below, the melody is provided a simple accompaniment in block chords.

Mozart: *Sonata,* K 545 (altered)

---

*The examples contain harmonic materials presented primarily in *Harmonic Materials in Tonal Music,* Parts I and II and may be useful in helping to facilitate simple compositional projects with additional guidance by the class instructor. They are intended only as a supplement if class time permits some supervised creative activity.

Block chords are easy to play because the left hand does not move over the keyboard. Care should be taken that principles of doubling and voice leading are applied. Active tones (the leading tone and chord sevenths) should not be doubled and should be resolved properly. Notice in measure two, for example, that the leading tone (B) is omitted from the left hand and also that the chord seventh (F) is resolved down by step to E.

Figuration patterns give rhythmic interest to block chords.

Mozart: *Sonata,* K 545

The way that the three notes of the block chords are transcribed into the figuration pattern is clear.

This technique of providing rhythmic animation for block chords is called "Alberti bass," after the Venetian composer Domenico Alberti (1710–1740?), who used such patterns extensively, perhaps even to excess.

Styles 3–12 show some of the many figurations that may be devised. The meter, as well as the degree of animation desired, affects the choice of pattern.

II. JUMP BASS (AFTERBEAT PATTERNS). In these styles the left hand jumps from bass notes to
block chords. The best sonority results when the block chords are set in the vicinity of middle C.

Schubert: *Waltz in A minor*

As in figurated block chords, care must be taken that principles of part writing are observed.
In the preceding example, there are four voices in the left hand. Notice how each of these traces a
smooth line; notice also the way active tones resolve properly.

Of course, the relation of the accompanying voices to the melody must also be considered. *Undesirable doubling and incorrect parallel motion must be avoided.*

Jump bass patterns are exploited mostly in waltzes and mazurkas but are also useful in duple or quadruple meter for marchlike effects. Some typical patterns are shown in styles 14–18.

III. ARPEGGIATION. While being similar to the Alberti bass, the successive sounding of chord tones over a more or less extended range is called *arpeggiation*. Compared with previously presented styles, arpeggiation generally produces more sonorous effects. This is due to the vibration of more strings. Rhythmic animation and richer texture also result from arpeggiation.

There is scarcely any limit to the arpeggiation patterns that can be devised. The examples that follow demonstrate a few typical patterns; these may suggest others that satisfy specific expressive needs as they arise.

In style 19, arpeggiation is used exclusively throughout the entire composition. The effect is of figurated harmonies.

Schumann: *Album für die Jugend* ("Kleine Studie"), Op. 26

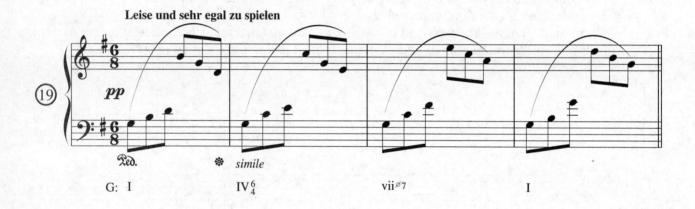

The example below shows fairly simple left-hand arpeggiation, which supports a melody in the right hand.

Chopin: *Nocturne,* Posthumous

V/iv   –   ii^ø7   –

The arpeggiation in the next example is more extended in range.

Leybach: *Nocturne*, Op. 52

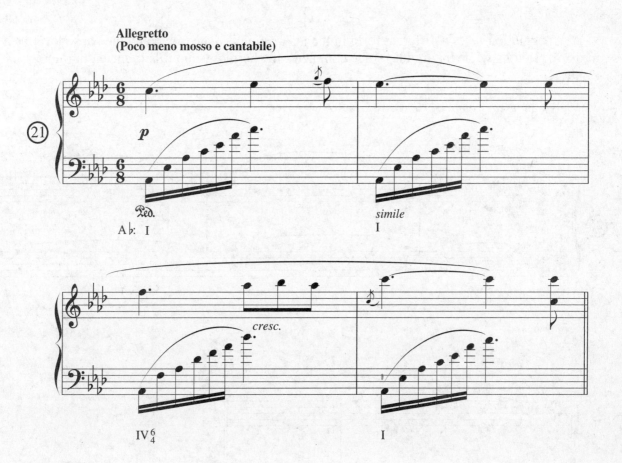

Style 22 has an arpeggiation pattern in the left hand while the right hand not only plays the melody but also fills in the harmony for additional sonority.

Brahms: *Intermezzo,* Op. 119, No. 2

Arpeggiation takes a different form in the next example. The treble and the bass move mostly in parallel tenths while the middle voice completes the harmony and fills in the eighth-note rhythm.

Mendelssohn, *Lieder ohne Worte,* Op. 85, No. 2

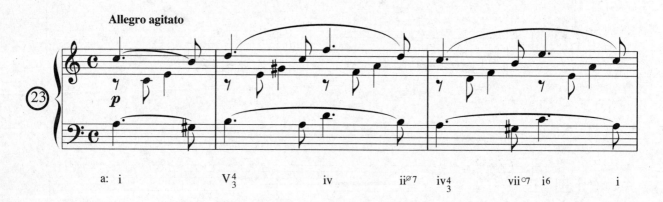

In style 24, the arpeggiation is in the tenor register, divided between the right and left hands.

Schumann: *Kinderszenen* ("Von Fremden Ländern und Menschen"), Op. 15

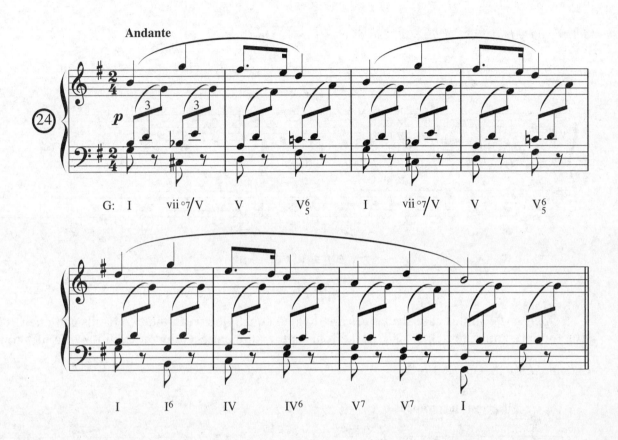

G: I   vii °7/V   V   V⁶₅   I   vii °7/V   V   V⁶₅

I   I⁶   IV   IV⁶   V⁷   V⁷   I

In the next example, the arpeggiation is in descending motion, divided between the two hands.

Burgmüller: *Lullaby*

F: I   I   V⁷   I

IV.   HYMN STYLE. For serious, dignified, or stately effects, melodies may be accompanied in a fashion similar to vocal settings of hymns. In this style, chords change for almost every melody note. The resulting rapid harmonic rhythm makes figuration impractical. The number of voices may be consistent or may fluctuate to produce the desired sonorities.

   Close style: The example below shows octave doubling of the bass, with the remaining voices in the right hand.

Schumann: *Album für die Jugend* ("Nordisches Lied"), Op. 26

   Open style: In this case the voices are divided equally between the two hands and open structure predominates. Only once is the four-part texture enriched by the addition of a fifth tone.

Chopin: *Mazurka,* Op. 68, No. 3

V. **RIGHT-HAND PATTERNS.** Of the several typical ways to treat the right hand, the single-line melody is the simplest. This style has been amply demonstrated in previous examples (see styles 2, 13, 20, and 21). A few others are shown in the remaining examples.

Added alto in thirds and sixths:

Mozart: *Sonata,* K 333

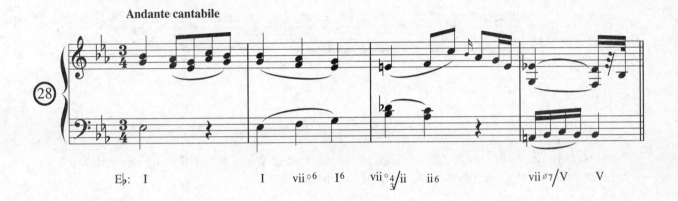

Filled-in chords:

Schubert: *Waltz in B-flat Major*

Melody in octaves: Increased sonority and prominence for the melodic line can be supplied by octave doubling.

Beethoven: *Sonata,* Op. 10, No. 1

Melody with afterbeats: This technique is used when fuller sonorities are desired. Such patterns also produce a more intricate rhythmic texture.

Mendelssohn: *Lieder ohne Worte,* Op. 102, No. 1

Polyphonic texture has not been touched on here, but even casual use of imitation between melodic and accompaniment elements is effective. In addition, placement of the melody in the tenor or bass register with the accompaniment above provides variety. Above all, avoid using only a limited range. The compass of the piano is more than seven octaves, and effective writing requires that the hands range rather widely over the keyboard. In this way, the color contrasts of the various registers are exploited.

Appendix C
Orchestration Chart;
Note/Octave, MIDI Charts

Note that conservative, practical ranges have been given here. In compositional assignments the extreme ranges of the instruments would probably be best avoided to facilitate classroom performances. See orchestration books in the Bibliography for information on instruments not listed here. The sounding range of the instrument is given first in whole notes, followed by the written range in quarter notes. The transposition interval, if needed, is given just to the right of the range staff. For more information on special performance techniques for any of the instruments, please see the Orchestration section of the *Bibliography for Further Study*, p. 382.

WOODWINDS

BRASS

* *The C trumpet's sounding and written range is the same as the B♭ trumpet's written range.*

\+ *If the baritone is written in treble clef, then it is written as a B♭ transposition; always check with your player to see which clef should be used for your part.*

STRINGS

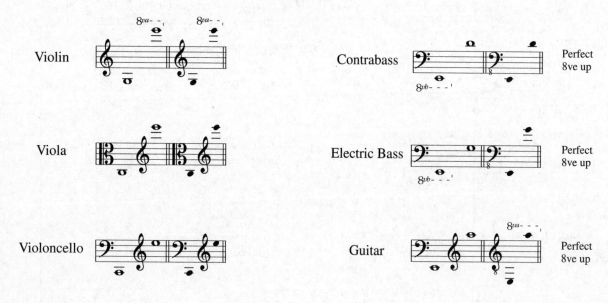

KEYBOARD RELATED*

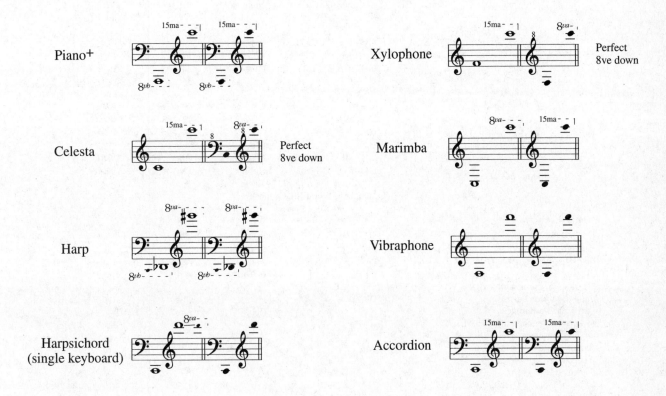

* For organ (pipe or electric) or synthesizers, check with instrument/performer available to you for ranges.

+ Electric or synthesized piano ranges may vary from this normal piano range.

CHORAL VOICES*

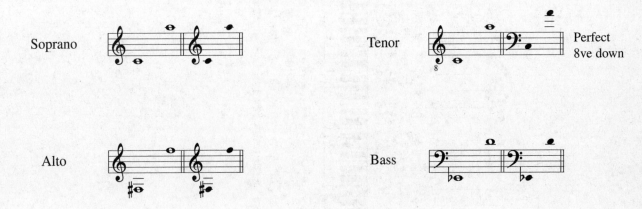

* Less experienced singers may be limited to a range approximately a major second below the top notes and a major second above the low notes listed here.

Octave Naming systems

Traditional	Shorthand 1	Shorthand 2	Numbered	MIDI nr	Frequency of A (Hz)
subsubcontra	$C_3 - B_3$	$C_{,,,} - B_{,,,}$ (CCCC–BBBB)	C-1 – B-1	0 – 11	13.75
sub-contra	$C_2 - B_2$	$C_{,,} - B_{,,}$ (CCC–BBB)	C0 – B0	12 – 23	27.5
contra	$C_1 - B_1$	$C_{,} - B_{,}$ (CC – BB)	C1 – B1	24 – 35	55
great	C – B	C – B	C2 – B2	36 – 47	110
small	c – b	c – b	C3 – B3	48 – 59	220
one-lined	$c^1 - b^1$	c' – b'	C4 – B4	60 – 71	440
two-lined	$c^2 - b^2$	c'' – b''	C5 – B5	72 – 83	880
three-lined	$c^3 - b^3$	c''' – b'''	C6 – B6	84 – 95	1760
four-lined	$c^4 - b^3$	c'''' – b''''	C7 – B7	96 – 107	3520
five-lined	$c^5 - b^5$	c''''' – b'''''	C8 – B8	108 – 119	7040
six-lined	$c^6 - b^6$	c'''''' – b''''''	C9 – G9	120 – 127	1408

Sample of World Note Names

Name	prime	second	third	fourth	fifth	sixth	seventh
Natural (English)	C	D	E	F	G	A	B
Sharp (symbol)		C♯	D♯	F♯	G♯	A♯	
Flat (symbol)		D♭	E♭	G♭	A♭	B♭	
Sharp (English name)		C sharp	D sharp	F sharp	G sharp	A sharp	
Flat (English name)		D flat	E flat	G flat	A flat	B flat	
Natural (No. European)	C	D	E	F	G	A	H
Sharp (Northern European)		Cis	Dis	Fis	Gis	Ais	
Flat (Northern European)		Des	Es	Ges	As	B	
Variant (Flat & Natural) (BE, NL)	-	-	-	-	-	-	Bes / B
Southern European	Do	Re	Mi	Fa	Sol	La	Si
Variant names	Ut	-	-	So	-	Ti	
Indian style	Sa	Re	Ga	Ma	Pa	Da	Ni
Korean style	Da	Ra	Ma	Ba	Sa	Ga	Na
Approx. Frequency [Hz]	262	277	294	311	330	349	370	392	415	440	466	494
MIDI note number	60	61	62	63	64	65	66	67	68	69	70	71

Reprinted from
http://en.wikipedia.org/wiki/Note

Frequency	Keyboard	Note name	MIDI number
		C8	108
4186.0			
3951.1		B7	107
3729.3 3520.0		A7	106 105
3322.4 3136.0		G7	104 103
2960.0 2703.8		F7	102 101
2637.0		E7	100
2489.0 2349.3		D7	99 98
2217.5 2093.0		C7	97 96
1975.5		B6	95
1864.7 1760.0		A6	94 93
1661.2 1568.0		G6	92 91
1480.0 1396.9		F6	90 89
1318.5		E6	88
1244.5 1174.7		D6	87 86
1108.7 1046.5		C6	85 84
987.77		B5	83
932.33 880.00		A5	82 81
830.61 783.99		G5	80 79
739.99 698.46		F5	78 77
659.26		E5	76
622.25 587.33		D5	75 74
554.37 523.25		C5	73 72
493.88		B4	71
466.16 440.0		A4	70 69
415.30 392.00		G4	68 67
369.99 349.23		F4	66 65
329.63		E4	64
311.13 293.67		D4	63 62
277.18 261.6		C4	61 60
246.94		B3	59
233.08 220.00		A3	58 57
207.65 196.00		G3	56 55
185.00 174.61		F3	54 53
164.81		E3	52
155.56 146.83		D3	51 50
138.59 130.81		C3	49 48
123.47		B2	47
116.54 110.00		A2	46 45
103.83 97.999		G2	44 43
92.499 87.307		F2	42 41
82.407		E2	40
77.782 73.416		D2	39 38
69.296 65.406		C2	37 36
61.735		B1	34
58.270 55.000		A1	33
51.913 48.999		G1	32 31
46.249 43.654		F1	30 29
41.203		E1	28
38.891 36.708		D1	27 26
34.648 32.703		C1	25 24
30.868		B0	23
29.135 27.500		A0	22 21

J. Wolfe, UNSW

From "Music Acoustics,"
http://www.phys.unsw.edu.au/jw/notes.html.
Reprinted by permission

Glossary of Musical Terms

A (It., Fr.)—At, to, by, in, with.
A battuta (It.)—In strict time.
Aber (Ger.)—But.
Accelerando (It.)—Gradually growing faster.
Adagio (It.)—Slowly, smoothly, gently.
Ad libitum (Lat.)—At pleasure, freely.
Affettuosamente (It.)—Affectionately, tenderly.
Affrettando (It.)—Becoming faster, excited.
Affrettoso (It.)—Hurried.
Agevole (It.)—Light, easy, smooth, facile.
Agitato (It.)—Agitated, excited.
Aimable (Fr.)—Pleasant, agreeable.
Aisément (Fr.)—Easily, comfortably.
Al (It.)—At the, to the, on the.
Al fine (It.)—To the end.
Alla (It.)—In the style of.
Alla breve (It.)—Rapid duple-simple meter in which the half note is the unit.
Alla marcia (It.)—In march style.
Allargando (It.)—Growing gradually slower.
Alla turca (It.)—In Turkish style.
Allegretto (It.)—Fast, but slower than *allegro*.
Allegro (It.)—Fast.
Al segno (It.)—To the sign.
Am (Ger.)—On, by, near.
Amabile (It.)—Agreeable, tender, lovely.
Amoroso (It.)—Amorous.
Ancora (It.)—Again, yet, still, more.
Ancora una volta (It.)—Once more.
Andante (It.)—Moderately slow.
Andantino (It.)—Diminutive of *andante*. Usually interpreted as slightly quicker than *andante,* but may also have the opposite meaning.
Animato (It.)—Animated, spirited, brisk, buoyant.
Animé (Fr.)—Animated.
Anmutig (Ger.)—Graceful, charming, pleasant.
A piacere (It.)—At pleasure, in free time.
Appassionata (It.)—With passion.
Aria (It.)—Air, song.
Arioso (It.)—Melodious.
Assai (It.)—Much, very much.
Assez (Fr.)—Enough, quite.
A tempo (It.)—Return to original tempo.
Attacca (It.)—Join, attach, bind.
Au (Fr.)—To the, in the, at, for.
Aufhalten (Ger.)—To retard.
Au mouvement (Fr.)—Return to the original tempo.

Ausdruck (Ger.)—Expression.
Avec (Fr.)—With.
A volonta (It.)—At pleasure.
A volonté (Fr.)—At pleasure.

Battuta (It.)—Beat (see *A battuta*).
Beaucoup (Fr.)—Very, considerably.
Behaglich (Ger.)—Without haste, placid, comfortable.
Bei (Ger.)—With, at, for.
Belebt (Ger.)—Lively, animated.
Ben (It.)—Well, very.
Beruhigend (Ger.)—Calming.
Bewegter (Ger.)—Faster, more animated.
Bien (Fr.)—Well, very.
Bis (Ger.)—Until, up to.
Bis zu Ende (Ger.)—Until the end.
Bravura (It.)—Spirit, dash, skill.
Breit (Ger.)—Broad, stately.
Brillante (It.)—Sparkling, brilliant, glittering.
Brio (It.)—Vigor, spirit, animation.
Brioso (It.)—Vivacious, sprightly, animated.
Buffa (It.)—Comic, burlesque.

Cadenza (It.)—An ornamental unaccompanied passage, cadence.
Calando (It.)—Growing softer.
Calore (It.)—Warmth, ardor.
Cantabile (It.)—In a singing style.
Capo (It.)—Head, beginning.
Capriccioso (It.)—Whimsical, capricious.
Cedendo (It.)—Growing gradually slower.
Cidez (Fr.)—Growing gradually slower.
Clair (Fr.)—Light, clear, bright.
Coda (It.)—Literally "tail," the closing section of a composition or movement.
Codetta (It.)—A short *coda*.
Col, coll, colla (It.)—With the.
Colla parte (It.)—With the principal part.
Collera (It.)—Anger, rage.
Come (It.)—As, like.
Come prima (It.)—As before.
Come sopra (It.)—As above.
Commodo (It.)—Easy, without haste.
Con (It.)—With.
Con animo (It.)—With animation.
Con moto (It.)—With motion.

373

Con spirito (It.)—With spirit.
Corto (It.)—Short, brief.
Coulé (Fr.)—Smoothly.
Crescendo (Cresc.) (It.)—Gradually growing louder
    (often notated: _____).
Cuivré (Fr.)—Play in a "brassy" way.

Da, dal, dallo, dalla (It.)—From, at, by, to, for, like.
Da capo (D.C.) (It.)—From the beginning.
Dal segno (D.S.) (It.)—From the sign.
Dans (Fr.)—In, within.
Décidé (Fr.)—Decided, resolute.
Deciso (It.)—Decided, bold.
Decrescendo (Decresc.) (It.)—Gradually growing
    softer (often notated: _____).
Del, dell', della, delle, dello (It.)—Of the, than the.
Demi (Fr.)—Half.
Desto (It.)—Sprightly, lively.
Détaché (Fr.)—Detached, short.
Deutlich (Ger.)—Clear, distinct.
Di (It.)—To, by, of, for, with.
Diminuendo (Dim.) (It.)—Gradually growing softer
    (often notated: _____).
Di molto (It.)—Extremely.
Dolce (It.)—Sweet, soft, pleasant, mild, charming.
Dolente (It.)—Sad, painful, sorrowful.
Dolore (It.)—Sorrow, pain, grief, regret.
Doppio (It.)—Double, twice as much.
Doppio movimento (It.)—Twice as fast.
Doppio più lento (It.)—Twice as slow.
Douce (Fr.)—Sweet, soft, mild, calm, charming.
Drängend (Ger.)—Hastening, pressing ahead.
Drückend (Ger.)—Heavy, stressed.

E, ed (It.)—And.
Edelmütig (Ger.)—Noble, lofty.
Eifrig (Ger.)—Ardently.
Eilig (Ger.)—Hurried.
Einfach (Ger.)—Simple.
En (Fr.)—In, into, as, like, in the form of.
En cédant (Fr.)—Growing gradually slower.
En dehors (Fr.)—Outside of, to be brought out.
En mouvement (Fr.)—Return to original tempo.
Espressione (It.)—Expression, feeling.
Espressivo (It.)—Expressive, vivid.
Et (Fr.)—And.
Etwas (Ger.)—Somewhat.

Facile (It., Fr.)—Easy, simple.
Feirlich (Ger.)—Festive.
Fermamente (It.)—Firmly, resolutely.
Fermata (⌢) (It.)—Pause.
Feroce (It.)—Wild, fierce, savage.
Festevole (It.)—Festive, joyful, gay.
Feu (Fr.)—Fire, ardor, passion, spirit.

Feuer (Ger.)—Fire, ardor, spirit.
Fière (Fr.)—Proud, lofty.
Fin (Fr.)—End, close.
Fine (It.)—End, close.
Flautando (It.)—Flutelike, clear.
Flüchtig (Ger.)—Delicately, airily.
Forte (f) (It.)—Loud, strong.
Fortissimo (ff) (It.)—Very loud.
Forzando (sfz) (It.)—With force.
Forzato (It.)—Forced.
Frei (Ger.)—Free.
Freimütig (Ger.)—Frankly, broad.
Frisch (Ger.)—Brisk, lively.
Fröhlich (Ger.)—Joyful, gay.
Früheres Zeitmass (Ger.)—The original tempo.
Funebre (It., Fr.)—Funereal, gloomy, dismal.
Fuoco (It.)—Fire.
Furente (It.)—Furious, frantic.
Furioso (It.)—Furious, violent, frantic.

Gai (Fr.)—Gay, cheerful, lively, pleasant.
Gefühl (Ger.)—Feeling, expression.
Gehend (Ger.)—Moderately slow (at a "walking"
    tempo).
Geist (Ger.)—Spirit.
Gemächlich (Ger.)—Comfortably, without haste.
Gewichtig (Ger.)—Ponderous, heavy.
Giocoso (It.)—Playful, gay, humorous.
Giusto (It.)—Strict, exact, precise.
Glänzend (Ger.)—Sparkling, brilliant.
Gracieux (Fr.)—Graceful, gracious.
Grave (It., Fr.)—Solemn, heavy, serious.
Grazioso (It.)—Graceful, charming, pretty.

Heftig (Ger.)—Impetuous, intense, furious.
Heimlich (Ger.)—Mysterious, stealthy.
Heiter (Ger.)—Serene, bright, cheerful.
Hübsch (Ger.)—Charming, pretty.
Hurtig (Ger.)—Rapid.

I, il (It.)—The.
Im ersten Zeitmass (Ger.)—In original tempo.
Immer (Ger.)—Always, ever.
Immer belebter (Ger.)—Growing more lively.
Immer langsamer werden (Ger.)—Growing gradually
    slower.
Innig (Ger.)—Intimate, heartfelt, ardent.
Istesso (It.)—Same, like.
Istesso tempo (It.)—The same tempo.

Kräftig (Ger.)—Strong, powerful.

Lacrimoso (It.)—Mournful, plaintive, tearful.
Lamentoso (It.)—Mournful, plaintive, doleful.
Ländlich (Ger.)—Rustic, simple.

Langsam (Ger.)—Slow.
Largamente (It.)—Broadly.
Larghetto (It.)—Slow, but quicker than *largo*.
Largo (It.)—Extremely slow, broad.
Lebhaft (Ger.)—Lively, animated, brilliant.
Legato (It.)—Smooth, connected.
Léger (Fr.)—Light, delicate, nimble.
Leggiero (It.)—Light, delicate, nimble, quick.
Leicht (Ger.)—Light, easy.
Leicht bewegt (Ger.)—Light, agitated.
Leise (Ger.)—Soft, gentle.
Le même mouvement (Fr.)—The same tempo.
Lent (Fr.)—Slow.
Lento (It.)—Slow.
Lesto (It.)—Quick, nimble, lively.
Licenza (It.)—Freedom, license.
Lieblich (Ger.)—Charming, sweet.
L'istesso tempo (It.)—The same tempo.
Lontano (It.)—Distant, soft.
Lungo (It.)—Long.
Lustig (Ger.)—Playful, merry.

Ma (It.)—But, however.
Mächtig (Ger.)—Powerful.
Maestoso (It.)—Majestic, stately, grand.
Mais (Fr.)—But.
Mais pas trop (Fr.)—But not too much.
Mal (Ger.)—Time, occurrence.
Mancando (It.)—Decreasing, dying away.
Ma non troppo (It.)—But not too much.
Marcato (It.)—Marked, accentuated, pronounced.
Marcia (It.)—March.
Marcia funebre (It.)—Funeral march.
Marziale (It.)—Martial, warlike.
Mässig (Ger.)—Moderate, the equivalent of *andante*.
Mässig bewegt (Ger.)—With moderate animation.
Mehr (Ger.)—More.
Même (Fr.)—Same.
Même mouvement (Fr.)—The same tempo.
Meno (It.)—Less.
Mesto (It.)—Sad, mournful, gloomy.
Mezzo (It.)—Half, middle.
Mezzo forte (*mf*) (It.)—Moderately loud.
Mezzo piano (*mp*) (It.)—Moderately soft.
Misura (It.)—Measure.
Mit (Ger.)—With.
Moderato (It.)—At a moderate tempo.
Modéré (Fr.)—Moderate, reasonable.
Möglich (Ger.)—Possible.
Möglichst (Ger.)—As much as possible.
Moins (Fr.)—Less
Molto (It.)—Very, greatly, well.
Morendo (It.)—Dying away.
Mosso (It.)—Rapid, animated.

Moto (It.)—Motion, movement.
Munter (Ger.)—Lively, vigorous, the equivalent of *allegro*.

Nicht (Ger.)—Not.
Nicht zu schnell (Ger.)—Not too fast.
Nicht zu viel (Ger.)—Not too much.
Nieder (Ger.)—Low.
Niente (It.)—Nothing.
Noch (Ger.)—Yet, still.
Noch einmal (Ger.)—Once more.
Non (It.)—Not, no.
Non tanto; Non troppo (It.)—Not too much.
Nur (Ger.)—Only, merely.

Oder (Ger.)—Or, or else.
Ohne (Ger.)—Without.
Opus (Lat.)—Work.
Oscuro (It.)—Dark, dim, mysterious.
Ossia (It.)—Or, or rather.
Ou (Fr.)—Or.

Parlando (It.)—In a speaking manner.
Pas (1) (Fr.)—Step, pace, dance.
Pas (2) (Fr.)—Not, no.
Pas beaucoup (Fr.)—Not too much.
Pas du tout (Fr.)—Not at all.
Pausa (It.)—Pause, rest.
Perdendosi (It.)—Dying away.
Pesante (It.)—Heavy, ponderous.
Peu (Fr.)—Little, not much, not very.
Peu à peu (Fr.)—Little by little, gradually.
Piacere (It.)—Pleasure, delight (see *A piacere*).
Piacevole (It.)—Agreeable.
Pianissimo (*pp*) (It.)—Very soft.
Piano (*p*) (It.)—Soft, quiet.
Pietoso (It.)—Doleful, pitiful, plaintive.
Più (It.)—More.
Più mosso (It.)—Faster.
Più moto (It.)—More motion, faster.
Placabile (It.)—Placid, mild.
Plötzlich (Ger.)—Sudden, abrupt.
Plus (Fr.)—More.
Po (It.)—Little.
Pochissimo (It.)—Very little.
Poco (It.)—Little.
Poco a poco (It.)—Little by little.
Poi (It.)—Then, afterwards.
Portamento (It.)—Connected, very legato.
Portato (It.)—Sustained, lengthened.
Precipitato (It.)—Sudden, hurried.
Pressé (Fr.)—Hurried, in haste.
Pressez (Fr.)—Hurry, press ahead.
Prestissimo (It.)—Extremely fast.
Presto (It.)—Very fast.

Prima (It.)—First.
Prima volta (It.)—The first time.

Quasi (It.)—Almost, as if, nearly.

Rallentando (It.)—Gradually becoming slower.
Rasch (Ger.)—Rapid, lively.
Recitativo (It.)—A speechlike passage.
Retenir (Fr.)—To hold back, to moderate.
Risoluto (It.)—Resolute, energetic, determined.
Ritardando (rit., ritard.) (It.)—Gradually becoming slower.
Ritenendo (It.)—Becoming slower.
Ritenuto (It.)—Held back.
Rubato (It.)—Robbed, irregular time.
Ruhig (Ger.)—Quiet, tranquil.

Sans (Fr.)—Without, free form.
Scherzando (It.)—Joking, playful.
Scherzo (It.)—Joke, jest.
Schnell (Ger.)—Rapid, equivalent of *presto.*
Schwer (Ger.)—Heavy, ponderous.
Secco (It.)—Dry, hard, short.
Segno (It.)—The sign.
Segue (It.)—Follows.
Sehr (Ger.)—Very, much, greatly.
Semplice (It.)—Simple, easy, unpretentious.
Semplicemente (It.)—Simply, plainly.
Sempre (It.)—Always, ever.
Senza (It.)—Without, free from.
Sforzando (sf or sfz) (It.)—A sudden, strong accent.
Sforzata (It.)—Forced.
Simile (It.)—Similar, in the same manner.
Sin' al fine (It.)—Until the end.
Sin' al segno (It.)—Until the sign.
Singend (Ger.)—In a singing style.
Slancio (It.)—With dash, boldly.
Smorzando (It.)—Extinguishing, the sound, growing softer.
Sostenuto (It.)—Sustained.
Sotto (It.)—Under, below.
Sotto voce (It.)—In a low, soft voice.
Später (Ger.)—Later, after.
Spirito (It.)—Spirit.
Spiritoso (It.)—Spirited, vivacious, jocular.
Staccato (It.)—Detached, short.
Stark (Ger.)—Strong, heavy, loud.
Streng (Ger.)—Strict.
Stretto (It.)—Pressed, hurried.
Stringendo (It.)—Hastening, accelerating.

Stürmisch (Ger.)—Stormy, impetuous.
Subito (It.)—Sudden, quick, at once.

Tacet (It.)—To be silent.
Takt (Ger.)—Measure, beat, tempo.
Takthalten (Ger.)—In strict time.
Tanto (It.)—So much, as much (*Non tanto*—Not too much).
Tempo (It.)—Time, movement, rate of speed.
Tempo primo (It.)—The original tempo.
Tenir (Fr.)—To hold.
Tenuto (It.)—Sustained, held.
Toujours (Fr.)—Always, ever.
Tranquillo (It.)—Tranquil, quiet, peaceful, calm.
Traurig (Ger.)—Sad, pensive.
Très (Fr.)—Very, greatly.
Triste (It., Fr.)—Sorrowful, mournful, sad.
Trop (Fr.)—Too, too much.
Troppo (It.)—Too, too much (*Non troppo*—Not too much).
Tutti (It.)—All, whole.

Übermütig (Ger.)—Gay, playful.
Un, una, uno (It.)—One.
Un, une (Fr.)—One.
Ungefähr (Ger.)—Approximate.
Un peu (Fr.)—A little.
Unruhig (Ger.)—Restless, agitated.

Va (It.)—Continue.
Veloce (It.)—Rapid, quick, nimble.
Vif (Fr.)—Brisk, lively, animated.
Vigoroso (It.)—Vigorous, robust.
Vivace (It.)—Lively, vivacious.
Vivo (It.)—Lively, brisk, animated.
Voce (It.)—Voice.
Voix (Fr.)—Voice, tone, sound.
Volante (It.)—With delicate, rapid execution.
Volta (It.)—Time occurrence.

Wehmütig (Ger.)—Doleful.
Wenig (Ger.)—Little.
Weniger (Ger.)—Less.
Wie (Ger.)—As, like.
Wütend (Ger.)—Furious.

Zart (Ger.)—Tender, soft, delicate.
Zeitmass (Ger.)—Tempo, time.
Ziemlich (Ger.)—Moderately.
Zögernd (Ger.)—Growing gradually slower.
Zurückhalten (Ger.)—Hold back.

Bibliography for Further Study

ACOUSTICS

Backus, John. *Acoustical Foundations of Music.* 2nd ed. 1977. New York: W. W. Norton.

Benade, A. H. *Fundamentals of Musical Acoustics.* 2nd rev. ed. 1990. Mineaola, N.Y.: Dover Publications, Inc.

———. *Horns, Strings & Harmony.* 1992. Mineaola, N.Y.: Dover Publications, Inc.

Bienvenue, Gordon F. & Prout, James H. *Acoustics for You.* 1990. Malabar, Fla.: R. E. Krieger Pub. Co.

Campbell, D. W. & Greated, Clive A. *The Musicians Guide to Acoustics.* 1987. New York: Schirmer Books.

Erickson, Robert. *Sound Structure in Music.* 1975. Berkeley: University of California Press.

Moravcsik, Michael J. *Musical Sound. An Introduction to the Physics of Music.* 1987. New York: Paragon House.

Pierce, John R. *The Science of Musical Sound.* 1983. New York: W. H. Freeman.

Slawson, Wayne. *Sound Color.* 1985. Berkeley: University of California Press.

Wagner, Michael J. *Introductory Musical Acoustics.* 3rd ed. 1994. Raleigh, N.C.: Contemporary Publishing Company.

COMPOSITION

Adams, Robert T. *Electronic Music Composition for Beginners.* 2nd ed. 1992. Boston: McGraw-Hill Higher Ed.

Austin, Larry & Clark, Thomas. *Learning to Compose: Modes, Materials and Models of Musical Invention.* 1989. Madison, Wis.: WCB Brown & Benchmark.

Brindle, Reginald Smith. *Musical Composition.* 1986. New York: Oxford University Press.

———. *Serial Composition.* 1968. New York: Oxford University Press.

Carter, Elliott. *Harmony Book.* Hopkins, Nicholas & Link, John F., eds. 2002. Paoli, Penn.: Carl Fischer.

Cope, David. *New Music Composition.* 1977. New York: Schirmer Books.

———. *Techniques of the Contemporary Composer.* 1997. Belmont, Calif.: Schirmer/Thompson Learning.

Dallin, Leon. *Techniques of Twentieth Century Composition: A Guide to the Materials of Modern Music.* 3rd ed. 1974. Boston: McGraw-Hill Higher Ed.

Dodge, Charles & Thomas A. Jerse. *Computer Music: Synthesis, Composition, and Performance.* 1997. Belmont, Calif.: Schirmer/Thompson Learning.

Hanson, Howard. *Harmonic Materials of Modern Music: Resources of the Tempered Scale.* 1960. New York: Appleton-Century-Crofts.

Kohs, Ellis. *Musical Composition.* 1980. Lanham, Md.: Scarecrow Press.

Marquis, G. Welton. *Twentieth-Century Music Idioms.* Reprint of 1964 ed. 1981. Westport, Conn.: Greenwood Press.

Mitchell, Kevin M. *Essential Songwriters Rhyming Dictionary.* 1996. Van Nuys, Calif.: Alfred Publishing Company.

Pellman, Samuel. *An Introduction to the Creation of Electroacoustic Music.* 1994. Belmont, Calif.: Schirmer/Thompson Learning.

Persichetti, Vincent. *Twentieth-Century Harmony: Creative Aspects and Practice.* 1961. New York: W. W. Norton.

Russo, William & Ainis, Jeffrey. *Composing Music: A New Approach.* 1988. Chicago: University of Chicago Press.

Wuorinen, Charles. *Simple Composition.* 1979. New York: Longman.

COUNTERPOINT

Benjamin, Thomas. *Counterpoint in the Style of J. S. Bach.* 1986. New York: Schirmer Books.

———. *The Craft of Modal Counterpoint: A Practical Approach.* 1979. New York: Schirmer Books.

Counterpointer 1.0 (counterpoint software for MAC/ WIN) Redmond, Wash.: Ars Nova Software LLC, P.O. Box 3770, Redmond, WA 98073. (http://www.ars-nova.com)

Gauldin, Robert. *A Practical Approach to Sixteenth Century Counterpoint.* 1995. Prospect Heights, Ill.: Waveland Press, Inc.

———. *A Practical Approach to Eighteenth Century Counterpoint.* 1995. Prospect Heights, Ill.: Waveland Press, Inc.

Kennan, Kent. *Counterpoint.* 4th ed. 1999. Upper Saddle River, N.J.: Prentice Hall.

Mason, Neale B. *Essentials of Eighteenth-Century Counterpoint.* 1968. Madison, Wis.: WCB Brown & Benchmark.

Merriman, Margarita. *A New Look at Sixteenth-Century Counterpoint.* 1982. Lanham, Md.: University Press of America.

Owen, Harold. *Modal and Tonal Counterpoint.* 1992. Belmont, Calif.: Schirmer/Thompson Learning.

Parks, Richard S. *Eighteenth Century Counterpoint and Tonal Structure.* 1984. Englewood Cliffs, N.J.: Prentice Hall.

Piston, Walter. *Counterpoint.* 1947. New York: W. W. Norton.

Reed, H. Owen & Steinke, Greg A. *Basic Contrapuntal Techniques: An Introduction to Linear Style Through Creative Writing.* Rev. ed. 2003. Miami, Fla.: Alfred Publishing.

Schenker, Heinrich. *Counterpoint.* 2 Vols. Rothgeb, John & Thym, Jurgen, trans. 1986. New York: Schirmer Books.

Schoenberg, Arnold. *Preliminary Exercises in Counterpoint.* Stein, Leonard, ed. 1982. Winchester, Mass.: Faber & Faber.

Schubert, Peter. *Modal Counterpoint, Renaissance Style.* 1999. New York: Oxford University Press.

Schubert, Peter & Neidhöfer, Christolph. *Baroque Counterpoint.* 2006. Upper Saddle River, N.J.: Prentice Hall.

Searle, Humphrey. *Twentieth-Century Counterpoint: A Guide for Students.* Reprint of 1954 ed. 1986. Westport, Conn.: Hyperion Press.

Smith, Charlotte. *A Manual of Sixteenth-Century Contrapuntal Style.* 1989. Newark, NJ: University of Delaware Press.

Stewart, Robert. *An Introduction to Sixteenth Century Counterpoint and Palestrina's Musical Style.* 1994. New York: Ardsley House Publishers, Inc.

Thakar, Markand. *Fundamentals of Music Making.* 1990. New Haven, Conn.: Yale University Press.

Trythall, H. Gilbert. E*ighteenth Century Counterpoint.* 1993. Boston: McGraw-Hill Higher Ed.

———. *Sixteenth Century Counterpoint.* 1993. Boston: McGraw-Hill Higher Ed.

Westergaard, Peter. *Introduction to Tonal Theory.* 1976. New York: W. W. Norton.

EAR TRAINING/SIGHT SINGING

Adler, Samuel. *Sight Singing: Pitch, Interval, Rhythm.* 2nd ed. 1997. New York: W. W. Norton.

Auralia 2 (MAC) 3 (WIN) (Interactive ear training for MAC/WIN) 2008. Walnut Creek, Calif.: Sibelius USA Inc., 1407 Oakland Blvd., Ste. 103, Walnut Creek, CA 94596. (http://www.sibelius.com/products/auralia/index.html)

Benjamin, Thomas E., Horvit, Michael, & Nelson, Robert. *Music for Sight Singing.* 3rd ed. 2000. Belmont, Calif.: Schirmer/Thompson Learning.

Benward, Bruce & Carr, Maureen. *Sight Singing Complete.* 7th ed. 2007. Boston: McGraw-Hill Higher Ed.

Benward, Bruce & Kolosick, J. Timothy. *Ear Training: A Technique for Listening.* 7th ed. 2005. Boston: McGraw-Hill Higher Ed.

Berkowitz, Sol, Fontrier, Gabriel, & Kraft, Leo. A *New Approach to Sight Singing.* 4th ed. 1997. New York: W. W. Norton.

Blombach, Ann K. *MacGAMUT 2000.* 2000. Columbus, Ohio: MacGAMUT Music Software International. (http://www.macgamut.com)

Campbell, Patricia Sheehan. *Lessons from the World.* 1st ed. 2001 Boston: McGraw-Hill Higher Ed.

Damschroder, David. *Listen and Sing: Lessons in Ear-Training and Sight-Singing.* 1995. Belmont, Calif.: Schirmer/Thompson Learning.

Durham, Thomas. *Beginning Tonal Dictation.* 1994. Prospect Heights, Ill.: Waveland Press, Inc.

Fish, Arnold & Lloyd, Norman. *Fundamentals of Sight Singing and Ear Training.* 1994. Prospect Heights, Ill.: Waveland Press, Inc.

Friedmann, Michael L. *Ear Training for Twentieth-Century Music.* 1990. New Haven: Yale University Press.

Ghezzo, Marta A. *Solfege, Ear Training, Rhythm, Dictation & Music Theory: A Comprehensive Course.* 1980. University (Tuscaloosa): University of Alabama Press.

Gregory, David. *Melodic Dictator* (Macintosh program). 1988. Ann Arbor: University of Michigan Center for Performing Arts and Technology.

Hall, Anne C. *Studying Rhythm.* 2005. Upper Saddle River, N.J.: Prentice Hall.

Henry, Earl. *Sight Singing.* 1997. Upper Saddle River, N.J.: Prentice Hall.

Hindemith, Paul. *Elementary Training for Musicians.* 2nd ed. 1949. New York: Associated Music Publishers.

Hoffman, Richard. *The Rhythm Book.* 2008. Nashville, Tenn.: Smith Creek Music. (http://www.smithcreekmusic.com).

Horvit, Michael, Koozin, Timothy, & Nelson, Robert. *Music for Ear Training: CD-ROM and Workbook.* 2001. Belmont, Calif.: Schirmer/Thompson Learning.

Karpinski, Gary S. *Aural Skills Acquisition, The Development of Listening, Reading, and Performing Skills in College-Level Musicians.* 2000. New York: Oxford University Press.

———. *Manual for Ear Training and Sight Singing.* 2006. New York: W. W. Norton.

Karpinski, Gary S. & Kram, Richard. *Anthology for Sight Singing.* 2006. New York: W. W. Norton.

Kazez, Daniel. *Rhythm Reading: Elementary Through Advanced Training.* 1997. New York: W. W. Norton.

Kraft, Leo. *A New Approach to Ear Training.* 1999. New York: W. W. Norton.

Lund, Eric, Terry, Brett, & Bork, David. *Norton Interactive Aural Skills.* 2006. New York: W. W. Norton.

Marcozzi, Rudy T. *Strategies and Patterns for Ear Training.* 2009. Upper Saddle River, N.J.: Prentice Hall.

Ottman, Robert W. *Basic Ear Training Skills.* 1991. Upper Saddle River, N.J.: Prentice Hall.

———. *Music for Sight Singing.* 5th ed. 2001. Upper Saddle River, N.J.: Prentice Hall.

Practica Musica 5.0 (Ear Training Software for MAC/WIN). 2005. Redmond, Wash.: Ars Nova Software LLC, P.O. Box 3770, Redmond, WA 98073. (http://www.ars-nova.com)

Trubitt, Allen R. & Hines, Robert S. *Ear Training & Sight-Singing: An Integrated Approach.* 1979. New York: Schirmer Books.

FORM/ANALYSIS

Berry, Wallace. *Form in Music.* 2nd ed. 1986. Englewood Cliffs, N.J.: Prentice Hall.

Cadwallader, Allen & Gagné, David. *Analysis of Tonal Music: A Schenkerian Approach.* 1998. New York: Oxford University Press.

Caplin, William E. *Classical Form, A Theory of Formal Functions for the Instrumental Music of Haydn, Mozart, and Beethoven.* 2001. New York: Oxford University Press.

Cook, Nicholas. *A Guide to Musical Analysis.* 1987. New York: W. W. Norton.

———. *Analysing Musical Multimedia.* 1998. New York: Oxford University Press.

———. *Analysis Through Composition.* 1997. New York: Oxford University Press.

Cooper, Paul. *Perspectives in Music Theory: An Historical-Analytical Approach.* 1973. New York: Harper & Row.

Dunsby, Jonathan & Whittal, Arnold. *Musical Analysis.* 1987. New Haven, Conn.: Yale University Press.

Epstein, David. *Beyond Orpheus: Studies in Musical Structure.* 1987. Fairlawn, N.J.: Oxford University Press.

Forte, Allen & Gilbert, Steven E. *Introduction to Schenkerian Analysis: Form & Content in Tonal Music.* 1982. New York: W. W. Norton.

Gordon, Christopher. *Form and Content in Commercial Music.* 1992. New York: Ardsley House Publishers, Inc.

Green, Douglas M. *Form in Tonal Music: An Introduction to Analysis.* 2nd ed. 1979. New York: Holt, Rinehart & Winston.

Hutcheson, Jere T. *Musical Form & Analysis.* 2 Vols. 1972, 1977. Boston: Taplinger.

Lester, Joel. *Analytic Approaches to Twentieth Century Music.* 1989. New York: W. W. Norton.

Mason, Robert M. *Modern Methods of Music Analysis Using Computers.* 1985. Peterborough, N. H.: Schoolhouse Press.

Mathes, James R. *The Analysis of Musical Form.* 2007. Upper Saddle River, N.J.: Prentice Hall.

Narmour, Eugene. *Beyond Schenkerism: The Need for Alternatives in Music Analysis.* 1980. Chicago: University of Chicago Press.

Neumeyer, David & Susan Tepping. *A Guide to Schenkerian Analysis.* 1996. Upper Saddle River, N.J.: Prentice Hall.

Perone, James E. *Form and Analysis Theory: A Bibliography.* 1998. Westport, Conn.: Greenwood Press.

Spencer, Peter & Temko, Peter M. *A Practical Approach to the Study of Form in Music.* 1994. Prospect Heights, Ill.: Waveland Press, Inc.

Spring, Glenn & Hutcheson, Jere T. *Musical Form and Analysis.* 1995. Boston: McGraw-Hill Higher Ed.

Wade, Graham. *The Shape of Music: An Introduction to Musical Form.* 1982. New York: Schocken Books, Inc.

Walton, Charles W. *Basic Forms in Music.* 1974. Sherman Oaks, Calif.: Alfred Publishing.

Warfield, Gerald. *Layer Analysis: A Primer of Elementary Tonal Structures.* 1978. New York: Longman.

White, John D. *The Analysis of Music.* 2nd ed. 1984. Metuchen, N.J.: Scarecrow Press.

Williams, J. Kent. *Theories and Analyses of Twentieth-Century Music.* 1997. Fort Worth, Tex.: Harcourt Brace College Publishers.

GENERAL

Alten, Stanley R. *Audio in Media: The Recording Studio.* 1996. Belmont, Calif.: Schirmer/Thompson Learning.

Barra, Donald. *The Dynamic Performance: A Performer's Guide to Musical Expression & Interpretation.* 1983. Englewood Cliffs, N.J.: Prentice Hall.

Baur, John. *Music Theory Through Literature.* 2 Vols. 1985. Englewood Cliffs, N.J.: Prentice Hall.

Beach, David. *Aspects of Schenkerian Theory.* 1983. New Haven, Conn.: Yale University Press.

Boatwright, Howard. *Chromaticism: Theory and Practice.* 1995. Syracuse, N.Y.: Syracuse University Press.

Chadabe, Joel. *Electric Sound: The Past and Promise of Electronic Music.* 1997. Upper Saddle River, N.J.: Prentice Hall.

Clayton, Martin, Herbert, Trevor, & Middleton, Richard, ed. *The Cultural Study of Music.* 2003. New York: Routledge.

Cogan, Robert. *New Images of Musical Sound.* 1984. Cambridge: Harvard University Press.

Cogan, Robert & Escot, Pozzi. *Sonic Design: The Nature of Sound & Music.* 1976. Englewood Cliffs, N.J.: Prentice Hall; reprint Cambridge, Mass.: Publication Contact International, 1985.

Cohen, Allen. *Howard Hanson in Theory and Practice.* 2003. Westport, Conn.: Praeger Publishers.

Cook, Nicholas & Mark Everist. *Rethinking Music.* 1998. New York: Oxford University Press.

Cooper, Grosvenor & Meyer, Leonard B. *The Rhythmic Structure of Music.* 1960. Chicago: University of Chicago Press.

Cope, David H. *New Directions in Music.* 7th ed. 1997. Prospect Heights, Ill.: Waveland Press, Inc.

Creston, Paul. *Principles of Rhythm.* 1964. New York: Franco Columbo.

Dell'Antonio, Andrew. *Beyond Structural Listening?: Postmodern Modes of Hearing.* 2004. Berkeley, Calif.: University of California Press.

Etler, Alvin. *Making Music: An Introduction to Theory.* 1974. New York: Harcourt Brace Jovanovich.

Fink, Michael. *Inside the Music Industry: Creativity, Process, and Business.* 2nd ed. 1996. Belmont, Calif.: Schirmer/Thompson Learning.

Forte, Allen. *The Structure of Atonal Music.* 1977. New Haven: Yale University Press.

Fotine, Larry. *Contemporary Musician's Handbook & Dictionary.* 1984. Sepulveda, Calif.: Poly Tone Press.

Gordon, Christopher P. *Form and Content in Commercial Music.* 1992. New York: Ardsley House Publishers, Inc.

Halloran, Mark, ed. and comp. *The Musician's Business and Legal Guide.* 3rd ed. 2000. Upper Saddle River, N.J.: Prentice Hall.

Harnsberger, Lindsey C. *Essential Dictionary of Music.* 1997. Van Nuys, Calif.: Alfred Publishing Company.

Harrison, Lou. *Music Primer.* 1970. New York: C. F. Peters.

Helm, Eugene & Luper, Albert T. *Words & Music: Form & Procedure in Theses, Dissertations, Research Papers, Book Reports, Programs, & Theses in Composition.* 1971. Valley Forge, Pa.: European American Music.

Hofstetter, Fred T. *Computer Literacy for Musicians.* 1988. Englewood Cliffs, N.J.: Prentice Hall.

Jablonsky, Stephen. *Tonal Facts and Tonal Theories.* 2005. Dubuque, Iowa: Kendall/Hunt Publishing Company.

Karlin, Fred & Wright, Rayburn. *On the Track, A Guide to Contemporary Film Scoring.* 1990. New York: Schirmer Books.

Kostelanetz, Richard & Darby, Joseph. *Classic Essays on Twentieth-Century Music: A Continuing Symposium.* 1999. Belmont, Calif.: Schirmer/Thompson Learning.

Kostka, Steven. *Materials & Techniques of 20th Century Music.* 3rd ed. 2006. Upper Saddle River, N.J.: Prentice Hall.

Latarski, Don. *An Introduction to Chord Theory.* 1991. Van Nuys: Alfred Publishing Company.

Marin, Deborah S. & Wittlich, Gary E. *Tonal Harmony for the Keyboard: With an Introduction to Improvisation.* 1989. New York: Schirmer Books.

Middleton, Richard. *Reading Pop: Approaches to Textual Analysis in Popular Music.* 2000. New York: Oxford University Press.

_____. *Studying Popular Music.* 1990. Berkshire, England: Open University Press, McGraw-Hill Education.

Middleton, Richard, & Horn, David, eds. *Popular Music 4. Performers and Audiences.* 1984. New York: Cambridge University Press.

Moore, F. Richard. *Elements of Computer Music.* 1990. Englewood Cliffs, N.J.: Prentice Hall.

Pratt, George. *The Dynamics of Harmony, Principles, and Practice.* 1997. New York: Oxford University Press.

Rahn, Jay. *A Theory for All Music: Problems & Solutions in the Analysis of Non-Western Forms.* 1983. Toronto: University of Toronto Press.

Rahn, John. *Basic Atonal Theory.* 1987. Belmont, Calif.: Schirmer/Thompson Learning.

Randel, Don Michael, ed. *The Harvard Dictionary of Music,* 4th ed. 2003. Cambridge, Mass.: The Belknap Press of Harvard University Press.

Rapaport, Diane. *How to Make and Sell Your Own Recording.* 5th ed. 2000. Upper Saddle River, N.J.: Prentice Hall.

Reti, Rudolph R. *The Thematic Process in Music.* Reprint of 1951 ed. 1978. Westport, Conn.: Greenwood Press, Inc.

_____. *Tonality, Atonality, Pantonality: A Study of Some Trends in Twentieth-Century Music.* Reprint of 1958 ed. 1978. Westport, Conn.: Greenwood Press, Inc.

Roig-Francoli, Miguel A. *Understanding Post Tonal Music.* 1st ed. 2008. Boston: McGraw-Hill Higher Ed.

_____. *Anthology of Post Tonal Music.* 2008. Boston: McGraw-Hill Higher Ed.

Salzman, Eric & Sahl, Michael. *Making Changes: A Practical Guide to Vernacular Harmony.* 1977. New York: McGraw-Hill.

Samson, Jim. *Music in Transition: A Study of Tonal Expansion and Atonality, 1900–1920.* 1995. New York: Oxford University Press.

Schafer, R. Murray. *The Thinking Ear.* 1986. (C86-093409-8). Arcana ed., Indian River, Ontario, Canada, K0L 2B0.

Schwartz, Elliott & Godfrey, Daniel. *Music Since 1945.* 1993. Belmont, Calif.: Schirmer/Thompson Learning.

Simms, Bryan R. *Composers on Modern Musical Culture: An Anthology of Source Readings on 20th Century*

Music. 1999. Belmont, Calif.: Schirmer/Thompson Learning.

————. *Music of the 20th Century.* 1996. Belmont, Calif.: Schirmer/Thompson Learning.

Sorce, Richard. *Music Theory for The Music Professional: A Comparison of Common-Practice and Popular Genres.* 1995. New York: Ardsley House Publishers.

Steinke, Greg A. *Bridge to 20th-Century Music,* rev. ed., 1999. Upper Saddle River, N.J.: Prentice Hall.

Steinke, Greg A. *Harmonic Materials in Tonal Music,* Pts. I & II. 10th ed., 2010. Upper Saddle River, N.J.: Prentice Hall.

Strange, Allen. *Electronic Music,* 1st ed. 2000. Boston: McGraw-Hill Higher Ed.

Straus, Joseph N. *Introduction to Post-Tonal Theory.* 3rd ed. 2005. Upper Saddle River, N.J.: Prentice Hall.

Taylor, Clifford. *Musical Idea and the Design Aesthetic in Contemporary Music: A Text for Discerning Appraisal of Musical Thought in Western Culture.* 1990. Lewiston, N.Y.: Edwin Mellon Press.

Toch, Ernst. *The Shaping Forces in Music: An Inquiry into the Nature of Harmony, Melody, Counterpoint, Form.* 1977. Mineola, N.Y.: Dover Publications.

Watkins, Glenn. *Soundings: Music in the Twentieth Century.* 1995. Belmont, Calif.: Schirmer/Thompson Learning.

MUSICAL ANTHOLOGIES

Benjamin, Thomas E., Horvit, Michael, & Nelson, Robert. *Music for Analysis: Examples from the Common Practice Period & the Twentieth Century.* 5th ed. 2001. Belmont, Calif.: Schirmer/Thompson Learning.

Berry, Wallace & Chudacoff, Edward. *Eighteenth Century Imitative Counterpoint: Music for Analysis.* 1969. Englewood Cliffs, N.J.: Prentice Hall.

Bockmon, Guy A. & Starr, William J. *Scored for Listening: A Guide to Music.* 2nd ed. 1972. records (ISBN 0-15-579056-0). San Diego, Calif.: Harcourt Brace Jovanovich.

Brandt, William, Arthur, Corra, William, Christ, Richard DeLeone, & Winold, Allen. *The Comprehensive Study of Music.* 1976. New York: Harper & Row.

Burkhart, Charles. *Anthology for Musical Analysis.* 5th ed. 1994. Fort Worth, Tex.: Harcourt College Publishers.

De Lio, Thomas & Smith, Stuart Saunders. *Twentieth Century Music Scores.* 1989. Englewood Cliffs, N.J.: Prentice Hall.

DeVoto, Mark. *Mostly Short Pieces: An Anthology for Harmonic Analysis.* 1992. New York: W. W. Norton.

Forney, Kristine. ed. *The Norton Scores: An Anthology for Listening.* 8th ed. 2 Vols. [2000]. New York: W. W. Norton.

Hardy, Gordon & Fish, Arnold. *Music Literature: A Workbook for Analysis.* 2 Vols. 1966. New York: Harper & Row.

Melcher, Robert A., Warch, Willard F., & Mast, Paul B. *Music for Study.* 3rd ed. 1988. Upper Saddle River, N.J.: Prentice Hall.

Owen, Harold. *Music Theory Resource Book.* 2000. New York: Oxford University Press.

Palisca, Claude V., ed. *Norton Anthology of Western Music.* 4th ed. 2 Vols. [2000]. New York: W. W. Norton.

Soderlund, Gustave & Scott, Samuel H. *Examples of Gregorian Chant and Sacred Music of the 16th Century.* 1996. Prospect Heights, Ill.: Waveland Press, Inc.

Straus, Joe. *Music by Women for Study and Analysis.* 1993. Upper Saddle River, N.J.: Prentice Hall.

Turek, Ralph. *Analytical Anthology of Music.* 2nd ed. 1992. Boston: McGraw-Hill Higher Ed.

Ward-Steinman, David & Ward-Steinman, Susan L. *Comparative Anthology of Musical Forms.* 2 Vols. Reprint of 1976 ed. 1987. Lanham, Md: University Press of America.

Wennerstrom, Mary H. *Anthology of Musical Structure and Style.* 2nd ed. 1988. Upper Saddle River, N.J.: Prentice Hall.

MUSICAL NOTATION

General listing site for notation programs: ace.acadiau.ca/score/others.htm#M

Ballora, Mark. *Essentials of Music Technology.* 2003. Upper Saddle River, N.J.: Prentice Hall.

Finale 2009, Allegro, Print Music!, Smart Music Finale Notepad (computer programs for MAC/ WIN). 2009. Eden Prairie, Minn.: MakeMusic! Inc. (http://www.finalemusic.com).

Gerou, Tom & Lusk, Linda. *Essential Dictionary of Music Notation.* 1996. Van Nuys, Calif.: Alfred Publishing Company.

Harder, Paul O. *Music Manuscript Techniques, A Programmed Approach.* 2 Parts. 1984. Boston: Allyn & Bacon, Inc.

Heussenstamm, George. *Norton Manual of Music Notation.* 1987. New York: W. W. Norton.

Metronome and *MetTimes* (music fonts to use directly in word processing for MAC/WIN). 2008. Haverford, Pa.: DVM Publications, 104 Woodside Rd., Haverford, PA 19041. (http://www.dvmpublications.com/)

Music Press 9.1 (computer program for MAC/WIN). 2003. Wilder, Vt.: Graphire Corp., 2706 NE 53rd St., Seattle, WA 98105-3114. (http://www.graphire.com)

NoteAbility Pro (MAC OSX). 2008. Vancouver, B.C., Canada.: Opus 1 Music, Inc., P.O. Box 39045, Vancouver, B.C., Canada V6R 1G0. (http://debussy.music.ubc.ca/download.html)

NoteWriter II (computer program for MAC OS9.2). 2008. Vancouver, B.C., Canada: Opus 1 Music, Inc., P.O. Box 39045, Vancouver, B.C., Canada V6R 1G0. (http://debussy.music.ubc.ca/ download.html)

Notion, Progression, Protege (computer programs for MAC/WIN). Greensboro, N.C.: Notion Music. (http://www.notionmusic.com)

Overture 4.1, Scorewriter 4.1 (computer programs for MAC/WIN). 2008. Mt. Pleasant, S.C.: Genie Soft, Inc., P.O. Box 1503, Mt. Pleasant, SC 29465. (http://www.geniesoft.om)

Powell, Steven. *Music Engraving Today*. 2nd ed. 2007. New York: Brichtmark Music, Inc.

Read, Gardner. *Music Notation*. 1979. Boston: Taplinger.

———. *Pictographic Score Notation: A Compendium.* 1998. Westport, Conn.: Greenwood Press.

Score (computer program for WIN). 2003. Palo Alto, Calif.: San Andreas Press, P.O. Box 60247, Palo Alto, CA 94306. (http://www.scoremus.com/)

Songworks II (computer program for MAC/WIN) Redmond, Wash.: Ars Nova Software LLC, P.O. Box 3770, Redmond, WA 98073. (http://www.ars-nova.com)

Stone, Kurt. *Music Notation in the Twentieth Century: A Practical Guidebook*. 1980. New York: W. W. Norton.

Warfield, Gerald. *How to Write Music Manuscript in Pencil*. 1977. New York: Longman.

MUSICAL TECHNOLOGY

Hill, Brad. *Going Digital: A Musician's Guide to Technology*. 1998. Belmont, Calif.: Schirmer/ Thompson Learning.

Williams, David & Webster, Peter R. *Experiencing Music Technology: Software, Data, and Hardware*. 1999. Belmont, Calif.: Schirmer/ThompsonLearning.

ORCHESTRATION

Adler, Samuel. *The Study of Orchestration*. 2nd ed. 1989. New York: W. W. Norton.

Black, Dave & Gerou, Tom. *Essential Dictionary of Orchestration*. 1998. Van Nuys, Calif.: Alfred Publishing Company.

Blatter, Alfred. *Instrumentation-Orchestration*. 2nd ed. 1985. Belmont, Calif.: Schirmer/Thompson Learning.

Burton, Steven D. *Orchestration*. 1982. Englewood Cliffs, N.J.: Prentice Hall.

Kennan, Kent & Grantham, Donald. *The Technique of Orchestration*. 6th ed. 2002. Upper Saddle River, N.J.: Prentice Hall.

Ostrander, Arthur E. & Dana Wilson. *Contemporary Choral Arranging*. 1986. Upper Saddle River, N.J.: Prentice Hall.

Piston, Walter. *Orchestration*. 1955. New York: W. W. Norton.

Polansky, Larry. *New Instrumentation & Orchestration: An Outline for Study*. 1986. Oakland, Calif.: Frog Peak Music.

Ray, Don B. *The Orchestration Handbook*. 2000. Hal Leonard Pub. Corp.

Read, Gardner. *Contemporary Instrumental Techniques*. 1976. New York: Schirmer Books.

———. *Style & Orchestration*. 1979. Belmont, Calif.: Schirmer/Thompson Learning.

Rogers, Bernard. *The Art of Orchestration*. 1951. New York: Appleton-Century-Crofts.

Schotzkin, Merton. *Writing for the Orchestra: An Introduction to Orchestration*. 1992. Upper Saddle River, N.J.: Prentice Hall.

Stiller, Andrew. *Handbook of Instrumentation*. 1985. Berkeley: University of California Press.

White, Gary. *Instrumental Arranging*. 1992. Boston: McGraw-Hill Higher Ed.

Please note that there are many musical computer programs based on both Mac and Windows operating systems appearing all the time that may relate to one or more of the preceding bibliographical areas. Please check with an instructor or musical computer listings for what might be currently available.

Also note that there are many musical Web sites on the Internet that may provide many helpful resources. The primary resource is the Web site for the Society of Music Theory (SMT); use your Web browser search engine to seek out their latest correct site address and for other resources as well.

Index

NOTES

NOTES

NOTES

NOTES

NOTES